Advance Praise

This book advances a provocative thesis about populism in India. Unlike Western polities, where populism is seen as a threat to democracy, Ayyangar analyses Indian cases to show that populism may not be a form of democratic deviance, but may actually contribute to the articulation of a democratic political condition. Deploying an innovative methodological framework to study numerous political leaders at the state and national levels, he argues the distinctiveness of Indian populisms, and their diverse and contingent relationships to democracy.

Niraja Gopal Jayal, King's College London

A Logic of Populism is a substantive and methodological masterpiece. Srikrishna Ayyangar expertly uses set-theoretic methods to identify the extent to which political leaders in India qualify as populists. Employing systematic comparative methods, he then uncovers the different pathways that they followed to become populists at the subnational and national levels. This book reveals the power of configurational analysis with fuzzy sets for conducting nuanced measurement and discovering general patterns in complex data. It offers a strikingly successful model for other scholars who seek to rigorously study populist politicians around the world.

James Mahoney, Northwestern University

Srikrishna Ayyangar's major contribution comes from understanding that populism wears several hats. India's populism debate was historically too fixated on fiscal handouts to the low-income groups. In the larger body of populism theory, this view is labelled "left-wing populism." Another concept has a long tradition in Europe and the US, "right-wing populism," which covers majoritarianism based on race, ethnicity, or religion. Ayyangar not only looks at right-wing populism and its impact on democracy, but also regional populisms of India (Tamil Nadu, Andhra Pradesh, Maharashtra, and post-CPM Bengal), which do not, he argues, threaten democracy, often making it deeper instead. These arguments are made in elaborate detail, with methodological dexterity and felicitous prose. With the publication of this book, Ayyangar will become the leading scholar of populism in India.

Ashutosh Varshney, Brown University

A Logic of Populism

What is the logic of populism that makes it both a threat and a corrective to democracy to India, and therefore distinct from other parts of the world? Using for the first time a set theoretic methodology and a comprehensive set of populists across India and its states, the book identifies populists as those that set the boundaries to parse divisions among people, and it is the democratic arenas that provide the political colour to such divisions. Populists divide—people within democracies collide—for the greater common good.

This book will be useful to those who want to understand democracy in India, and also the role of populism in political modernization beyond the Americas and Europe. It will be useful to researchers interested in qualitative methodologies to theory building in the social sciences. It can also provide conceptual insights about populism as a matter of contemporary public affairs.

Srikrishna Ayyangar is Associate Professor at National Law School of India University (NLSIU), Bengaluru. He has taught at Azim Premji University, Bengaluru, the University of the South – Sewanee, and the University of Hartford, and worked at the Centre for Policy Research, New Delhi. His research has been published in journals including the *Studies in International Comparative Development* and *Studies in Indian Politics*.

A Logic of Populism

India and Its States

Srikrishna Ayyangar

CAMBRIDGE
UNIVERSITY PRESS

CAMBRIDGE
UNIVERSITY PRESS

Shaftesbury Road, Cambridge CB2 8EA, United Kingdom

One Liberty Plaza, 20th Floor, New York, NY 10006, USA

477 Williamstown Road, Port Melbourne, VIC 3207, Australia

314–321, 3rd Floor, Plot 3, Splendor Forum, Jasola District Centre, New Delhi – 110025, India

103 Penang Road, #05–06/07, Visioncrest Commercial, Singapore 238467

Cambridge University Press is part of Cambridge University Press & Assessment, a department of the University of Cambridge.

We share the University's mission to contribute to society through the pursuit of education, learning and research at the highest international levels of excellence.

www.cambridge.org
Information on this title: www.cambridge.org/9781009605427

First published 2025

Printed in India by Avantika Printers Pvt. Ltd.

Cover illustration: *Kolam*, a traditional art form in Tamil Nadu, India. Illustration credit: Lakshmi Srikrishna.

A catalogue record for this publication is available from the British Library

ISBN 978-1-009-60542-7 Hardback

For EU product safety concerns, contact us at Calle de José Abascal, 56, 1°, 28003 Madrid, Spain, or email eugpsr@cambridge.org.

For
Lakshmi

Contents

Tables and Figures

Tables

Figures

Acknowledgments

This book has taken many, many years and it has been worth the wait. There are many whose insights and encouragement have helped me through these years.

The first person I wish to thank is Niraja Gopal Jayal. As a young student at Jawaharlal Nehru University (JNU), and in the throes of Mandal, *masjid* and the market, Niraja instilled in me the confidence of belonging in the academy and has unflinchingly been an encouraging and inspiring teacher for the past thirty years.

The Maxwell School at Syracuse was my second home. I had the best of both the worlds that I inhabit—public policy and political science. Craig Parsons was the first teacher who literally sat down with me and wrote out a map of causation for my dissertation and it was not so much the map as the moment of a teacher sitting next to me and teaching me that I am grateful for. Pablo Beramendi, over several rounds of coffee and TA sessions, taught me that theory mattered more than method, as he worked his magic on STATA. He shepherded me through the ups and downs of dissertation writing for which I am thankful. Mitchell Orenstein showed me the first form of argumentation, "under what conditions ...", and taught me the importance of institutions. Jeremy Shiffman taught me the importance of alternate arguments, Katrina Burgess that the forest matters more than the trees, and Larry Schroeder that sometimes tables speak as much if not more than words. These are perhaps fleeting moments in the life of a teacher, but they were pivotal. While I was at Syracuse, reading Ken Roberts gave me the first glimpse of populism. I thank him for inviting me to a conference where I saw the best comparativists of Latin America at work concerned about the rise of populism at that time. My roommates and friends,

Ian Wilson and Cyril Ghosh, thank you for being there and I think of our times with other friends fondly.

Bangalore is my home, and Azim Premji University made it possible to return to India. But first, I want to thank Michael Clancy at the University of Hartford, who gave me the reassurance that returning to India was worth doing because it was the right thing to do.

This book owes everything that makes an intellectual inquiry such as this possible to the generosity of the Azim Premji Foundation. I owe special mention to Manoj and Indu, who have with all the professional affection possible provided the space and the time over the past ten years and more to pull this together. I could not have done this if you were not there. I have had the fortunate privilege of working with one of India's brightest minds and academic leaders, Sudhir Krishnaswamy, where I learnt why and how we build institutions for a public purpose. My colleagues at the School of Policy and Governance—Narayan, Malini, Ram, Sham, Sasidhar, Abhay, Vishnu, and all the others who were part of it at some time—thank you for patiently listening and responding to various versions of this research. The latter includes many students who have patiently sat through problem statements, Ishikawa diagrams, and QCA puzzles—thanks to all of you. I am grateful to my friend Siddharth Swaminathan for helping me construct the populist outcome, but more importantly the many conversations around Political Science, belonging and data. I would also like to thank Suhas Palshikar and other regional experts who reviewed the particulars of specific cases for comments on early drafts of this project, and CSDS–Lokniti and TCPD, Ashoka University, for sharing their political datasets. I also thank Mimi Choudhury for providing editorial support at a crucial phase, and for Anwesha, Koyena, Aniruddha, and others at Cambridge University Press for overall support and seeing this book through.

I need to account for two other collaborators who helped me move this project along. I consider Suraj Jacob a fellow traveler who has seen me work on populism for the longest time, thank you for always being enthusiastic to think and work through ideas. I am immensely grateful to Ashutosh Varshney, who observed that I think visually and should consider looking at sets as a methodological entry into my questions around populism.

Earning the stripes to do a QCA did not take long only because of the intellectual generosity of those who drive it. I am grateful for the Summer School at Lugano, the European conference at Zurich, and the American AQCA at Evanston in 2024 for the numerous opportunities to present my work. Patrick Mello taught me QCA and has guided this project through and I thank him for his enduring support. Thanks are owed to Adrian Dusa, Claude Rubinson, Peer Fiss, Roel Rutten, Benoit Rihoux, and Gary Goertz for their timely encouragement and support. Their conviviality and their collegiality are infectious. I owe a special thanks to Jim Mahoney because his scholarship and advice have helped me better understand my approach to the social world.

Personally, thanks are owed to the many friends I made while doing field work in the villages near Kuppam town in Andhra Pradesh. Much thanks are owed to Srinivas Murthy, Arunachalam Gowda, Manjunatha Murthy, Srinivas, and their families, and to all the others who belong to Chinnaparthikunta village and to the Krishnegowda family at Bathlahalli. Thanks are also owed to Mr Kulandei Francis who opened up IVDP to several opportunities for my students and who shared his wisdom of ground realities and populist regimes. I also want to thank Rajesh Dubey who has been my source of jest and joy over the many years.

I wish to thank my extended family for welcoming me to their fold— Jayalakshmi Natarajan, Vijaya, Mahesh, Anita, Vamsi, little Tara, and Arjun. Thanks to my sister Bharathi—always spreading joy and good cheer despite her myriad challenges. Thanks to my brother Mohan—exemplary human being, who has inspired so many, including me, to do the right thing. Sadly, my father, A. Balakrishna, passed away many years ago and Achala more recently, and we are bereft because they were the ballasts to my family. To my mother, Hemalatha, I owe the deepest love and gratitude—her fortitude, faith, and smile have helped me finish this book. To my spiritual guide, the late Parthasarathi Rajagopalachari, I have been blessed to have grown under you, you added life to our years. To Kamlesh Patel, I owe thanks for creating opportunities that have helped me understand things in a different light.

To our little sparkle of joy, Lakshmi. You are our morning sun, always. I thank you for watching this with quiet pride and patience as your father struggled to write this book. Finally, to Rajani. You are mine and have been a part of this journey the closest, and whatever it means to me, I know also means the same to you. Thank you.

1

Populism

Conundrum and Context in India

For a Sunday morning drive sometime in May 2023, the busy Outer Ring Road in Bengaluru seemed much more congested than usual. Vehicles were coming from everywhere and spilling into and out of this main road, and what was surreal was that this congestion was without the usual levels of nudging, shoving, shouting, and scraping on the road. For one, the road was crawling with traffic police, being, I should add, ably assisted by burly Bharatiya Janata Party (BJP) party workers. For another, it was one among Narendra Modi's several visits to the state as part of his campaigning for the assembly elections, and so it looked like everyone knew the reason behind the congestion and everyone seemed resigned to it, happily or otherwise. Modi was going to go through one of the perpendicular roads as part of his Bengaluru road show.

And as is typical of most Bengaluru drivers, I also took the chance of exiting the main road, into the narrow alleyways, hoping that I could get to another road that I presumed would be out of the vicinity of the road show. At the end of this alleyway maze, I suddenly found myself in the middle of a much wider road, again overflowing with cops and BJP party workers. With no traffic around, strangely, they casually gave me a glance as if my car was intruding upon something. Clearly it looked like I was.

I found myself on the road that Modi's procession had just crossed barely a few minutes ago, and those public officials were possibly breathing a sigh of relief when my car came in as an unwelcome pull back to reality. It was very quiet, with absolutely no traffic on the road. But what struck me was that the road, the adjoining walls of the apartment, the overhanging branches of trees and electric poles—all were bedecked with marigold garlands and flowers. The whole place was redolent, in a blaze of bright orange, and with the lingering odors of a procession gone by. Elevated souls or divine beings would have gotten a more routine welcome. Modi has now been elected to a third term, the only prime minister after Jawaharlal Nehru to have been elected to power after two successive full terms. What is it about Modi that makes him such an intensely attractive and powerful political figure?

This book seeks to disentangle populism from democracy to understand its place in political modernization outside the Americas and Europe. It relies on the vast, complicated, and rich democratic experience of India and its states to understand what populism means in India and whether democracy in India is all the better for it.

Every comparative project will involve comparing attributes among cases, identifying preceding explanatory conditions, and explaining consequent emergent outcomes of interest. In a classic book on development and democracy in early twentieth-century Latin America, Collier and Collier suggest that any such comparative project that involves the steps outlined will follow one of the two approaches: "splitters" and "lumpers." Splitters see contrasts and distinctive attributes among cases, while lumpers have an eye for generalizations and commonalities for fitting particular cases into broad categories. Both are essential according to them because splitters "bring to light new information, for generating new hypotheses and theories, and for providing the basic data on which all comparative analysis depends" and lumpers "play an important role in synthesizing the details presented in case studies" (Collier and Collier 2002: 13–14).[1]

Both approaches have been used to explain India's democratic experience. For instance, Varshney (2013) argues that India's improbable democracy emerged from four predominant reasons: the strategies and commitments of India's civic nationalist movement, a Nehruvian model of development that favored democratic deepening over economic development, multiple cross-cutting ethnic cleavages that contest (excepting Hindu nationalism, which can tear India apart) and not necessarily undermine elections, and, finally, the nation-building temper of its first generation of leaders. Varshney shows that India's democracy has grown more democratic by deepening enfranchisement and welfare enhancements to lower castes and groups notwithstanding recent liberal deficits (Varshney 2013, 2019a). Contrariwise, Mehta makes a splitter kind of argument about Indian democracy, arguing that "[t]he experience of democracy in India has opened up numerous points of dissent, new conflicts

of values and identities, a permanent antagonism of meaning and interest."
Making his argument more explicit, he says:

> It is true that one of the reasons for the relative success of its democracy,
> and its hanging together as a nation has been the profoundly cross
> cutting character of cleavages within Indian society that has made
> collective action on a large scale, to overthrow the state, quite difficult
> to mount.... India has worked not because of "unity in diversity", the
> presence of a locus of identity beneath differences, as the state is fond
> of telling us. We have flourished rather because we are "diverse in our
> unities" each able to imagine the connection with others in his/her own
> way. (Mehta 2003: 15)

This book argues that populism in India is primarily a plebiscitarian
strategy, and it is democracy that provides the context and indeed the
political color for such mobilization. India is made up of multiple diversities
characterized by multiple tensions—some confrontational and others
conversational—that populists use to make their case for political ascent.
And so, first, populism should be seen as a distinct form of mobilization and
not as a deviant incongruity of democracy. Liberal democrats accommodate
and unite—and populists parse and divide—for the greater common good.
Drawing insights from the Indian experience, I argue that populism is not just
a thin ideology, an unmediated political strategy, or a performative act, but
can also be understood as a rupture of the status quo articulated by a political
leader for the people and against the "other," which usually constitutes the
elites.

Second, the book also departs from the conventional association of
populism with the idea of a "people." Populism, more recently, is understood
essentially as an invocation to the people (with or without a demagogic
leader) wherein the "othering" serves to sharpen and polarize the difference
between groups. In this prevalent sense, the Manichean polarizations are a
natural extension but not a central feature of populism. Evidence from India
shows that the opposite is also true—Manichean polarizations are the core
feature of populism wherein the notion of the "people" helps to sharpen
the distinctions. Such polarizations are mostly construed as "bad" because
they can reinforce majoritarian prejudices (nationalist chauvinism, for
instance). However, it can also be a "good" force because it can articulate lived
experiences that people are inured to as acceptable conditions (colonialism,

inequality, even party system cartelization, into problems that require public interventions). Populism is a splitters approach to understanding political modernization in India.

India's experiences with populisms are so much a part of its democratic heritage,[2] ideologically diverse (because populists of all stripes can be found here[3]), contradictory (a democratic subnational version can run simultaneously with an authoritarian version at the national level[4]), and disparate (leading to false equivalences around the populist label[5]) that it does not fit well with the received political understandings originating from the Americas or Europe even if the cases peremptorily concur with contemporary approaches. Populism has been used to describe ethnolinguistic assertion, regionalism, market reforms, social movements, and political leaders belonging to both the left and the right of the political divide[6] in India, but intriguingly, the overall story of what is populism in India remains mostly untold. Also, it is not like India is going through and coming out of populist waves, every once in a while, leaving the country scathed, but seems more like populists emerge intermittently across its states, leaving the larger country relatively unperturbed while the smaller cleavages compete under the nationalist surface.

This description of populism in India is quite distinct from the descriptions prevalent in the Americas and Europe because populism in India is much more complex, diverse, and so baked into the political fabric of the nation that it cannot be treated as only an anomaly that threatens democracy. Methodologically, one could characterize the distinction of populism in India as various smaller clusters of attributes across the different cases in India, chosen from a larger consolidated list of attributes that collectively describe populism outside India—which is to say that to describe the logic of populism in India, all one would have to know is which attributes matter in which case and when, chosen from a list derived from extant scholarship. Such an exercise would certainly be a fair attempt, akin to the family resemblance method of concept building (Goertz 2006), whereby attributes that underlie a concept are substitutable and thereby a natural way to account for diversity. But there seems to be a real need to go deeper into—rather, to go behind—the attributes so as to better understand the intrinsic nature of populism in India, its constitutive ontology, or the structural glue that binds the various attributes together. The need seems to arise because the more convinced I am of its intrinsic nature (which I explain later is configurational rather than essential), the better I can explain its functionality and outward relationships, such as with democracy, polarization, and such. Such a curiosity is obviously not novel and, in fact, is the classical approach going back to Aristotle and built around the structure of necessary and sufficient conditions or some combination thereof.

The following sections have been organized along the following three steps: I first survey contemporary approaches to populism and critically explain their relevance and their limitations to the Indian cases. In the next section, akin to a boundary-setting exercise, I explain what populism is not, thereby helping to avoid the inadvertent conceptual stretching that populism is prone to. These sections help to understand what populism can be and is not. The third section is a short overview of the evolution of populism in India, which helps to set the ground upon which this analytical project is built. The next section in this chapter provides a short description of the design and methodology of the study. Finally, I summarize the organization of the subsequent chapters in the book.

Available Approaches to Populism

Conceptualizing a version of populism that is relevant to cases across India is a challenging puzzle for three reasons. First, as mentioned earlier, the diverse cross-cutting cleavages across the cases do not lend themselves easily into coherent comparative categories that speak to the context. Second, even if one were to fit in the cases because all available approaches seem to explain the various cases in India, the approaches themselves cannot be combined as explained subsequently because they are seemingly poised against each other as incommensurable frameworks. We have multiple concurrent conceptual approaches that purportedly may not speak to each other. And third, as mentioned earlier, if all the Indian cases fit all approaches that are also incommensurable, then are we really explaining anything at all?

Following is a brief discussion of the three dominant approaches— ideational, strategic, and cultural—and their relevance to India.

Ideational Approach

The ideational approach to populism has gained traction most recently, perhaps because of the emergence during this decade of populists who rally the "folk" around the threats to a national identity relying on an ideology motivated by chauvinistic and conservative ideas. In this approach, populism is viewed as a "thin" ideology "that considers society to be ultimately separated into two homogenous and antagonistic groups, 'the pure people' versus the 'corrupt elite' and argues that politics should be an expression of the 'volonte generale' (general will) of the people" (Mudde 2004: 543; 2017).

The ideational approach to populism has four core attributes (Mudde 2017). The first attribute is that it is an ideology that is thin-centered. Thin-centered can mean two things. One, it has little to no programmatic content within itself and is more like a latent attitude that is quiet but nevertheless restive and tends to hitch on to more full-blown resonating ideologies when triggered by some exogenous shock or anything that ruptures the status quo. Second, a thin-centered ideology comprises a narrow range of concepts— "empty signifiers"—which are essentially like latent attitudes that resonate with the people and can be filled with relevant programmatic content by a populist leader.

The second attribute is the idea of "the people." "The people" in this approach is not just a reference to the existence of a living and present community or an abstract intergenerational imagined community, but a necessarily vague idea that the people are pure, and which is given some cultural determination in the political context in which the approach is used. While the people are a politically imagined community, it is a timeless image of a community existing across *space*, distinct from the idea of another politically imagined community, nation, which is an image of a community across *time* (Canovan 2005: 40).[7] It will not necessarily have any ascriptive characteristics, except that the community is common and pure.

The third attribute is a contradistinction from the idea of the people, which is that the elite are corrupt. The division between the people and the elite is seen as a Manichean division wherein the people are considered virtuous and pure, and the elite are self-serving and corrupt.

Lastly, populist politics will reflect a fidelity to the general will of the people. The belief in the general will of the people is linked to two important concepts in populist ideology—common sense and special interests. Populists often claim to base their policies on common sense, that is, the result of the honest and logical priorities of the people, and anyone who opposes this, by definition, falls into the group of the special interests, which usually comprises the devious elite.

The ideational approach has become the predominant approach to populism because the emergence and growing popularity of right-wing political parties rest on threats to the people, and "people" are the central analytical category for ideational approach theorists. As an approach it is fairly settled, pervasive, diverse, and eclectic (Hawkins et al. 2019; Hawkins and Kaltwasser 2017), with a broad and shared understanding that people matter most, and more than other attributes within populism.

Akin to the ideational approach are three other related approaches where the people are at the center.[8] The first is a discursively articulated version of the people that comes from Laclau, who identified the people as those disparate individuals who experience grievances that are similar but not distinct, and these experiences help them to concatenate together, creating the idea of the "people." He clarifies that one cannot find which social group expresses itself through these populist symbols because these chains of equivalence cut across many social groups and the radicalism they signify could be articulated by movements of entirely opposite political signs (Laclau 2005). The second related approach is based on the psychology of decision making known as prospect theory, according to which people make decisions based not on absolute levels of value, but in terms of relative gains and losses, using the status quo as their normal point of reference. They are risk averse when dealing with gains and risk acceptant when confronted with prospects of loss. Describing economic reforms during the 1990s in select Latin American countries, Weyland (2002) shows how deep crises made possible the rise of charismatic, neo-populist leadership and the initiation of drastic adjustment and structural reform. Embracing bold economic reforms bolstered the power of these populist leaders, and thus an interesting synergy was built between political populism and economic liberalism (Weyland 2002: 37–66). The third approach that I think fits the ideational theme because it focuses on the people is to understand and measure populist attitudes. Instead of focusing on the supply side—political narratives and strategic connections from a leader—the focus is on understanding the depth and scope of populist attitudes among the people and thereon their background characteristics, impact upon party systems, electoral choices, and so on. Here populist attitudes are considered latent attitudes toward politics that are given content and direction by populist leaders—when such citizens say that the leader "gets them," perhaps this is what they mean (Akkerman et al. 2014; Hawkins et al. 2012; Hawkins and Kaltwasser 2017).

The Strategic Approach

The strategic approach, prevalent in the 1990s, preceded the ideational approach. Populists emerged during this period as a reaction to ISI[9] obsolescence and comprised both neoliberal and left-of-center reformists with a mass-based redistributive agenda across Europe and Latin America. The approach was called the strategic approach because the populists in this era were strategic in their approach to undertaking the dual transitions into market economies and democratic reforms (Barr 2017). They were mostly strategic primarily because there was no standard reform playbook to follow; they had to display a gumption to challenge the venal establishment by taking up heterodox approaches to hyperinflation, regime transition, and other forms of crises. In other words, they had to follow a pragmatic approach because dual transitions were fraught with risks, and they had to simultaneously remain popular to follow through on their reforms, rather than an approach that was ideationally coherent or logical, however thin-centered it may be. The strategic approach was defined as a "political strategy through which a personalistic leader seeks or exercises government power based on direct, unmediated, un-institutionalized support from large numbers of mostly unorganized followers" (Weyland 2001: 14; 2017: 59). The strategic approach also aligns with the idealist approach in arguing that populists claim to advance the general will of the people as embodied in the leader. Thus, the core attributes under the strategic approach are, first, a personalistic leader that has a direct, unmediated connection with the masses (charisma intensifies such bonds wherein people are convinced of the leader's salvational and redemptive qualities) and, second, the capacity to draw power through large crowds of people. Mass support is the only legitimate basis of political rule.

The strategic approach was a particularly insightful approach to understanding dual transitions in Latin America and Eastern Europe[10] but has since been overshadowed by the ideational approach as it seems to grasp the idea of the populist radical right better. However, a variation of the strategic approach can be seen in the sociocultural approach.

The Sociocultural Approach

The sociocultural approach is construed as being relational, particularly between popular sociocultural identities or traits and ways of doing, which can then be articulated as identities, and an asserting (or flaunting) leadership. The leader can use culturally high or low symbols, but such populist appeals are transgressive, improper, and antagonistic in the sense that they are intended to shock or provoke (Ostiguy 2017). The cultural approach helps analyze those populists who use a coarse register comprising words, gestures, humor, style, and so on, to identify with and thereby connect with the masses. Such a performance is deliberately coarse because it is enacted as a subversion of the establishment status quo by challenging its propriety. Moffit, for example, defines this form of populism as a "political style that features an appeal to 'the people' versus 'the elite', 'bad manners', and the performance of crisis, breakdown or threat" (Docx 2021; Moffitt 2016: 45). Another form that the sociocultural takes is tied to religion; it proclaims to be following or fulfilling the will and the plans of the Almighty, with whom the groups feel, and believe, they have a privileged relationship. In sum, these populists are doing God's work here on earth against its Godless enemies, possibly by fundamentally changing the mundane everyday evil politics as they are the absolute and transcendental force (Ostiguy and Roberts 2016; Zúquete 2017).

How Relevant Are These Approaches to India?

All the aforementioned approaches can find suitable cases in India. For example, populism is used to describe Dravidian politics, a well-known progressive ethnolinguistic movement that was dominant for more than seven decades but has now become routinized into several splintered political parties that dominate the subnational electoral system (Rudolph 1961; Subramanian 1999; Wyatt 2013). Populism has also been the primary motif of some regional political leaders in the 1980s, to assert the cause of regional identities or of a dominant caste group against the domination of national political elites[11] (Kohli 1988; Manor 1980). Akin to the dual transition in Latin America, the deepening of economic liberalization in the 1990s into the states led to the emergence of some subnational political leaders to adopt neo-populist strategies to simultaneously deepen market penetration and sustain their electoral legitimacy (Ayyangar 2007; Jaffrelot 2013; Reddy 2002). In addition, some social movements have also been described as populist movements, that is, those whose adherents belong to neither fixed nor determinate categories (such as class), in the past (Dhanagre 1988) and not so distant past (Nigam 2011; Sarkar 2011). At the national level, Indira Gandhi and Narendra Modi have been described as populists belonging to the left (Kenny 2021) and the right (Varshney 2019b) respectively. Thus, populism in India has been used to label political mobilization that is majoritarian, redistributive, regional, ethno-linguist, radical, and so on.

The ideational approach can fit very well with the ethnocentric kind of populists who could argue that the time has come to give primacy to an imagined community (Hindu nationalists, ethnic regionalists such as the Marathas under the Shiv Sena). The strategic approach can well explain the political maneuvers of reformists such as Chandrababu Naidu in the 1990s or Narendra Modi (as the chief minister of Gujarat). And in the case of the cultural approach, we find both high and low ends of cultural registers being used by populists. We do have the coarse rustic (Laloo Yadav) and we have the distant technocrat (Naidu), and both are cultural tropes used for mobilization and making that connection. And there are some other contemporary cases that may not fully fit the three approaches, such as an Arvind Kejriwal or a Mamata Banerjee, quite apart from the well-known established cases of Tamil populists such as M. G. Ramachandran (MGR), M. Karunanidhi, and Jayalalitha. But the larger point is that if all approaches are valid, how can we then identify what is distinctive about the rich history of populism in India when all these populists are within the same sovereign democratic system?

While the strength of the ideational approach relies on its discursive nature that makes it valid across contexts and across ideological affiliations, its critics argue that it can generate false positives. For instance, critics have shown that the ideational approach has lumped together cases that are ontologically alien: Chavez with Putin, the French Yellow Vests with the Occupy Movement (Sanders 2020), or have stretched the concept to include cases such as George Bush, Italian Fascism and National Socialism as populism (Weyland 2017: 53). Although Sanders does not identify the specific scholars, it would not be out of the ordinary to expect that a recent and thoughtful approach to a topical problem, such as the ideational approach, runs the risk of being stretched. Moreover, strategic approach theorists argue that since the focus is on the behavior of leaders, their approach becomes more real (more valid) as the leader has to make real choices and show their true colors more clearly than in speeches and other forms of discussion that can display vagueness, rhetorical license, and opportunistic dissimulation (Weyland 2017: 61). Critics of the strategic approach point to the narrow nature of looking at political leaders as strategic rational actors, which seems a myth because they do function in party, institutional, and within historical contexts, which the ideational approach is better able to capture (Rueda 2021).

The quandary that core attributes of populism face in India is not new to comparative scholarship because using approaches or definitions to explain concepts is generally fraught with contestations. For instance, many would recall the spurt of neoliberal populists in Latin America and Europe in the 1990s as a reaction to the failed dirigisme of the postwar years. At the time, Weyland pointed out that, on the one hand, a cumulative definition (that identifies attributes across domains by using the logical "and") can avoid false positives and allow for intensive small N analysis. And, on the other hand, linking attributes across domains can be questionable if they are determined by definitional fiat rather than being open to empirical research. Instead, he argued for a classical approach to arrive at a minimal definition, because the approach does not demand the simultaneous presence of attributes from different domains (Weyland 2001b).

The classical approach argues for identifying a core property(s) to concepts from which other subsidiary dimensions can intersect or radiate outwards according to the empirical context. However, methodological and technological advances have made it possible to rethink the overbearing of natural science essentialism—such as the classical approach—upon the social sciences. The approach adopted here, which was made possible because of the advances mentioned earlier, is akin to the idea of articulation described within discursive theory—to produce a structure of meaning that resonates with populism in India and with the three approaches. Articulation is the process of bringing discursive elements together and consequently constructing a more or less original structure of meaning (Cleen 2017: 343). Identifying attributes from the different approaches and then rearticulating them into various configurations is promising because it allows one to construct various structures of meaning that collectively describe the context. As I explain later in this chapter, using the language of necessary and sufficient conditions under set theory and the qualitative comparative analysis (QCA) approach, this book rearticulates populism in India. The later chapters will show the various conjunctural conditions derived from the QCA analysis as the rearticulated pathways that help us describe populism in India.

This section identified the limitations within contemporary conceptual approaches. I will now turn to another group of scholarship, mostly with reference to experiences from India, that also requires certain clarificatory responses to avoid conceptual stretching or false equivalences among the cases. This scholarship mostly associates populism with a wide variety of politics, ranging from social movements to authoritarian leaders.

What Populism Is Not

Political mobilization can vary greatly in the public arena, and unsurprisingly populism is used to describe such diverse forms because they are about transformative politics on behalf of the people. Populism has been used to label social movements, authoritarian leaders, and personality-based politicians that compete in elections in India and elsewhere. This book, however, uses only the cases of populist leaders that have won elections in India even though they may share some qualities with other forms of political mobilization that can be labeled as "populism." While these forms of political mobilization share affinities, describing differentiating characteristics helps to sharpen the meaning of the concept that we are interested in. Knowing the boundaries of what we think populism is helps in case selection.[12] Populist leaders are selected from among elected political leaders in this study, and I make the case here as to why other forms are not considered here.[13]

First, social movements. Because populist mobilization shares some generic traits with social movements, scholars point out that the bottom-up forms of political mobilization can also be considered populism, and not limit populism to top-down perspectives that are usually narratives of outsider politicians lambasting corrupt establishments (Aslandis 2017). All populists emerge from a sense of democratic disenchantment as seen in the political arena and therefore seek to re-envision the same. They seek to represent and wrest power back to the "people," away from the self-serving interests of the establishment. These grievances can remain latent, unless someone infuses them with political importance, and they cultivate an appetite for action, and this kind of origin can be common to both populist leaders and social movements. Many social movement leaders in India have also been described as populists, such as Gandhi and the nationalist movement (Subramaniam 2007), Periyar as the heretical articulator of the Dravidian movement (1999), thereafter the farmers movements in Maharashtra and also as an alternative to the framing of various other tribal, ethnic, and farmers protests as subaltern movements (Dhanagare 1988), and more recently the moral authority exerted by Anna Hazare during the movement against corruption (Chatterjee 2012).

Conceptually though, I think there is an inflection point that differentiates social movements from populists, which is when political leaders seek to compete and emerge victorious in elections. Populists in India seek to win elections as there is nothing more than this legitimate rite of passage in India that vindicates their direct connection with the masses. Electoral processes in India have mostly been robust, with high voter turnouts and regular electoral cycles demonstrating both their efficacy and legitimacy. Pragmatically speaking then, it makes little sense for populists to rail against elections when popular sentiment endorses the opposite. Populists would also want to contest elections, as it is the fairest contest to demonstrate their connection with the "people." They may want to display their authenticity by jumping into the contest and yet stand above the fray by exposing the weak connections that other potential aspirants may have with the masses compared to their own connect with the "people." Their pursuit of political power is precisely to bring power back to the people; by engaging with other aspirants on the same footing, they are able to show that they are more connected than others. Electoral contests can help them display how close they are to the people relative to other politicians.

However, political leaders contesting elections are a starker instantiation of populism compared to charismatic leaders of social movements for two other reasons. There is a difference, say, between Arvind Kejriwal and his erstwhile colleague Yogendra Yadav, who moved out of the Aam Aadmi Party to establish a social movement called Swaraj Abhiyan. First, populist leaders are primarily interested in bringing power back to the people to reform governing institutions, because they presume that the people are "pure" the way they are and the real malaise does not lie within the social attributes of the people but in the atrophy of our public institutions (which is because of evil/ self-serving elites, perhaps) where policy concessions or institutional reforms may prove inadequate. The focus is on public institutions and systemic reform. Social movement leaders, on the other hand, draw attention to issues that can be particular to the social strata (working class, farmers, displaced, and so on) that seek redressal of specific grievances. Their focus is not on public institutions but on the groups and their grievances. For example, neither Periyar nor Gandhi or for that matter, in recent years, even Yogendra Yadav were interested in furthering their cause through political parties or elections, as they felt the problem and the solutions were in the societal and not in the political arena. Second, social movements may have charismatic leaders and direct connections with masses, but they are not populists of the first order because they seek to draw attention to an agenda that puts the spotlight on either the people or the issue and do not seek to draw attention to themselves. They also might have a purist approach to politics, arguing that they do not want to "soil" their hands in the dirty world of politics and thereby besmirch the purity of their cause.[14]

Put another way, populists, on the other hand, are vague about causes, choosing to use "empty signifiers," as that puts them squarely in the center of attention more than the causes or the people affected by such causes. The populists we have in mind are not preoccupied with societal issues that warrant reform or with some public issue that merits agenda setting; they are centrally concerned with representational deficiencies stemming from the party oligarchies, party system cartelization, or programmatic convergence and seek to bring power back to the people to reform the public institutions and demonstrate that they and they alone have the gumption to bring about that change.

Some but not all social movements transition, to use a phrase from social movement theorists, from barricades to ballots. Aslandis distinguishes three ways by which such a transition may occur—as a new political organization within the electoral arena originating from a populist movement, being associated with existing political parties that sympathize with the populist cause, and by being co-opted by a political party exogenous to the movement (Aslandis 2017). Many cases in this book, as the latter chapters will describe, have originated from social movements, but the point being made here is that conceptually, populism would more fully describe political leaders competing in elections than it could describe social movements because competing in elections inflects the distinction between the two.

Thus, on the one hand, populist leaders do not like to self-efface for the larger social cause under a social movement. And on the other hand, they seek to remain front and center and as the leader of the people, and so are keen to always remain larger than their political party.

Because they like to remain front and center of political representation, the term "populism" is also used to describe personality-based parties and their extreme version of authoritarian leaders. Hence, a second distinction must be made between elected populist leaders and personality-based politics.

It is almost a corollary in electoral politics that those who seek electoral legitimacy would also ordinarily seek to build parties because of the inherent advantages associated with party organizations. Political parties help to mobilize voters on scale over successive electoral cycles, smoothen the process of executive–legislative relations, and incorporate diverse interests within a single organizational frame (Levitsky and Cameron 2003). However, while populists seek electoral legitimacy, they are rarely interested in building party organizations and, in fact, are almost keen to ensure that it never overshadows their personalized, unmediated access to the people. We can argue that they seek to remain taller than their party for two reasons. First, they would not want the charismatic connection with the masses to be overshadowed by party organizations. Part of the charismatic connection relies on the fact that such leaders would like to remain connected with people as political outsiders that are untainted by the political trappings of electoral politics and parties even if they have to compete in elections. Second, to retain their charisma and to retain control over the legislature, it is necessary that they retain control and leadership over the party organization. Thus, populists do launch political parties and create an organizational machinery that will mobilize support during elections and in the legislature, but they will always ensure that their persona is larger than the party image or any of its insiders.

There are several political parties in India that are primarily organized around personalistic leadership, and rarely do such parties ever evolve into any other form of stable organization. Much like non-governmental organizations (NGOs) initially established by charismatic leaders and who rarely think about leadership succession, such personalistic parties are content in their scope and power in the electoral landscape. Naveen Patnaik, S. Ramadoss, and P. A. Sangma, for example, are not audaciously charismatic, but they have nevertheless retained tight control over their parties.

On the face of it, populism seems to share strong affinities with a particular mythopoeic motif of political mobilization in India—the personalist, Gandhian kind—whereby political leaders are seen as having mass appeal and having moral authority, and only reluctantly agree to take on political authority and statecraft to provide "selfless devotion to constructive work for the good of society...." (Brass 1992: 14). However, the distinction between personality-based parties versus populist-leader-based parties might be that the former mass affiliation is cultural, that is, as the vestige of some form of monarchical or feudal political culture, and the latter political as mobilization that is essentially democratic and contemporaneous with the extant party politics. That is, personality-based parties are typically established on some form of patron–client relations that are considered sacred based on affiliations of caste, kinship, royal lineage, or such. Thus, it could be the case that these parties are mostly parties that owe their allegiance to a "dynasty."

Populist-leader-based parties, on the other hand, establish affiliations that are essentially constructed, not a priori culturally constituted, as part of the discourses of the contemporary electoral arena. For example, one may argue that Naveen Patnaik's popularity (and that of his father) may partly be because he is a descendant of a royal family. S. Ramadoss was able to stitch together a lower-caste-based federation around the Vanniyars and was reverentially addressed as "Maruthuvar Ayya." Mulayam Singh Yadav was the archetype "goonda" to many, exploiting state resources for personal benefit, but was a modern-day "Lord Krishna" to his Yadav followers, who saw in him both masculinity and humanity to serve their greater collective good (Michelutti 2010). However, contrast these leaders with M. G. Ramachandran (MGR) and N. T. Rama Rao (NTR), who entered mainstream politics having established mass popularity through movies and constructed affiliations that countered contemporary established political discourses. Their popularity cut across social and historically affiliated ties, and their discourse was constructed around contemporary electoral and governance issues.

Concurrently, one should also distinguish populist leaders from authoritarian leaders, as the latter is an extreme form of personality-based leadership, and populism is often equated with Big Men politics. Populists and authoritarians govern in almost similar fashion. It is true that both populist and authoritarian leaders are averse to any form of oversight from non-elected institutions. Populists believe that their ascendance to power is essentially to bring power back to the people to reassert control over institutions that have been vitiated by establishment control.[15] Thus, institutional veto players, ordinarily considered necessary to check majoritarian excess or hold executive power accountable, such as the judiciary, the bureaucracy, the press, or other civil society groups, are treated with disdain, intimidated, suppressed, and relentlessly brow beaten to submission. Those institutions that are more pliable and servile are encouraged and given access to such leaders. Thus, they tend to rule through executive decree, emaciate institutions by implanting pliable actors, block access to the media, and even harass powerful public actors and extensively regulate the civil services. And they do just the opposite with those functionaries that toe their line.

While on the face of it, both populists and authoritarian leaders seem to share the same antipathy toward non-elected institutions, there is a crucial difference. Populist leaders come to power because of populist majorities, and so they undermine liberal checks at the behest and with the blessings of such majorities. Authoritarian leaders undermine liberal checks to legitimize their rule because they may have been foisted upon a silent and possibly recalcitrant population. In other words, authoritarian leaders do not necessarily come to power because of elected popular majorities, but actually seek to manufacture them after coming to power so as to sustain their rule. Populists, on the other hand, having first manufactured such majorities that brought them to power, now claim to follow through on various measures at their behest. For example, Yogi Adityanath did not become the chief minister based on a popular mandate for him, but was appointed to the same by the party hierarchy. Nevertheless, many of his measures have mostly been authoritarian, such as his drives against slaughterhouses or vigilante measures against consenting youth. But these myopic measures pale in comparison to the nefarious and draconian threats to the public, who were reeling under the second wave of the pandemic because of the lack of oxygen, medication, or even testing facilities in the public health system. Yogi Adityanath was blatantly authoritarian, living in his own fantasy of power, and certainly does not come across as having any connect with the people as a populist either, but in fact, like any other authoritarian, he governs through a reign of terror.[16]

Having indicated the conceptual limitations of contemporary approaches to populism and distinguishing it from other possible affiliates of political representation, I now turn to provide a very short survey of populism in India. Most studies that we know of are usually based on single cases or of state-level politics but a survey of cases over time has not been done yet. The following section is necessarily a short introduction surveying the emergence of populist leaders in India.

A Short Survey of Populism in India

Over the past 75 years, India has had a fair share of populists, some of whom are well known among those familiar with Indian politics. Notably, Gandhi in the national political arena has been identified as populist, though one can certainly argue that Gandhi had a much larger persona and contribution to India and it would indeed be narrow to equate his politics only to the populist label. Thereafter, with the demise of Nehru, Indira Gandhi was the quintessential ISI classical populist as she centralized political, economic, and administrative control and reached out to the "people" through massive redistributive programs. Her revisions to the constitution to centralize fundamental control that threatened the basic features of the Indian constitution, and her brazen use of Emergency powers to destabilize state-level governments, provoked a backlash from several regional leaders, some of whom adopted populist tactics to challenge establishment politics. Modi is the other populist candidate at the national level. While his emergence early on had mostly to do with the anti-incumbent sentiment of the preceding United Progressive Alliance (UPA) regime, he is now clearly established as the tallest political leader in his party and a formidable challenge to the political opposition. However, with multiple political cleavages and multiparty competition at all levels, and well-established federal and administrative structures, it is atypical for a populist to emerge at the national level.

At the state level, however, populists have emerged far more often. They have emerged across India's subnational landscape over more than five decades across its various states, usually to fill a crisis of representation arising from a gap that cannot be filled by candidates from existing party systems. Mirroring the only possibly public arenas—the social, the economic, and the political—populisms have emerged in each of these arenas at the subnational level. In the social arena, populists have emerged in the context of ethnic assertion (with and without self-determination claims) and have taken on both inclusive and exclusive colors. In the economic realm, populists have emerged mostly to both deepen market reforms and simultaneously try to retain political legitimacy. More recently, a more novel and recent form of populism, concentrated on urban governance spaces, has emerged that has threatened party cartels and the establishment. The following narrative will describe each of these sequentially, and while there is some credibility to look at them in the manner they have evolved in the history of democratic politics in India, it would be over-deterministic to presume that the three forms cannot emerge independently, concurrently, or in any other way. In any case, the following narrative provides a quick overview of the emergence of populisms as phases at the state level in India.

Regional Populism

The first phase of the national party system was from the 1950s till around 1967, corresponding with the predominance of the Congress across all party systems in India until it was defeated in many states in the 1967 Lok Sabha and state assembly elections. Linguistic mobilization could very well have provided the necessary canvas for populists to emerge, but this was preempted perhaps because linguistic reorganization took mostly a pluralistic form under Nehru, whereby mutual agreements among contending groups within a state were secured before the central government provided a solution. Thus, regions that were organized into the states of Andhra Pradesh, Gujarat, Maharashtra, Karnataka, Punjab, and the northeastern states were in closer conformity with the grievances of the principal large language communities in the respective states, and thereby seem to have preempted the mobilization of language as a populist agenda (Sarangi 2013).

However, in many such linguistically reorganized states, regionalism did subsequently emerge in the second phase of the party system that lasted from around 1967 till around the mid-1990s. Thus, states like Kashmir, Punjab, Mizoram, Nagaland, and Assam, apart from Tamil Nadu and Andhra Pradesh, saw more assertive, almost insurrectionist levels of regionalism than earlier (Chadda 2013). One can attribute three reasons for the violent regionalism during this period. First, in order to bolster her ascendancy at the national level after Nehru's death, Indira Gandhi intervened in state-level politics in many states so as to either drive a wedge among competing groups within the Congress party and thereby ensure that her rivals in the Congress were defeated (such as in Devraj Urs in Karnataka) or she intervened to stoke the flames of regionalist sentiment among already mobilized regionalist groups to embarrass other regional contenders that were able to challenge Congress hegemony in the respective states—Bhindranwale versus the Akali Dal and Laldenga versus T. Sailo in Mizoram, for example (Brass 1992: 132). Second, the centralization of all political authority under Indira Gandhi and the egregious imposition of President's rule across India's states by both national parties (Janata Party in 1977 and Congress in 1980), numbering to around 100 instances by the early 1990s, spurred some states to reinvoke their regional identities to restore dignity to their states (Sadanandan 2012). And third, the consequence of the two interrelated conditions—Indira Gandhi's politicking and the use of President's rule—seems to have been to basically weaken regional party systems, which brought to the fore issues of government legitimacy and democratic representation.

However, populist mobilization was not the natural response to assert regional statehood to counter national-level domination. Populist leaders emerged primarily in Tamil Nadu and Andhra Pradesh, while in other states political leaders either took to secessionism or adapted to the extant party system. One could make some speculations as to why populist leaders emerged in these two southern states and not others. First, the leaders in these states were able to mobilize the non-brahmin castes, which were the majority, along the lines of a traditional regional identity. Except for caste, no other cleavage was cross-cutting. In the other states there were multiple cross-cutting cleavages that not only stopped an easy majoritarian coalition from being constructed, but also allowed the central government to drive a wedge between local political actors and thereby retain central control. For instance, in Punjab and Kashmir it was religion (Sikh or Muslim versus Hindu), and in the northeastern states it was language (native versus migrant), religion, and also topography (hills people versus plains people), and in all these states, Indira Gandhi intervened to ensure that moderate regional interests were undermined by insurrectionist interests that dealt directly with the centre (Chadda 2013). Second, populist leaders, particularly in Tamil Nadu and Andhra Pradesh, established connections with the masses through mythological movies or as larger-than-life heroes with common-folk backgrounds, wherein they established their personas as virtuous, egalitarian leaders. Leaders in other states rarely had that level of popularity garnered through films or the cultivated larger-than-life persona that wielded moral authority.

Regionalism after the 1990s (particularly following the Bommai judgment[17]) no longer remained the backdrop for populist mobilization. The growth of regional parties led to the formation of competing coalition fronts on the national stage wherein such regional leaders could use coalition platforms to assert their regional aspirations and otherwise act as veto players when necessary. In other words, they did not have to polarize subnational electorates against national governments to get their interests represented. They could simply aim to win the minimum number of seats necessary to gain a place at the coalition table and play the game of political brinkmanship. Some states were also formed in the late 1990s without populist mobilization, such as Chhattisgarh, or their populist movements were co-opted by nationalist parties, such as in Uttarakhand (Kumar 2011). Thus, it would seem as if regionalism and populism had parted ways by the early 1990s. Regionalism found itself a niche within the national-level party system and no longer had to act as a counter to the same.[18]

Reformist Populism/Neo-Populism

Coincidentally, the 1990s was also the period of the beginning of market reforms, apart from democratic deepening as seen through the increasing participation of regional interests. Literature from many countries that went through contemporaneous dual transitions has pointed out the intriguing capacity of populism to reinvent itself on the political landscape, from that of a patronage-based populism in the ISI era to re-appear as a neoliberal technocratic version that vilified the former. Some Indian states followed a similar script (Andhra Pradesh under Naidu, Gujarat under Modi, West Bengal under Banerjee).

One could argue for some other potential reasons behind the emergence of market populists, apart from the mainstreaming of regional politics. The first has to do with the ability of transnational institutions to directly affiliate with subnational governments to promote market reforms. Subnational lending by the World Bank was authorized around 1996, which created the opportunity for the bank to scope for potential regional chief ministers as liberalizing partners to legitimize and deepen market reforms in a context where some early experiments had failed (Odisha electricity sector privatization) and threatened to undermine the bank's nascent legitimacy in the Indian state (Kirk 2005).

The second reason has to do with the rising aspirations of the urbanizing middle class (Mooij 2007). The proliferation of technical education and ostensibly associated upwardly mobile economic opportunities that were now accessible to ascendant dominant castes, coupled with the rise of the informal sector that frayed agrarian affiliations, and the growing influence of regional business elites who allowed only partial liberalization so as to capture and protect their own interests against more powerful market forces (Kohli 2006) seem to have converged to create an electorate that squarely focused on the governance capacity of states to promote a better quality of life, starting with economic opportunities. Thus, while Mandal and *masjid*[19] were well-established concurrent agendas, markets were also now ripe for the picking.

The third reason has to do with the institutionalization of the state-level party system. Scholarship has shown that where parties tend to get frozen or cartelized, that is, when parties alternate in public office to collude and share public resources and monopolize access to public institutions, their voter linkages tend to weaken over time when social cleavages become more fluid as a result of social mobility, middle class expansion, and societal secularization. Arguably, Mamata Banerjee would be such an example. That is, parties "are no longer what they once were" as the political system looks more like a "partyarchy," and consequently become more susceptible to orthogonal claims by party outsiders. In such a situation, come election time, one speculates that parties tend to rely on candidates more than their programs, thus encouraging electoral switching. Electoral switching seems also to occur where there are negative economic shocks, as it further legitimizes the idea of "throwing the rascals out of office" and forces parties and candidates to switch alliances to diffuse responsibility and potentially avoid economic voting. Under such circumstances, established parties and their candidates could potentially create the perception of a political class that has to be challenged by a political outsider. Put another way, populists bring to the fore reform issues that remained hitherto orthogonal in the political arena and are able to come to office because of under-institutionalized party systems wherein both candidate selection and voter choice are volatile.

Urban Populism

The third phase that has emerged belongs clearly to the urban politics space—the populist of the city state. In the larger canvas of Indian politics, Kejriwal's emergence may well be seen as a one-off event. However, the day is perhaps not far away when the politics of urban spaces may well overshadow the staple canvas of agrarian Indian politics. Such urban politics is characterized by fraying social hierarchical relations, loose party affiliations, greater inequality than poverty, and greater exposure to unmediated forms of political mobilization, which altogether would make proximate causes for the emergence of what can be described as urban populisms. The populism identified with Kejriwal was mostly targeted against the chokehold that established national parties had over Delhi, but the division is fundamentally between the powerbrokers in the city and the informal sector. With the expansion of urban spaces, Kejriwal's case is one such instance of perhaps more to come when urban politics becomes as important if not more important than rural politics.

In sum, while the aforementioned three kinds of populisms—regional, economic, and urban—are overarching themes that have occurred sequentially in India but can also occur concurrently, the subsequent chapters will discuss variations within each of them by comparing them across common attributes of populism.

Design and Methodology

This work takes a set theoretic approach using qualitative comparative analysis (QCA) to understand the attributes that constitute populism in India. Since the study is an attempt to identify and explain the configurations of attributes that constitute a concept, it is important to distinguish this study from those studies that causally frame problems in the social world and explain how that distinction contributes to our understanding of knowledge in general and populism in this instance.

At a time when Latin American and European countries were electing populists to handle the tumult of democratic and economic transitions in the 1990s, populism was being scrutinized for its meanings and implications. Weyland's (2001) landmark essay argued for understanding the concept as having an attribute at its core (classical view) instead of seeing it as having a combination of attributes related with each other either by an "And" (cumulative) or "Or" (radial) conjunction. And in that vein, he argued that populism is essentially a plebiscitarian strategy by an authoritarian leader.

Using the essential properties as an approach to concept building in populism seems to run the risk of reinforcing the core when the actual problem is at the boundaries of the concept. For example, Mudde states that the ideational approach "does not deny the importance of leadership or organizational structures … but it is neither a necessary condition for electoral breakthrough nor a sufficient condition for electoral persistence…. It has an elective affinity with charismatic leadership and weak formal organizations, but these are not defining features of populism" (2017: 40). On the other side, Weyland agrees that the ideational approach has seen a revival, but apart from the false positives problem, he argues that the invocation to the people inevitably ends up vesting the power with the leader, and so the invocation is essentially a means for the goals determined by the leader on her own (Weyland 2017: 54). And so, for Weyland, "contrary to discursive and ideology centered notions, Manichean rhetoric does not form the core of populism as a potentially bottom-up movement but serves as a top-down instrument for personalistic leaders." (2017: 59).

This boundary reinforcing predilection is not just an academic challenge but also reflects in the public commentary on populism. Building an argument that focusses on the core tends to reinforce positions. One should question, really, whether such reinforcements can lead to a commensurable and shared perspective. For instance, with the rise of Modi, a think tank downgraded India's status as a democracy, concurrent with the backsliding of other big democracies in the world witnessing the emergence of the populist radical right in the recent past (Alizada et al. 2021). Under Modi's watch, there have been arrests of human rights activists and political leaders, including chief ministers; journalists have been silenced or attacked; Muslims have been killed and tormented for eating beef, wearing the hijab to college, or falling in love with Hindu girls; and crony capitalists have been given free reign, altogether threatening the liberal foundations, indeed the very idea of India itself. However, under Modi's watch one has also seen the streamlining of the goods and services tax (GST), the popular hawkish approach to Pakistan, the promotion and successful reach of various welfare schemes, some would argue demonetization, the rise to become a global power, and so on.

I think the point is whether going down an ever-lengthening list of merits and demerits is the approach to empirical analysis that is most persuasive because it brings to bear evidence to a question, and if it is, whether that form of persuasion is the way to think of inquiry in the social world. An emphasis to reinforce the core repeatedly through various instantiations does not sound convincing because it may very well be an argument on a loop, reinforcing what are some core positions wrapped up in alternate forms and argumentation. The question as to whether populism is a threat or corrective cannot depend on who you ask. What we are really interested in knowing is the "thinking"—or the wiring, if I may—of the persons we ask so that we can establish some level of coherence that is behind the core of these concepts.

The problem with an essentialist approach is that the polarized points of view are comprehensible but inscrutable because the "wiring" is not that visible. The approach to understanding intention within the social world has become contiguous with what Mahoney terms as essentialist reasoning in the natural world and argues that it is not appropriate for the scientific study of social reality (Mahoney 2021). Derived from Lakoff (1987), which summarized two decades of research across various disciplines showing that categories do not derive meanings from their correspondence to entities in the natural world, Mahoney argues that social scientists seem to have no choice other than at least acknowledging an inescapable role for human minds in creating and sustaining social categories. He is not arguing for relativism, where logic is assumed to be "an artifact of the kind of bodies and brains that human beings happen to possess" (Mahoney 2021: 5), but for a conceptual space that reflects the meanings of the category for the individuals who use and understand the category. This is not about a consensus around the meaning but the coherence around a category. The existence and utility of a concept depend on shared knowledge and shared understandings of its meanings among communities of individuals (Mahoney 2021: 7). Under this perspective, social categories refer to "particular entanglements of human understanding and aspects of objective reality. They are interactions between conceptual spaces in human minds and entities from the natural world" (Mahoney 2021: 7).

These interactions between conceptual spaces are perhaps best approached through the set theoretic method. Like causal methods, the approach is interested in explaining a relationship between conditions and outcomes, but unlike causal methods, the relationship is sought to be understood as constituting configurative relationships. In understanding the relationship between conditions and outcomes, the attributes are not looked at as variables but as members belonging to certain sets. That is, variables are commonly measured by indexing them according to some standard (say, central tendency) that is derived internally from the data. Membership, on the other hand, is a measure that indexes whether one is a member or not by deciding boundaries that are external to the data. That is, measurements are calibrated by standards external to the data and not internal (as a derivation from some average or such). Chapter 4 of this book deals with the distinctiveness of this method compared to quantitative approaches.

Thus, the research design is set theoretic based, because populism is right now an under-explored concept that does not seem amenable to tether to any core attribute because of the diversity across contexts, and instead seems more adaptive to understanding the same as a concept discursively constructed in the social world. Further, two distinctive features of the QCA method make it the appropriate method to analyze populist attributes.

First, the study recognizes the existence of equifinality—that is, a scenario in which alternate factors can produce the same outcome—and is not really interested in isolating causal variables from one another to purify the estimate of each variable's separate effect. There is no single factor or even single combination of factors that can cause or constitute populism, but can do so only together with other conditions that are now well known as conjunctural causation—many of these conditions can be understood as SUIN or INUS[20] conditions and are explained later in the book.

Second, the study recognizes the asymmetry of concepts to embrace social complexity, and therefore they are mostly amenable to a set relation rather than a co-relation. A correlational concept is a purely symmetric concept because when it tests for the presence of a cause and the presence of an effect, it tests equally for a connection between the absence of the cause and the absence of the effect. Because it is symmetric, it is blind to set theoretic relationships. Set theoretic relationships can test for both the presence and the absence of the cause and effect and they are not symmetric. For example, development and democracy can be correlated, but in a set theoretic relation, the assertion "developed countries are democratic" does not require that not developed countries be not democratic. There can be, and are, many not-developed countries that are democratic, and their existence does not count against the initial claim, and so such a claim is asymmetric (Ragin 2014: xxvi).

It is important to mention that QCA shares a deceptive affinity with quantitative methods because it, more recently, relies on the numerical and computational capacity of software to provide insights into the social world. But, to clarify, it is essentially a comparative approach that relies on the algorithmic capacity of computers, and so one has to resort to numbers because that is the language that computers understand. However, the computational capacity has also helped to address certain standard criticisms of the approach, and these will be dealt with in the chapter on the data and its results.

Overall, this book opens a new front in populist scholarship by arguing that populism is not a mobilization of the people or a mobilization by a leader, but a mobilization *against* someone. The people and the leader are well-established axes to understand populism, whereby the elite are an additional feature to distinguish the people. This book makes the case that the other can be the third axis around which populism is mobilized. Populism is a construction achieved by drawing a boundary against someone and leaving open a capacious, rolling invitation to whoever wants to join the "us" group. It is a rallying against some group, around whom many people who are anxious about the future cohere, because it resonates with their lived experiences. The other can be from above, such as Congress party bosses, Delhi Khan Market elites, liberal secular groups, or can be from below – Tamil and Bihari migrants, religious minorities, urban Naxals, and such. Further, this kind of populist strategy can emerge only when people are anxious about their futures such that they are willing to take risks of voting in populists, or only when there are latent populist attitudes that get triggered by programmatic content offered by populist leaders.

This book arrives at this conclusion through a process akin to solving a jigsaw puzzle. When confronted with a brand new puzzle, all the pieces seem very different at first. But then, we first identify some common principles (boundary pieces, recognizable features, color patterns, and so on), and thereafter we identify the pieces that either fully or partly reflect these principles. Next, we work on organizing these pieces into smaller groups as logical clusters by fitting them with each other, and slowly a pattern may emerge. Perhaps one can describe this process of puzzling as a sequence comprising principles, pieces, clusters, and patterns.

Similarly, this book identifies five principles that are commonly used to describe populism and explains their relevance in the Indian context in Chapter 2. Invocations to the people, the setting of boundaries, political leadership, populist attitudes, and anxieties about the future are the five parameters discussed within the comparative and the Indian scholarship. Considerable attention is paid to the invocations to the people characteristic because of its unquestioned primacy in Western democracies owing to its particular genealogy there, but I argue that it is a sufficient and not a necessary condition in the Indian context because of its particular history here. Next, we identify the pieces, that is, the cases of populist leaders, that fully or partly reflect these principles and explain their membership in each of these principles in Chapter 4. The research identifies around 16 leaders responsible for 37 populist instances that can be considered fully populist or otherwise, and the cases in between, and justifies their membership in each of these buckets. Chapter 3 is an introduction to the formal method that is referred to as puzzling here—the set-theoretic comparative methodology using the QCA method. Those unfamiliar with the methodology and the method and want to learn to do a QCA will find this chapter useful. Chapter 5 reports the results and identifies the patterns (the necessary and sufficient conditions) and the cases and how they cluster to create particular configurations that describe the logic underlying the pathways to populism in India. Chapter 6 rounds off the analysis by identifying cases that would remain robust even when circumstances (data, conditions, parameters, and so on) change and concludes by arguing why this argument is important now because many challenges pertaining to the Indian condition remain unresolved by the extant theory.

What this book does not do in arriving at the conclusions is provide an in-depth analysis of each of the cases, and so those looking for rich case study descriptions of these leaders may be disappointed. This book is not a comparative history of populists, as such a task would be beyond the scope of this book, but instead is a comparative analysis using narratives of such leaders that provide a sound but nevertheless basic description of the leaders.

Much public commentary around populists, or similarly polarizing topics, eventually competes into shouting matches that rely on a drumming of facts, personalities, and talking points where basic questions often remain marginal because they are seen as being of academic and therefore marginal interest. We need to, for instance, understand what populism is and what its relationship is with democracy and its constituents before we make up our minds as to whether populism is a threat or corrective to democracy. This book will be of interest to those who are interested in these theoretical questions and are keen to learn the means to unpack such questions, especially when it is known that the answers to such questions are inherently configurational or intersectional.

Notes

1. The authors refer to a similar parallel by Theda Skocpol and Margaret Somers, who describe splitters as those who generally follow their method of "contrast of contexts" and lumpers as those who follow their method of "parallel demonstration of theory" (Skocpol and Somers 1980).
2. Mahatma Gandhi (Ionescu and Gellner 1969; Subramanian 2007) and Periyar (Subramanian 1999) have been referred to as populists when they were politically active from 1915 till around the mid-1940s. Arguably, and ironic when we think of how populists are viewed now, it was these populists who sought greater democratic participation within the imperial democratic institutions.
3. India's experience has its share of populists from the right, left, sub-national, national, neoliberal, anti-political, and so on.
4. Those familiar with Indian politics will be familiar with the cases of Chandrasekhar Rao (Telangana) and Mamata Banerjee (West Bengal), being subnational democratic populists currently while Modi is the prime minister.
5. A Narendra Modi in Gujarat and a Chandrababu Naidu in Andhra Pradesh are not the same kind of neo-populists, though they were similar in their disposition to market reforms.
6. Jaffrelot and Tillin have been the first to categorize the various strains across India into anti-establishment (against the political machine and an agrarian type), Hindu nationalism, and regional version (Jaffrelot and Tillin 2017). However, as they point out, the list is not exhaustive, and the examples and the categories might require further iterations before one settles the question of framing the varieties of populisms in India.
7. That is why populism and nationalism go very well together; the latter provides the former with the foil of history and the former gives the latter the

platform for legitimacy. Survey research shows that they are co-occurrent and the people do not see them as the same (Jenne et al. 2021). For an excellent discussion on the distinctions between the two, see Varshney (2021).

8. A distinct opinion that shares the same degree of valence associating people with populism comes from Mueller. But, acknowledging that every politician invokes people, he points out that the populist is distinctive because they cast this idea against elites and for, and only for, the *plebs*, who are the real and true people (Muller, 2016).

9. ISI stands for import substituting industrialization—a dirigiste economic strategy followed by most developing countries that allowed the importation of capital goods to build capacity to produce cheap exportable consumer goods such as electronics and vehicles. Politicians in this era sustained their power through patronage and subsidies (whereby this kind of fiscal redistribution, or profligacy, was referred to as populism) under authoritarian forms of control (Dornbusch and Edwards, 1990).

10. Much of the scholarship that described the neoliberal reformers during the 1990s in Latin America was aligned with this approach (Levitsky and Cameron, 2003; Levitsky and Loxton, 2013; Weyland, 1996).

11. There were many political leaders and parties that emerged in the early 1980s that asserted themselves against the one-party dominant system of the Congress party, but only some among them took the populist turn.

12. Goertz suggests that the basic level of a concept is best understood when we identify the positive pole and explicitly analyze the negative pole and the tipping point between them, as that would help identify the concept and justify the empirical distribution of the cases (rather than have the distribution of the cases presume the concept) (Goertz, 2006: 43).

13. Following Goertz (2006), I should have ideally identified a single continuum wherein I can demonstrate social movements, personality-based leaders, and authoritarian leaders on a single negative pole and then identify and select cases under these labels as negative and irrelevant or some other version thereof. Suffice it to say that these concepts are considered "NOT" populism cases, and the path chosen for now is a concept structure based on necessary and sufficient conditions. It does, however, seem possible to conceive an alternate populist research project where the scope conditions are broader and the attributes across these concepts are substitutable as part of a family resemblance concept structure.

14. Bal Thackeray is probably a clear example of this kind of sentiment. However, I do consider him among the cases under study here as an exception because, as I explain in the chapter, he is too central a figure in the politics of Maharashtra to be excluded because he did not put his name on the ballot.

15. For example, in an interview to her alma mater explaining Trump's rise to power, journalist Megyn Kelly pointed to this quite pithily. "When you have people controlling the newspapers and the airwaves, not to mention Hollywood and other circles of power, who are judgmental of and dismissive of the points of view of those in fly-over country, it leads fly-over country to want to revolt," she says. "And they get to the point where they don't really care about ideology. They just care that they have somebody who's going to crush these institutions that they know do not respect them" (Rodgers 2018).

16. One has only to look at the press coverage on "love jehad" and slaughterhouses and the reports that came out during the second wave of the pandemic in March 2021 to understand the extent of the bigotry, delusion, and the resultant draconian tactics unleashed by the regime (for example, see the articles here: https://caravanmagazine.in/tag/uttar-pradesh). Also see Jha (2022).

17. In 1988–89, the S.R. Bommai government in Karnataka had an unstable legislative majority because of splits, mergers, and defections among legislators in the state assembly, prompting the governor to impose President's rule in the state. The Bommai judgment refers to a Supreme Court judgment responding to a writ petition challenging the validity of the imposition by the central government. Among other things, the judgment essentially validated that the legislative majority should be decided on the floor of the house, thereby curbing the arbitrary use of Article 356 justifying the imposition of President's rule (https://articles.manupatra.com/article-details/Case-Comment-on-the-Supreme-Court-Judgement-SR-Bommai-V-Union-Of-India).

    Additionally, on hindsight, it could be argued that the judgment blunted the ability of central governments at that time to drive a wedge between state-level political adversaries by playing one politician and his loyalists against others. The use of Article 356 has certainly reduced though contestations around legislative assembly majorities have generally continued.

18. However, one cannot discount the possibility of regional populism in the future. For instance, while I describe a version of populism that was pitted against the national elites in the 1980s here, regional populist claims could very well be pitted against subnational or city elites or state governments in

the future as newer versions of "people" are constituted, such as the eventual culmination of the Telangana movement into a state in the early 2000s.

19. Politics after the 1990s was predominantly preoccupied with two fundamental transformations that polarized the public. The first was related to the additional 27 percent reservations for the backward classes as suggested by the Mandal Commission and implemented by the V. P. Singh government that led to divisions for and against the reservation. The second was the destruction of the Babri Masjid in 1992 that deepened the divide around Hindu majoritarianism. That is, identity politics dominated the political arena in the early 1990s, but soon enough issues and opportunities associated with market reforms began to acquire political salience (Rudolph and Rudolph 2001).

20. SUIN stands for "A Sufficient and Unnecessary condition that is itself Insufficient but Necessary." INUS stands for "An Insufficient but Necessary condition that is itself Unnecessary but Sufficient." Both reflect combinations of necessary and sufficient conditions.

2

The Sufficient and Necessary Conditions of Populism

To compare is to "assimilate" and to discover deeper or fundamental similarities below the surface of secondary diversities (Sartori 1970). This chapter will discuss the underlying conceptual attributes of populism and how they have been constructed as they provide the background for indexing the cases in Chapter 4. The intention behind parsing populism into its underlying conceptual attributes is to be able to identify how they configure with each other to constitute the various populisms in India. And since set theoretic analysis is the approach adopted here to understand these configurations, this chapter will also translate these attributes and their constructs as necessary and sufficient conditions.

At this point, it may be helpful to step back from populism and understand the construction and the kind of concept structure being used and why that justifies the need for sufficient and necessary conditions and the downstream analysis that follows. The description provided here is a simple adaptation of the framework outlined by Goertz (2006). The concept structure being used here is multilevel and multidimensional. A multilevel concept has a basic structure, reflected through the secondary level as visible attributes whereby each attribute in turn can be measured through indicators as membership scores (in this project) or as variables in projects with a quantitative design. A multidimensional concept has different dimensions that constitute the basic level of the concept. The nature of the relationship between the attributes and the basic level can be causal, ontological, and substitutable.[1] In this project, the attributes share an ontological relationship with the basic concept, according to which the various attributes are not just the defining features of the basic concept but in fact are the elements that compose the basic level. The logic by which these attributes conjoin with each other to constitute the concept is based on necessary and sufficient relations as conditions to the outcome. Presented here is first a summary of the attributes of populism, followed by a discussion that characterizes them as sufficient or necessary conditions.

From the discussion in the earlier chapter, one can surmise that those who follow the ideational approach argue that the primary attribute of populism is the fundamental idea of popular sovereignty. For ideational scholars, the people and their will are supreme and are so inviolable that it can undermine the edifice of liberal democratic institutions if the people feel that the latter is not serving their interests. For the strategic scholars, the leader and his direct connection with the masses are supreme, and the leader can bypass intermediary public institutions and liberal safeguards if they interfere with this direct connection. Both approaches agree that the public is divided and polarized where one end represents the people and the other end is demonized as belonging to the "other."

Where they differ is in what they think is the primary attribute—people for the ideational approach and leader for the strategic approach. It is perhaps no coincidence that the strategic approach was the relevant approach in the 1990s when many populist leaders were undertaking the dual transitions of market reforms and democratization and so followed a mostly inclusive approach to legitimize what were essentially risky measures in and of themselves (Roberts 1995; Weyland 1996). The ideational approach was subsequent to this decade of reforms and mostly in Europe, as a conservative nativist backlash against economic anxieties exacerbated by immigrants and waves of refugees coming in from Africa and the Middle East (Mudde 2007).

Thus, from the two dominant approaches to populism, the ideational and the strategic approaches, we can consider the two attributes from the ideational approach to be:

1. People are sovereign
2. There is a fundamental divide between the people and the elitist "other"[2]

And from the strategic approach, the third attribute of populism would be:

3. A populist leader has an unmediated connection with the people

These attributes have been described more recently as "supply side" attributes because they are explicitly expressed by political actors that employ populist language. As mentioned in the previous chapter, this study is also motivated to get behind the wiring of how people understand populism, that is, to understand the political psychology behind the formation of political identities. Scholarship, particularly inspired by the ideational approach, has described the latter as the "demand side" of populism, focusing on innate and latent political attitudes that make people prone to holding the populist worldview (Kaltwasser 2021). This study will also add the demand side to the data analysis by incorporating perceptions such as populist political attitudes and the risk propensity of the electorate as additional attributes.

Thus, popular sovereignty, the divide, leadership as the key core attributes of populism, along with additional demand-side attributes such as political attitudes and risk propensity, altogether individually or as configurations underlie the concept of populism. While these terms have been used very often to describe populism, I use a slightly different set of labels to accurately capture the conditions of interest in this book. I will outline these different concepts and their constructions in the sections that follow in this chapter. Further, I will argue that all these attributes can be considered sufficient conditions,[3] excepting leadership, which I will argue is a necessary condition.

Electoral Invocations to Their People

Populist leaders base their core appeal upon the idea that people's aspirations are not being represented in the political establishment and therefore contemporary democratic representation requires a corrective because it is ultimately the people and not the state that are sovereign. That popular sovereignty is at the core is understandable, based on the experience of liberal democratization in the West, where liberal democracy and popular sovereignty are intrinsically linked. And so, when popular sovereignty disavows the liberal democratic experience by stating that it is elitist, then the unhinging of the two causes an anxiety that the liberal democracies are under threat. If popular sovereignty undermines liberal democracy, then the future of the polity will certainly look weak because illiberal democracy is synonymous with authoritarian rule. I first discuss the genealogy of popular sovereignty and its inextricability with liberal democracy in the West, which justifies thinking about popular sovereignty as a, if not the, core feature of populism.

I then argue, however, that popular sovereignty, liberal democracy, and political rule do not share such an intertwined relationship in India. To be clear, I am not arguing that this is a relationship that is as yet underdeveloped, akin to an anxiety that it needs to measure up to Western expectations. Instead, I will argue that the distances between the three are large enough to be able to accommodate and adapt to their idiosyncrasies such that it need not be considered a necessary concept in the Indian context although it is certainly a sufficient condition. Again, this is not to make an argument that popular sovereignty is a constitutive condition in the West and it is not a constitutive condition in India. Rather, it is to argue that it is a constitutive condition in India like in the West, but the nature of the relationship is not as a necessary condition like in the West but as a sufficient condition in India.

Two more caveats related to this condition have to be mentioned here. First, the more accurate terminology in this project is to identify the populist appeal as an invocation to the people rather than as an invocation to popular sovereignty. However, it is true that the former is deliberately vague, referring to people as a construction, at best as an interpretation (or simplification) of reality (Mudde and Kaltwasser 2017: 9). But this is exactly how it is being used by populists here because references to people are a contingent reflex by the various political leaders at different points in time—varying in ever-widening circles ranging from caste, community, nation to the idea of the "common man." And popular sovereignty is used in the context of a democracy to refer to the accepted notion that ultimate rulership rests with the people. Since most discussions in this project are about people in the context of a democracy, there may be instances when the terms are used interchangeably, though the reference is as an invocation to the people. In this project, the reference is to invocations to the people particularly during elections. Therefore, to be precise as a concept, the condition being referred to here is electoral invocations to their people,[4] thereby locating this condition within electoral politics and where invocations to the idea of people are also located within the frames of reference used by the political leader in that context.

Popular Sovereignty in the West

Democracy is the best form of political rule to promote popular sovereignty because democratic representation has made universal adult franchise possible to govern in the public interest. Consequently, democracy and popular sovereignty are often conflated even though they are not the same in meaning and genealogy.

Sovereignty was formulated in the early modern period between the late sixteenth and mid-seventeenth centuries as a power that, according to Bodin, was supreme, absolute, indivisible, and perpetual (Bourke 2016). In the Greek tradition, the idea of sovereignty also existed but it was understood at the time as tyrannical power. According to them, tyranny is not used in a pejorative sense but in a positive sense to mean to "proceed as one does who rules in the face of resistance," to be "tough and clear eyed about the imperatives of action in a context of resentment and hostility" (Hoekstra 2016: 28).[5] Thus sovereignty, though popular in form, was not termed so, even when in function it was clear that such sovereignty was understood as unaccountable rule (except to God) and meant to keep the leaders in check.

The centrality of popular sovereignty to political rule can be traced back to the origins of constitutional law in the Roman Republic. The first documentary evidence for popular sovereignty as the keystone for law can be found in a bronze tablet in the Church of St. John Lateran legally conferring full public authority of the Roman people upon the emperor (in this case, Emperor Vespasian). And it was this *Lex de Imperio Vespasiani* that was considered concrete historical evidence of the popular foundations of Roman Imperial Authority, known thereafter as Lex Regia. According to Lex Regia, the Roman populus have conferred their original law-making authority to a princeps and thereby legitimized the law-making authority of the emperor upon all Romans (Lee 2016: 8). Subsequent interpretations diverged as to whether this transfer of authority was an irrevocable transfer or a revocable investiture, which in some sense perhaps foreboded the subsequent tensions between popular sovereignty and the liberal democratic public institutions.

Ultimately, Rousseau is credited with weaving the public with ideas of sovereignty and therefore is the starting point for popular sovereignty. He argues that the general will should be obeyed in preference to individual wills because there is "invincible proof that the most general will is also the most just, and that the voice of the people is indeed the voice of God" (Rousseau 1997: 7, 8), thereby making popular sovereignty as sacred as personal faith. And if the general will is obeyed, "this act of association produces a moral and collective body made up of as many members as the assembly has voices, and which receives by this same act of its unity, its common self, its life and its will" (Rousseau 1997: 50).[6] What we have today therefore is the acceptance that people[7] hold a fundamental position in a community and in the political system. Societal conflicts would be primarily disagreements about identifying the common good, which can be overcome by rational discussion; the role of the political process would be epistemic, a search for the true general will (Przeworski 1991: 15).

Hidden in the search for the true general will is the original flaw that populists strike at and take advantage of. The present model of liberal democracy is a gap between how it is imagined to be (absolute power to the people) and how it functions (power being necessarily devolved to elites chosen by people through a competition). Populists expose this pathology by arguing that people's contribution to democracy is little more than participation in the selection of their rulers, and so they contest the form that democracy has taken (elitist capture) but not the principle because they believe that they are the pure democrats as they seek, ultimately, power to the people (Meny and Surel 2002).

It is no surprise then that populist scholarship from the Western world would consider popular sovereignty as the core attribute and consider it a necessary condition for populism. What happens though when popular sovereignty and democracy are not so historically intertwined and consequently are at some distance from each other?

Popular Sovereignty in India

Mapping the trajectory of the evolution of the Indian state upon its society, Kaviraj states, Political analysts often work with the wrong genealogy: the nation state in India is not a structural descendant of modern European states but of pre modern Indian empires" (Kaviraj 2018: 4). These pre-modern Indian empires had little to no connection with popular sovereignty either as an irrevocable transfer or as a revocable investiture. During that period, sovereignty or its analogous form was located in a supreme moral order (one can say religious order) that was considered immutable and beyond the foibles and frailties of human evolution. That is, Dharma was sovereign and not only transcendental in form but also immanent in all political and social arrangements that informed public and private life. Consequently, the content of Vedic kingship was "chiefly power, that could crush the enemies of Rta, uphold Dharma and afford protection to the people" (Sinha 1936: 30). Sovereign power is absolute in the sense that there is no human authority that can contest it, and not absolute in the sense that it is in the end subordinate to a moral framework. The king's power is simply the translation into the human scale of the law, the logic of a given natural and social order (Kaviraj 2018: 46–48).

The logic of subservience to a larger moral order continued during the medieval period under Mughal rule that preceded the British Empire. During the Mughal era, the creation of urban spaces created urban publics. Such urban publics "voted from the rooftops," which is to say that they used the idioms of Islam to question and assert themselves against imperial power, as opposed to just being inert objects inhabiting urban spaces that were principally fashioned out as a stage for the performance and celebration of imperial power (Kaicker 2020). Even though the medieval period was replete with instances of popular upheavals and unrest from time to time, wherein the 1857 revolt is often depicted as the apogee of such popular resistance, Kaicker is categorical in saying that he does not wish to paint it as "a stage in the emergence of popular sovereignty in India. To do so would be to chain it in a teleology towards some universal significance of European provenance" (Kaicker 2020: 307). Further, he reiterates the argument being made in this book that "[t]he nominal claim to sovereignty would not descend upon the people until the adoption of the Constitution of India, ninety-three years after the rebellion of 1857" (Kaicker 2020: 308).

Even in modern pre-Independence India, popular sovereignty was not the original moral core for the evolution of the national movement and a consequent awakening of a political consciousness against British imperialism. Initially, the nationalist movement comprised moderate elites, who sought to be interpreters of British rule to the masses. Their politics was mostly to appeal to the character of British rule "to liberalize it so that India can join a confederacy of Free states, English in their origin, English in their character and English in their institutions."[8] Furthermore, "despite moderate attempts to forge a common political platform and to conceive a common political secular identity, they did not regard the people as a source of sovereign authority. The ideal was their representation in the legislatures" (Sen 2007: 46).

The idea of popular sovereignty germinated in the political discourse in India with the emergence of "Swaraj" in the political discourse led by the Extremist group within the Indian National Congress. Their thinking was considered extremist because they radically departed from the Moderates' view that the British rule was the fulfilment of a providential mission in and for India. As the disparity between British ideals and the impact of their rule upon the lives of the Indians grew, it became clear that real effective control over the executive and legislative institutions should rest with the natives, and that Indians can no longer afford to be sanguine about British control over political power. Of course, such an articulation came with some neo-religious revivalism to deepen and legitimize the ethnos, the Indian political community, but eventually dovetailed into the idea of "Swaraj" as a natural right to have complete and early self-government and independence from Britain (Sen 2007: 55).[9]

Thus, even though popular sovereignty entered the lexicon of political discourse and mobilization in India, it was used to breach existing political order and not as the moral foundation to reinforce political rule. Popular sovereignty was a rallying cry to galvanize resistance against political rule and not yet an approach to political rule itself. This agitational approach took a moral and ethical form under Gandhi and an institutional form under Nehru, and both eventually provided the foundations for the framing of the Indian Constitution.

For Gandhi, popular sovereignty, or Swaraj (in the Indian context), also meant a reflexive practice in that it became defined as a part of the personal moral code to govern one's life.[10] The sovereign exercise of political authority by the people was a requirement of self-government. But he was also clear that by sovereign exercise, he meant direct exercise of political authority by the people. In this sense, he was a pure populist because he did not want people's aspirations to be tainted by centralization, hierarchy, party representatives, and their partisan considerations via the institutional scaffolding that comes with it. In order to keep the people's voice pure, he did not want it to be refracted through elites or through institutions and therefore was skeptical of the Parliament and industry and suchlike. Instead, he felt real freedom could only be achieved by effort from within, that is, by self-purification and self-help, and therefore by the strictest adherence to truth and non-violence (Gandhi 1938).[11]

Nehru was singularly important for leading the national movement and toward creating a political and public institutional scaffolding that was both liberal and democratic in its promise. Nehru seemed to see popular sovereignty in the strategic sense, by equating the idea of the people with the contemporaneous "mass struggle", and valorized Gandhian principles of satyagraha, as it provided both the moral impetus and the necessary conscientization for the creation of a political community. Nehru took the quintessentially Western liberal idea of popular sovereignty as being the constitutive foundation of statehood (irrevocable investiture) but made it his own narrative by arguing that it must be the Indian people and not the British people whose voices should resonate in the institutions.[12]

It was finally Ambedkar, being the architect of the Indian Constitution, who oversaw popular sovereignty acquiring its fullest expression in the Preamble to the Constitution. Skeptical of the obscurantist leanings of Swaraj toward a status quoist sociopolitical hierarchy, Ambedkar pointed out the paradoxical dimension of Swaraj—freedom from foreign domination, which meant destruction of the political order, but it kept intact the social order, which permitted one class to dominate the other and, indeed, on a hereditary basis. "Swaraj would be the substitution of the domination by the British for domination by the Hindus" (Rathore 2020: 44). Additionally, as Chairman of the Drafting Committee, apart from acknowledging the diverse meanings associated with the idea of Swaraj from various religious groups, Ambedkar was certain that abolishing untouchability had to precede Swaraj. In the end, popular sovereignty was no longer orthogonal to the idea of an Indian demos even though it continued to be daunted by Hindu majoritarianism (Ahmed 2022); rather, the project of popular sovereignty that was statist and nationalist in character emerged dominant relative to other contemporaneous projects of popular sovereignty.[13]

In conclusion, popular sovereignty and democracy have historically not been closely tethered to each other as in the West. There is enough space in the interstices between them to allow for alternative or even counter-narratives to emerge and thrive in the Indian postcolonial context. Populism, construed as a version of popular sovereignty, indeed even democracy, can survive within settings such as India, and will not be a source of anxiety such as found in the West, where the coupling of these terms of political order is almost airtight. In fact, viewed comparatively, Jalal has argued that the labels of democracy and authoritarianism obscure more the dynamics between the state structures and political processes than is revealed across India, Pakistan, and Bangladesh. In South Asia, democracy can and often does coexist with authoritarian tendencies of the state, and overt authoritarianism is shaped by power conflicts between elected and non-elected institutions rather than by changes in civil–military relations alone (Jalal 1995).

Based on the preceding discussion, if popular sovereignty is not as tightly tethered to the idea of democracy in India, the question for the purposes of this analysis that arises is whether this condition should be considered necessary, sufficient, or some configuration thereof to describe populism in India. There is no gainsaying that popular sovereignty is a constitutive condition of India's democracy—the question is whether the constitutive condition is a necessary or a sufficient condition. I propose that popular sovereignty in India cannot be considered a necessary condition because it is not the genealogical core of India's democratic evolution. One cannot say for certain, as the analysis will later show, that a populist will emerge only if it is based on a notion of their people in India. Populists can well emerge articulating the venality of the elite or some threat posed by an outsider where the question of popular representation is remedial to what is perceived to be at its core a problem of establishment capture. It is certainly a sufficient condition, because it is almost prosaic to argue now that where there is an invocation to the notion of popular sovereignty in a democracy, specifically some form of invoking the idea of people, one can expect that a populist will emerge.

The Setting of Antagonistic Boundaries

It is commonplace to understand that all social identities, including the idea of the people, are constructed relationally because the meaning of a particular unit within a system can arise in terms of its differentiation from other elements in the same system. In this sense, as Stravakakis (2017) suggests, people would function as markers of the internal division of any political community between the part and the whole, the few and the many, the governing and those governed, those inside and those outside, those above and those below (Stavrakakis 2017: 543). This book refers to the relational identity identifiable as those belonging inside and those outside, that is, those who belong inside a set, and its complement as those belonging outside a set, with the boundary dichotomizing the criteria of membership from non-membership. The boundary is crucial because it determines the size of a set vis-à-vis its complement (big and small; above and below) and its relationship with other sets and their complements (Mahoney 2021: 50). Thus, more than any other label (such as a Manichean ethic, polarization, the divide, and others commonly used in populist literature), boundary setting was the more accurate way to describe what politicians were doing. Of course, the act of setting boundaries is not naïve; it is intended to evoke, anticipate even, the kinds of responses that would come from the act of demarcation. And so, labeling this condition as "boundary setting" helps to accurately capture all the versions and interpretations of this act ranging from emancipatory to predatory.

In a pre-populist world, one could assume that the boundaries would inevitably map onto the standard cleavages that assert themselves during elections or protests and other forms of political mobilization. But in a populist world, the making of boundaries takes on a higher level of salience because it fundamentally can redefine heretofore democratic contestations. Laclau evocatively describes the making of these boundaries as the populist rupture (Laclau 2005). Since his argument is elaborate and terminologically dense, I will describe it by imagining an example of a lived experience.

Imagine that a Mr "X" lives in a multistoried apartment in a city much like everyone else and is relatively anonymous but has had his own share of distinctive life experiences, again, like everyone else. One day, Mr X visits the local motor vehicles department to get his driver's license renewed, where he quickly is given to learn that he will have to grease some palms if he wants to schedule an appointment, never mind getting the license renewed. Both frustrated and irritated because, despite all the talk of e-governance and general hoopla, he feels that nothing much has really changed on the ground. He returns home disappointed, unrelenting to give in, and with the hope that there may be a way out. Upon entering the elevator to go to his apartment, he meets a neighbor who asks him if everything was okay, as he seemed a bit "out of sorts" or chafed at something. He begins to tell his story about the license, but halfway through the story itself, the neighbor cuts him off, saying, "Oh! I know, I know ... I get it. Just the other day when I was going to get my electricity connection restored...," and repeats a similar conclusion to the story, to which Mr X knowingly nods as if he has heard that story before. They both do not have to end their stories—the connection of a shared and equivalent experience of governance has been made.

From my reading of Laclau, what has transpired, resulting from the conversation between the two acquaintances who otherwise are not in any way connected except as neighbors, is the establishment of a "chain of equivalences" with "empty signifiers" (Laclau 2005). Two disparate people are now interlinked or connected (chain) because they each perceive that they have gone through something similar (equivalences) even if the details are different (empty signifiers). This chain goes on and on connecting differentiated "people," where the details are not known, but they seem affiliated because of equivalent lived experiences, thereby rupturing traditional modes of political organization and mobilization. In other words, I may be very different from you, but that does not matter now because we both "get" what "Y" (a populist leader) is telling us. This connection that is experiential, subjective, and real gets articulated discursively by the leader, creating the divide between those who get it and those who do not, and consequently rupturing accepted alignments of standard political mobilization. Such an articulated division can align in concurrence with traditional cleavages, but really its objective is to straddle and overlay upon multiple cleavages and simultaneously differentiate this grouping howsoever vaguely but intuitively defined (flyover country, cattle class, and so on) from a common equally ill-defined enemy on the other side who does not seem to get it (Khan market gang, beltway bandits, and so on). Such a common other is usually part of the establishment and therefore part of the elite.

In essence, populist politics emerges when it ruptures from traditional lines of mobilization by drawing new lines of alignment that are articulated by the populist leader through a discursive construction with the people. Such discursive articulations of divides and consequent political mobilization would naturally fall somewhere within the arenas of the state, market, or civil society because the notion of "people" is invoked in three overlapping senses: as rightful sovereign, as downtrodden class, and as nation respectively (Canovan 2005: 80).

The rupture articulated by a populist will usually, perhaps inevitably, transform into a Manichean division between the people who are "in" with the equivalent lived experiences and those who are "out," that is, beyond the boundary articulated by the leader. Existent research around discursive political articulations of the Manichean divide[14] between the people and elite has shown that the divide can take either inclusive or exclusive approaches along material, political, and symbolic dimensions.

Most populisms in Latin America seem to be inclusionary because they seek to establish, and in Europe seem to be exclusionary because they seek to protect, conditions that are related to the distribution of material goods, political participation, and contestation, and more symbolically restoring the dignity of the people (Mudde and Kaltwasser 2013). In the inclusionary form, populist politics would aim to include hitherto marginalized populations by establishing conditions that redistribute a higher share of material resources to them, empower excluded communities by broadening the vote, and substantively dignify the existence of a people. In the exclusionary forms of populism, the motivations are to deepen nativist engagement by protecting conditions of the "pure people" that are threatened by immigrant incursions (illegal and legal) from above and below and from elite disconnect and/or venality from above. Such exclusionary forms tend to marginalize non-natives from citizenship-based entitlements such as jobs and welfare, preclude them from engaging with the state, and tend to characterize them as deviants and burdensome dependents upon the nation-state. In the inclusionary form, the motivations are to deepen and widen representation within corridors of state power, initiate redistributive programs to enhance coverage, and exclude the elites and other obstructionists through either some form of retribution or through compensatory payoffs.

While populist politics can be described as inclusionary or exclusionary, it does not seem to fully capture the power that populists wield because their connection is not just a matter of corralling the masses to one side or another. The binary does not capture the intensity and fervent nature of the divide. The dimensions on which these centrifugal and centripetal forces work can be more richly described using the logics of equivalence and difference, as first explained by Laclau and Mouffe (2014) in the context of political discourse theory.

The logic of equivalence is the process by which populist discourse typically involves the establishment of linkages between a series of initially heterogeneous unsatisfied demands that enter into relations of equivalence, thus forming a collective identity around the people and the leadership representing them. The equivalence linkages sublimating heterogeneity are achieved through the opposition toward a common enemy, usually the establishment. The term "the people" invariably becomes a marker that internally divides the population, an invisible frontier between the people and those who are not the people. In other words, the logic of equivalence works, perhaps only works, concurrently by articulating a logic of difference wherein the sublimation of differences at one side is accompanied by the creation of a frontier that dichotomizes the social space wherein the other side is occupied by the antagonistic other. And thereby the stage is set for a distinct political antagonism, of sometimes Manichean dimensions, between the populist and the anti-populist blocs (Stavrakakis 2017).[15]

As the latter chapters will show, these logics resonate directly within Indian populist politics because it is almost impossible to construct a logic of equivalence without a logic of difference. That is, considering the bewildering, multiple fragmentations within caste, class, religion, language, and ethnicity, it would be very challenging to construct impervious and clear coalitions unless the difference is made stark enough to make the division politically antagonistic. For instance, imagine two 1,000-piece jigsaw puzzle sets whose pieces are mixed; piecing them randomly together may not help us differentiate which group the pieces belong to because they will look almost indistinguishable. Differentiating the pieces would require a criterion of difference (theme, design, material, and so on) to distinguish the sets.

Similarly, piecing together a coalition would require a clear drawing of a line without which the boundaries of the groups will remain contestable and porous.

An illustration of the logic of equivalence in India is the classic example of Dravidian politics in Tamil Nadu. Historical accounts of Dravidian politics since the early 1900s show that Dravidianism was a construction agglomerated from various caste groups, evoking a resplendent past that was overshadowed and subjugated by Brahmin dominance whose genealogy was from the Aryans and whose provenance is in northern India.[16] Dravidian politics, in its early years that were prior to independence, sought to restore the self-respect of the Dravidians by seeking greater representation in the provincial assemblies, in education, and in the government. Non-Brahmins in the Dravidian movement comprised Tamil-speaking Sudras (other backward and most backward castes), with other groups such as Adi Dravidars, Muslims, and Christians as further concentric circles (Subramanian 1999). One could argue that the logic of equivalence was the dominant mobilizational logic in Dravidian politics, a lived experience antagonistic to the dominance of the Aryans generally and the Brahmins in particular. It was the logic of difference articulated first; the antagonistic boundary was set against the Brahmins, around which the logic of equivalence cohered various other castes by finding common ground from among the lived experiences.

Over the years, Dravidian politics have internally fragmented into several Dravidian parties and populist leaders and their successors after their demise, and the virulence toward the Aryans, north Indians, and Brahmins has muted. Although Dravidian parties have been part of national coalitions, the frontier that divides those who espouse the Dravidian cause from the others persists. Since 1967, neither the Congress nor the BJP, more recently, have governed Tamil Nadu, and this is not likely to change in the near or distant future because they are essentially not considered Dravidian parties.

Populism enmeshed in the vocabulary of the ethnos provides greater sharpness to the logic of difference in India. Narendra Modi as prime minister fronts the populist dimension by invoking a transformative persona bolstered by his majoritarian Hindu credentials within his party and affiliated organizations. Populism and nationalism unsurprisingly seem co-occurrent, akin to similar experiences in Europe and North America (Jenne, Hawkins, and Silva 2021). Bal Thackeray raised the banner of Marathi chauvinism and was for the purging of Muslims and Tamils primarily out of Maharashtra. Maratha sub-nationalism in the democratic sphere was primarily communal and privileged the logic of difference sharply represented by the violence toward the non-Marathas and others opposed to the Shiv Sena (Hansen 2001), even though Maratha consciousness more broadly emerged from a trove of "historical memory," a rich discourse evolving out of shared lived experiences across time in Maharashtra (Deshpande 2007).

While these two illustrations reify a dominant logic at work, as argued earlier, however, it is also possible that the populist is in fact bicephalous, where the divide is sharpened with both logics at work. Indira Gandhi would be such an example. Emerging out of the shadows of the regional party hierarchy, she appealed directly to the people to go over the heads of these party bosses. She constructed a majority by championing many heterodox policies that ostensibly spread patronage to the poor while persistently undercutting the power of regional leaders by splitting the party, undermining state governments through the constant invoking of President's rule and centralizing key constitutional powers to the office of the prime minister, indeed undermining democracy itself through the imposition of Emergency Rule. One could argue that in order to deploy the logic of difference to emerge politically powerful, she had to sustain the logic of equivalence—power through popularity, as she put it (Kenny 2021: 110).

In conclusion here, I would argue that the division is also a significant constitutive attribute of populism. It is created either by any or both the logics described earlier. The condition is titled here as "the setting of boundaries" or "boundary setting" and "Manichean" is often the adjective used in the scholarship to describe the nature of the divide. I am not sure if Manichean would be a consistent enough description across all the kinds of populist divides that exist in India, although they certainly can be antagonistic. An ascendant caste's antagonism toward the upper castes is quite different from Hindu hostility toward Muslims, and they are quite different from the despise toward Biharis or North-Eastern migrants by natives in Mumbai and Bengaluru. I am doubtful whether all of these can be equivalently labeled as being Manichean divides though they are undoubtedly antagonistic. Second, this condition requires an adjective because without it, the act of setting boundaries can be considered value free. But the condition is value laden; it is meant to antagonize, to provoke or to emancipate the people and the out-group.

In conclusion, one could presume that this division exists in configuration with both the idea of the people and the presence of a leader and cannot exist without either. If there is an idea of the people as constructed through the chain of equivalences described earlier, then there is a group that is not of the people. And its obverse, if there is a group that is culpable for democratic disenchantment, that disenchantment can be visible among the people who experience it. In both cases, that division is articulated by a leader, which I explain subsequently. And so, because this setting of boundaries hinges upon the notion of a people or a culpable group and a leader, I would propose that boundary setting is a sufficient condition or an INUS configuration thereof. Since it is configurationally related to other conditions, it can be argued that it may very well be an individually necessary part of a condition that is jointly sufficient for the outcome.

Political Leadership

Within the democratic multi-party system in India, political leadership has not been emphasized much compared to the party system and policies because there is perhaps an implicit recognition that political leaders under such systems are representative of the ideas and interests of the parties and are therefore of secondary interest. Despite much public commentary, analytical studies of political leadership are scarce in India, possibly with the sole exception of an edited volume published in the 1950s (Guha 2010). But the emergence of populist leadership is an exception to this norm, and although it is a crucial core concept, perhaps the dilemma now is whether political leaders create populism or populism creates them.

Populists are exceptions to standard analytical frameworks of political leadership because they are understood to be political outsiders and therefore are political outliers that one may usually ignore. Weyland shows that it was important for the populists to be identified as political outsiders during the period of the neoliberal reforms of the 1990s in Latin America because they did not want to be seen as part of established policies or tainted by earlier mistakes and instead as those with the gumption to cut through the establishment status quoists and undertake transitions. Political outsiders in these cases came as factions either outside the mainstream party elites or just outside of the political system itself, who challenged the established political leadership (Weyland 2002: 47). Ken Roberts argued that populists have usually emerged as orthogonal alternatives when party systems are cartelized and frozen around a narrow set of policy choices that do not allow for voters to differentiate among the parties (Roberts 2017). But the primary motivation that drives both descriptions, as a political outsider or as an orthogonal agenda setter, is that such a leader becomes central to resolving collective action problems (Weyland 2017), especially if the solutions being offered are either heterodox or orthogonal.

While being a political outsider that resolves collective action problems is an important feature, it does not really explain why populists cause such mass anxiety or a restive enthusiasm, depending on where one stands, and why they, among all the other forms of political leadership, are considered a threat or a corrective to democracy.

I argue that populists cannot be of secondary interest because they are not just representatives of larger popular forces, but in fact give it shape and meaning in a manner that undermines the status quo. Populists drive the wedge to create the populist rupture to solve the problems experienced by the people and exacerbated by the others. It is the leader who is responsible for articulating what is an acceptable circumstance that people have resigned themselves to, into that of a problem that ruptures the status quo.

An argument from the policy literature is useful here. A "problem" in the policy literature is primarily a gap between the world as it is and as it should be (Brest and Krieger 2010).[17] This gap is akin to a rupture described in the populist literature. That is, what is described as a problem in the policy literature seems akin to that being described as a rupture in the populist literature. To understand how a policy problem is created, it is worth quoting from the work by Andrews et. al:

> Work is often required to craft problems that can motivate such groups and draw awareness to failures that commonly fester but are routinely ignored or accepted as normal or unavoidable (or too difficult or risky to address)—as is the case with many challenges in development and in government in general. These challenges resemble what Kingdon (1995) calls "conditions" that agents complain about but also accept—like a nagging hip pain one learns to live with. One does nothing to resolve such pain as long as it is a condition one can endure. When one wakes up and cannot walk, however, the condition becomes a problem demanding attention and individuals find the strength to accept needed change (like a hip operation). Similar to this example, Kingdon notes that many social, political, and economic conditions have to be politically and socially constructed to gain attention as

"problems" before we should expect any real change. (Andrews, Pritchett, and Woolcock 2017: 143)

An articulation, as mentioned earlier, is to bring different elements together such that a new meaning is derived from this articulation. Thus, in this context, I am arguing that a populist is able to see a gap from the disparate elements that people accept as a condition, and thereby construct this as a problem and rupture the status quo around it by driving a wedge between the people and the establishment that are supportive of the status quo.

The following are two recent examples that make this point.

The starkest example here would be the initial days of the Aam Aadmi Party (AAP) during the early 2010s. One day in April 2014, people in Mumbai were surprised to see actors such as Ranvir Shorey, Vidya Malvade, and Ayub Khan walking in the streets holding AAP placards that read, "I am not Ranvir Shorey, I am an aam aadmi." Narrating this, Tripathy explains, "Not that these actors were part of India's box office elite, but the fact that they had crossed the threshold that separated celebrities from their fans, for a perceived sense of social commitment, made the exercise a spectacle of sorts" (Tripathy 2017: 77). The foundations of the AAP were on the performative constructs of the broom (its election symbol) that got transformed in AAP's hands from that of a mere cleaning tool to a polysemous symbol of social transformation to disinfect public spaces from mainstream political parties and politicians in general, and the muffler (a scarf used by Kejriwal) and the Wagon R (Kejriwal's vehicle) that resonated with the public as a process of de-elitization of politics and contributed to Kejriwal's charm, restraint, and simplicity (Tripathy 2017).

Another instance, related to Modi, comes to mind. In his first term as prime minister, one of his first acts was to urge the United Nations' member states to declare 21 June as International Yoga Day during the General Assembly session in 2014. Telecasting this day on 21 June 2015, Kedhar provides a description of the event, which is worth quoting:

June 21, 2015: Indian Prime Minister Narendra Modi sits in a cross-legged meditation position with his eyes closed on the lawn of Rajpath ("King's Way"), a tree-lined boulevard that runs from the Presidential Residence to India Gate in New Delhi, the capital of India. It is the first International Yoga Day. Modi is dressed in a crisp white cotton kurta top and matching white cotton pyjama bottom. Around his neck

is a loosely draped scarf in white, orange, and green—the colours of
the Indian flag. His choice of clothing indexes both purity and national
pride; he is at once [a] spiritual guru and political leader. Thousands of
people, all dressed in white T-shirts and dark coloured athletic pants,
are seated behind him on uniform red yoga mats ready to follow Modi's
lead. Modi's signature white beard and wispy hair stand out against the
darkhaired youth behind him. The juxtaposition affirms his position
as the supreme patriarch of the nation, while also being a man of the
people.... (Kedhar 2020: 42)

A broom, a muffler, Wagon R, and a regular practice of yoga are perhaps
staples of humdrum middle class living in India. The example from Kejriwal
is a rupture that brought the elites to the people, and Modi's Yoga Day was
a rupture that brought yoga to the center stage of both national and global
politics. In doing so, Kejriwal was able to rupture the distance between the
aloof celebrities and public places and replace it with a frontier that divided
the common and simple urban classes from those that were corrupt and aloof,
such as the mainstream parties. Modi purportedly ruptured the barriers
between global powers and the local underrecognized traditions of India and
replaced them with those who believe in the new India and those who do not
and continue to hold onto practices of the past.

   Populists tend to be distinct in their ability to create such transformative
ruptures, either inadvertently or otherwise, so much so that they perhaps
also become quite routine. The ones cited here are innocuous, but they are
a natural part of the constructions of populism, and only such leaders seem
to have the felicity to make such moments. Therefore, it would seem as if
populists are a necessary condition[18] for constituting populism because they
have the particular ability to transform conditions into opportunities for
political mobilization. Populism comes into existence perhaps if and only if
there is a populist who can give meaning to it.

   A final note of clarification by way of conclusion to this section to clarify the
adjective (populist) associated with the concept (leadership). This section began
by differentiating populist leadership from other forms of political leadership
by arguing that they are usually political system outsiders and even orthogonal
agenda setters. Populist leadership therefore is a subset of political leadership.
And populist leadership, argued earlier, is a necessary condition for populism,
and therefore is a superset of populism. Visually then, one should see populism
as a subset of populist leadership, which is a subset of political leadership.

Other Attributes: Populist Attitudes and Anxiety about the Future

Popular sovereignty, a populist division, and political leadership are commonly accepted key attributes of populism in extant scholarship. Recent research seems to suggest that these attributes are mostly from the supply side of populism, driven by concepts and opportunities available for agenda setting by political actors. Recent research, particularly from the ideational approach, shows that populism can exist at the demand side as well (Hawkins, Kaltwasser, and Andreadis 2020). They argue that populist attitudes are latent and are a layer underneath ideological and issue positions and are activated by external triggers such as intentional elite behavior, elite collusion, a crisis of moral or political legitimacy, or an economic recession or some such material crisis (Akkerman et al. 2014; Hawkins et al. 2020; Hawkins, Riding, and Mudde 2012). Prolific research nevertheless from European countries in the recent years suggests the following conclusions about populist attitudes. Psychologically, populist attitudes seem to be strongly associated with an anxiety related to the lack of control over a crisis, conspiracy beliefs, and feelings of nostalgia. Sociologically oriented studies of populist attitudes seem to show associations with perceptions of relative deprivation, distance from elites, and so on. Politically, evidence on whether populist attitudes shape vote choices is mixed and on overall support for democracy seems complex where the idea of populism being a threat to democracy is not that clear (Marcos-Marne et al. 2023).

There is no such corpus of literature from India yet from which we can ascertain the spread and depth of populist attitudes. What we do know so far is that among all the various cleavages that characterize Indian politics, survey results seem to show that anti-elitism has the largest and widest spread. Forty-eight percent of the respondents surveyed felt that elites were blocking the progress of people like them, followed by 21 percent for upper castes and 15 percent for minorities and such (Varshney et al. 2021).

Another demand-side attribute that is associated with populism can be broadly described as an individual's perception of uncertainty about the future or, simply put, an anxiety about the future. One analytical measure for perceptions about the future are discount rates. For instance, Kitschelt and Wilkinson argue that discount rates can explain clientelist linkages—higher the uncertainty and precariousness of future income flows (such as among the urban poor), discount rates on the future will be higher, favoring short-term material benefits and preferring targeted handouts rather than distant benefits of policy change (Kitschelt and Wilkinson 2007).

The other concept related to perceptions of the future that has been applied to understanding the emergence of populism comes from prospect theory, used by Weyland to understand the sustenance of neoliberal reforms and democratic transitions in Latin America (Weyland 2002). Innumerable experiments show that people take decisions not on absolute values but in terms of relative gains and losses, using the status quo as their normal point of reference. They are risk averse when better off and risk prone when worse off. Crisis triggers bold actions, while better times induce risk aversion (Weyland 2002: 39). Applied to populist voting, he argues that deep crisis made possible the rise of charismatic neo-populist outsiders who invoked the will of the people against special interests that defended their own privileges against the common good. Further, if such neo-populists were able to sustain the transitions, citizens continued to vote for them to sustain the momentum.

Populist attitudes and anxieties about the future, while distinct, seem to speak to the same idea. If the voters are confronted with a rupture that signals an uncertain future, then a candidate that provides redemption seems more attractive among the available alternatives. Where there are populist attitudes, one can expect the emergence of populism. And where there are perceptions of uncertain futures relative to their current situation, one can also expect the emergence of the same. Further, needless to add, being demand-side attributes, one can also anticipate some configuration thereof comprising the two conditions.[19] In conclusion, one can expect that these conditions are sufficient conditions that can constitute populism.

As far as I know, apart from the survey mentioned earlier, there has been no empirical study of these demand-side attributes of populism in India yet. But the material is available in the various public opinion pre-poll and post-poll surveys, and this study explores the possibility of these conditions being sufficient as a post hoc adaptation of some of the questions available in those surveys, which is explained in Chapter 5 of this book. In Chapter 6, populist attitudes are labeled as "A," and anxieties about the future as "F" in the analysis.

To conclude this chapter, I argue that invocations to the people, the setting of boundaries, and political leaders are commonly accepted core attributes that constitute populism in India. Keeping contextual considerations in mind, I argue that electoral invocations to their people and antagonistic boundary setting are sufficient conditions, and populist political leadership is a necessary condition. In addition, I argue that demand-side factors such as populist attitudes and anxieties about the future are other sufficient conditions that constitute populism. With these propositions in place, I now turn to the chapter that introduces set theory and comparative analysis and follow that up with the chapter on the cases.

Notes

1. A causal relationship between the basic- and secondary-level attributes indicates a "causes of causes" relationship. That is, the relationship between the two levels is such that the basic-level attributes are caused by secondary-level attributes. For instance, one could talk about more proximate causes and more remote causes to describe a causal relationship. A substitutable relationship is neither causal nor constitutive but a relationship where each secondary-level attribute is a substitutable means to a given basic level. For instance, labor can be incorporated via political parties in one way and via the state in another context, and therefore the nature of labor incorporation becomes a substitutable relationship (Goertz 2006: 237–44).

2. To be accurate, Mudde and Kaltwasser consider the people and the general will as distinct core concepts. However, they also mention that the notion of the people is often referred to in combination with other concepts such as sovereignty (Mudde and Kaltwasser 2017).

3. To put it more accurately, one should consider the first two attributes (popular sovereignty, Manichean divide) as belonging to the core basic level and therefore can be considered being individually necessary but as jointly sufficient conditions (INUS conditions). INUS stands for an insufficient but necessary part of an unnecessary but sufficient condition. Its meaning is explained in more detail in Chapter 3. I argue that leadership is a necessary condition, though the results show that it is actually an INUS condition. The last two attributes are sufficient conditions. These nuances are fully explained in the results in Chapter 6. For our current purposes, using sufficient and necessary conditions as a way to describe the relationships between the attributes seems adequate for now.

4. To understand the role that adjectives play in concepts, such as the word "electoral" to qualify invocations to the people, in this project, see the discussion in Goertz (2006: 75–82). I also thank James Mahoney for clarifications on this point.

5. This type of rule is referred to exactly as Anupeuthunos or Aneuthunos, or unaccountable rule, in Greek (Hoekstra 2016: 22).

6. Populists might want to appropriate Rousseau, but Rousseau himself seemed to have been wary of populist demagogues. In *Social Contract* he writes,

> But it is not up to just anyone to make the Gods speak or to have them believe him when he proclaims himself to be their interpreter. The great soul of the Lawgiver is the true miracle which must prove his mission. Any man can carve tablets of stone, bribe an oracle, feign secret dealings with some divinity, train a bird to speak in his ear, or find other crude ways to impress the people. Someone who can do only that much might even by chance succeed in assembling a flock of fools, but he will never found an empire…, the true politician admires in their institutions, the great and powerful genius which presides over enduring establishments. (Rousseau 1997, Book 2, Chapter 8: 71–72)

7. The people is used in two senses here: across time: intergenerational, transcending and outliving its members; and the immediate: living members, a collection of ordinary ever-changing people with their separate lives (Canovan 2005: 6).

8. Report of the Eleventh Indian National Congress 1895, as quoted in Sen (2007: 44).

9. Sen further states that the genealogical origins of the term lay in ancient Hindu sacred texts wherein Swaraj indicates the highest spiritual state where the individual is not merely free from all bondage but is established in perfect harmony with all else in the world. This sense of freedom based on release attained through a high spiritual state is considered equivalent to self-rule or being sovereign over one-self in the political sphere.

10. Gandhi's articulation that eventually focused on the self seems to have originated out of his experience in South Africa. His disappointment with the Crown and Parliament lay in the fact that the basic rights he and others like himself readily enjoyed in London were not protected in South Africa. Globally at the time, the transition from an integrated empire state with an attendant imperial citizenship to congeries of nation-states that circumscribed citizenship status based on birth or race, which South Africa was experiencing along with other parts of the world, disgruntled Gandhi out of South Africa and out of notions of imperial citizenship, mobility across the empire and legal protections, and into India with an original and politicized articulation of Swaraj (Mantena 2016).

11. For Gandhi and popular sovereignty, see Sen (2007: 64–73), and for Gandhi being the first populist in India, see Subramanian (2007).

12. As one of the objectives that went into the making of the Indian Constitution, Nehru introduced the following objective for voting in the Constituent Assembly: "(4) Wherein all power and authority of the Sovereign Independent India, its constituent parts and organs of government, are derived from the people." See Sen (2007: 79). Interestingly, not all members such as the rulers of Princely states were convinced about sovereignty residing among the people even when they were members of the Constituent Assembly, and Nehru was quite abrupt with them to much applause (Krishna 2018).

13. Referring to emerging historiographies of the nationalist movement, Mantena describes alternate projects of sovereignty. One that was prior to provincial nationalism was the idea of imperial citizenship within a federated structure whereby provincial citizens were considered on a par with those of the empire. Both the Moderates and the Princely States in India seemed the primary advocates, but this project was given up because of shifting global dynamics and emergent civic nationalisms which privileged provincial autonomy. The other sovereignty project was not linked to overcoming the empire or about imperial citizenship, but about the anxieties of majority rule under popular sovereignty. In this vein, Jinnah was concerned about majoritarian tyranny in both Hindu- and Muslim-dominated provinces and sought a federated structure with functional devolution and a strong center. Eventually, the Congress preference for the statist nationalist version of popular sovereignty and the preference for Partition over a dual-nation federation led to the disappearance of these alternate projects of popular sovereignty (Mantena 2016).

14. The word "Manichean" originates from the teachings of Mani, a mid-third-century Iranian prophet. Mani preached a form of Gnosticism, a belief in salvation through the acquisition of a body of revealed knowledge. He preached a dualistic religion in which the material world was evil and revealed knowledge was a method of releasing the soul from its imprisonment in matter (Mottahedeh 1985: 159).

    In this sense, the Manichean divide somewhat appropriately captures the yearnings of a populist and those who follow him—that the (political/civil) world is evil and its reality is revealed through the chain of equivalences felt or lived by its people, and given its clearest expression, of course, by the populist leader.

15. Of course, Stavrakakis points out that such binary logic makes sense to explain populism only when it is accompanied by an affective component. That is, there has to be an emotional connect that makes the cleavage

resonate; otherwise, a mere division between the two would remain just so. I agree, and I argue later on that that is why the leader is a necessary attribute because he provides the affective foil to the division. Without such a foil, such divisions are routine matters of redistributive politics. This strand of the argument has been developed in Gudavarthy (2023).

16. The British initially created the categories of Brahmin and Non-Brahmin, which by the turn of the century had become routine administrative categories. Among other aspects of its heritage, Dravidianism was also built upon the foundations of this British idea (Irschick 1986).

17. A similar argument can be found in philosophy and possible world semantics. Social scientists are known to study the actual world—that is, the spatiotemporal arena that we can, in principle, know and affect. They do not typically study non-actual worlds—that is, domains that lack any spatial, temporal, or causal connections to our own. However, non-actual worlds can be both possible and impossible worlds. Possible worlds are worlds that do not violate transcendental truths and are maximal domains that include all parts that have any spatiotemporal relationship with one another. They are as real as actual worlds in that they are hypothetical domains that exist in a person's imagination without corresponding to any natural kind in any real domain. For an excellent discussion, which is summarized here, see Mahoney (2021: 55–61). Populists invoke actual and possible worlds as they articulate the gap or the problem that people confront. I would argue that "Making America Great Again" or "Viksit Bharat" (Developed India) are propositions of possible worlds.

18. My results will show that populist leaders do not meet the standards required to fulfill the condition of necessity, and so this proposition does not hold in this project. The condition is, however, sufficient for the outcome. Nevertheless, I still retain the original proposition here because it seems to follow a logic that supports the idea of being a necessary condition. To argue that whenever there is a populist leader, one can expect populism, which is a sufficient condition, seems to be tautological.

19. It would be challenging to make the case for a necessary condition. For instance, to argue that populists emerge only when there is a populist attitude or uncertainty is problematic because they can very well remain inert until some candidate emerges and articulates their condition as being systemic and not relative, as their lived experience shows.

3

An Introduction to Set Theory Comparative Analysis

When we see data on a spreadsheet, concepts and methods associated with standard quantitative techniques inevitably come to mind. Usually and by default, we try to make sense of the data by deriving the summary statistics to understand what has gone up or down, we explore associations between factors by identifying correlations, and administer technical tests to see if the results confirm, reinterpret, or nullify our research questions and hypotheses.

But is it possible to look at a dataset "qualitatively"? And what would that imply? Is it possible to look at columns and rows and identify relations and configurations between them that are more than associational? At first glance, the possibility of this approach seems incongruous because we usually associate qualitative methods with text and quantitative methods with numbers.

This chapter introduces the reader to a qualitative approach by providing an overview of the set theoretic methodology and the QCA method. An introduction to the methodology and the method is important not just because it is mostly an unfamiliar method to many social scientists, particularly those who work in the Indian context, but also because, as a methodology, its philosophical and conceptual roots are somewhat distinct from standard social science approaches. And, equally important, because QCA relies on numbers and software codes for analysis, it misconstrues expectations since the use of numbers can inadvertently lead to interpretations based on quantitative reasoning.

The origins of the set theoretic methodology in the social sciences, and QCA in particular, are attributed to the work of Charles Ragin and his book *The Comparative Method* (2014), first published in 1987. Disenchanted with multicollinearity and variable-based thinking applied to social science problems, Ragin made the case for a comparative method that neither applies linear algebraic logic nor takes an interpretivist turn, and instead draws from Boolean algebraic logic to address research questions in the social sciences. There is probably no other foundational text that better introduces what is now collectively labeled as the set theoretic method. I would describe the set theoretic method as having undertaken three more substantive leaps. The second leap is, again, with Ragin's scholarship incorporating fuzzy scores and measures of fit as part of the set theoretic method in the early 2000s (Mello 2021: 6; Ragin 2008). The third, to my mind, is primarily the scholarship coming from Europe over the past few years, where we see substantive developments in (and critiques of) QCA and various other configurational techniques inspired by set theory and the enhanced convenience with the development of packages in R.[1] I would argue that James Mahoney's scientific constructivist approach is the fourth leap, making the audacious case to fundamentally question essentialist reasoning of social problems by adopting a scientific logical constructivist approach to social inquiry (Mahoney 2021).

The next section will explain the philosophical foundations behind the set theoretic method and how QCA is distinct from a standard quantitative approach. The subsequent section will introduce the reader to the various steps and concepts that are part of doing the QCA.

The Philosophical Foundations of Set Theory Comparative Methodology

The philosophical foundations of the set theoretic method are based on the idea that the mode of abstraction to explain the social world rests on categories that do not have inner essences of their own but are constructed by the social world. This form of thinking in social science methodology can be traced to Max Weber and to John Stuart Mill's joint method of agreement and difference (Mello 2021: 7).

The most recent validation for incorporating set theory in the social sciences comes from Mahoney, who makes a fundamental distinction between the social and the physical world. According to Mahoney, social science concepts are discursively constructed ideas, as opposed to having an ontology of their own, and cannot be understood through essentialist reasoning. Deriving insights from the scholarship of George Lakoff and from psychological research, Mahoney states that "category meanings are located in cognitive models that structure thought and that reflects both human culture and human sensorimotor constitution" (Mahoney 2021: 4). That is, the social world does not exist *a priori*, waiting for us to discover its essential properties; it exists in the neurological patterns in our heads as images, schemas, and metaphors and, therefore, requires us to derive meanings and establish categories from these patterns to achieve a coherent understanding of the social world. And because set theory is about sets, defined as "bounded entities located in space (mental space, if you will) in which these entities have membership (or not)" (Mahoney 2021: 49), the method is appropriate to constitute meanings and configure relationships from these bounded entities that exist in the social world. Nancy Cartwright summarized Mahoney's argument simplistically: according to him, when you do social science, you are doing sets even if you do not know it.[2] Quite obviously, a constructivist persuasion as a philosophical foundation for the social sciences is not, and may never be, a settled argument. But since it departs from conventional approaches, such a form of thinking and theorizing now can be useful to understand how lived experiences constitute concepts, and vice versa, thereby helping us to better understand the world we live in. For instance, democracy and populism are so conceptually entangled that we encounter the following conundrum: for those schooled in democracy, populism threatens liberal democracies because of its authoritarian and illiberal approach to governance (Levitsky and Ziblatt 2019); and for those schooled in populism, contemporary liberal democratic systems threaten popular aspirations because venal elites have captured and made institutions effete, thereby forsaking the original promise of our republics (Mounk 2018a, 2018b). Consequently, we seem to be at a conceptual quandary, where our register of meanings around democracy are divided, and we have no fresh approaches to cohere out of this polarized space. Understanding what is inside a concept and what is outside may be one way to start thinking about their relationship again.

Prior to the publication of Mahoney's book or what can now be termed the scientific constructivist approach, set theoretic methods traced the origins of this form of reasoning primarily to the Boolean approach to logical reasoning.[3] Correlational reasoning is the basis of much of the causal explanation, whereby social reality is disassembled into atomistic variables on the assumption that causal relationships exist independent of context. Linear algebra is the mathematical reflection of such correlational reasoning because it allows for the isolation of net effects. However, the set theoretic method is not based on correlational reasoning but on configurational reasoning using case-based analysis, wherein the cases are holistic social entities that are context driven. Factors that are common across these cases, albeit in varying degrees, are insufficient by themselves (hence there is no justification to isolating them), but are necessary parts of configurations explaining the outcome (Rutten and Rubinson 2022). And Boolean algebra allows for the identification of such configurations using "And," "Or," and "Not" relations to create such configurations.

The set theoretic method is a configurational approach that goes beyond not just identifying intersecting conditions, but also to understanding configurations that are equifinal, conjunctural, and where the outcomes are asymmetric. The method recognizes that sets can configure in ways that include the possibilities of equifinality (a scenario in which alternative factors can produce the same outcome), conjunctural causation (single conditions do not display their effect on their own but only in conjunction with other conditions), and asymmetry (the explanation for the non-occurrence of the outcome cannot be automatically derived from the explanation of the outcome) (Schneider and Wagemann 2012: 6). And to repeat, the recognition of the existence of these possibilities is through situations where they relate through the Boolean logic of "And," "Or," and "Not" relations, and can produce both the outcomes of interest (Y) and the non-outcomes of interest ($\sim$Y). Within set theoretic methods, QCA is the tool most associated with set theory methods because it allows for causal explanations, makes use of truth tables (which helps to visualize the various configurations and relevant cases), and the principle of logical minimization whereby empirical information can be summarized in a parsimonious manner to draw inferences from cases that share the same outcome (Schneider and Wagemann 2012: 9).

In sum, the philosophical foundations of set theoretic methods can be found ontologically in a constructivist perception of the world, which can be conceptualized using the Boolean approach to logical reasoning. Such form of reasoning inherently thinks of factors as being configurational, and the latter in turn facilitates social world explanations where the conditions (factors) are conjunctural, equifinal, and the outcomes are asymmetric. I now turn briefly to understanding the QCA better and how it is distinctive from a standard dataset.

How Is a QCA Dataset Different from a Quantitative Dataset?

A QCA dataset on a spreadsheet looks just like any other spreadsheet where the columns are features of the phenomenon being studied and the rows are the various instances of these features. In quantitative methods, the columns would be understood as variables and the rows would be the units of analysis of these variables. In QCA, the columns are understood as conditions and the rows as cases, but neither conditions nor cases are the same as variables or units.

A good method needs a good vocabulary because it signifies using precise words and phrases that express what the method does, and allows researchers to clearly articulate their findings in a way that is consistent with the method (Rutten and Rubinson 2022). The need for such a vocabulary is even more relevant for QCA. Because of the predominance of causal or correlational thinking when it comes to the use of numbers to research social realities, there is an automatic, mostly inadvertent, subsuming of QCA within a quantitative form of thinking. And so, vocabulary becomes crucial to make the point that QCA is fundamentally different from quantitative reasoning in both thinking and analysis of social problems.

Therefore, it becomes important to distinguish between variables, conditions, cases, and units to avoid these slippages. First, a variable is a distribution of a characteristic of a population, abstracted from cases, and is usually represented along columns. The distribution describes variation at the level of a population—that is, the extent to which the dimension varies from a base number—and various such distributions allow one to calculate correlations between them. The column in QCA, on the other hand, is a condition (not a variable) and is described not as a distribution, but as a "set." Sets can be imagined as container-like entities where things that belong to the entity are inside, and the rest are outside the containers. Another way is to understand sets as entities that are created by setting boundaries of inclusion (exclusion).[4] Both are ways of thinking of the space either as the line that divides or the content of each entity across the lines—a case can be inside or outside a bucket or a line. Either way, these sets constitute the conditions that can be related to an outcome. We make sense of the world and our relationship with it by looking at things and assessing whether they fit or do not fit our concepts (inside or outside of our concepts), and how they configure with each other, to derive meaning and provide explanations related to the world.

Second, the rows in a dataset in both the quantitative and the QCA methods are termed as cases and are the units of analysis. A case is a unit that is located in time and place. It is a spatially delimited phenomenon observed at a single point or over some period of time (Gerring 2011: 1137). Cases as units of analysis in quantitative methods are the rows that exhibit the various characteristics of the variables. They are also a sample of a larger population, which implies that the units should exhibit or replicate the diversity of the population that they represent. In the QCA method, cases are holistic entities with a variety of characteristics, some of which are captured as sets, but they are mostly entities that are reflective of a context. Cases are selected based on scope, conditions that define the population to which the findings may be generalized. That is, knowing what the case under consideration is a case of would reflect the scope of the findings (Rutten and Robinson 2022).

There are many more terms and concepts that feature as part of QCA and are better learnt while doing the method. The following section will walk the reader through how to do a QCA.

Doing a QCA

QCA is a case-based analysis of the various configurations that are related to an outcome. It is easily done using RStudio because of the functionality of R, though other software packages are also available.[5] There are some mandatory steps to doing a QCA:

1. Organizing the dataset
2. Calibration
3. Necessary and sufficient conditions
4. Parameters of fit: consistency and coverage tests
5. Truth table analysis
6. Logical minimization and solution terms
7. Robustness checks related to sensitivity to calibration, consistency thresholds, case fitness, and case parameters.

Presented here are the details of each step.

Organizing the Dataset

The first step in doing the QCA is to organize a dataset where the columns are the conditions of interest and the outcome, and the rows are the various cases. By this stage, one should have some theoretical premises to state that the conditions and their configurations will have some relationship with the outcome. Case selection can be done from a given population, from scope conditions that provide the parameters of what the cases are a case of, or through a purposeful selection of cases that have value for the outcome (Mello 2021: 24).

Knowing the cases well cannot be emphasized enough—as it is the principle upon which the remaining steps are scaffolded. Eventually, one would like to arrive at a case(s) that best describes the results of the configurations to be able to tell a story that contributes to our theoretical knowledge of concern (Oana, Schneider, and Thomann 2021) and also be able to discern the cases that suit the conditions but the outcome was absent (negative cases) from the irrelevant cases (Goertz and Mahoney 2006). How many cases should one have is a standard question; ideally, one should have as many cases as the number of configurations of conditions possible to allow for the possibility that all configurations can be accounted for, though getting that spread may not be possible (Schneider and Wagemann 2012). A more specific answer would be possibly around 4–5 cases per condition, and anything outside of 20–50 cases would make them amenable to other methods (Mello 2021).

Calibration: Boundary Setting for Making Sets

Calibration is the most crucial criterion that helps to decide the membership of cases. It is a theoretically informed judgment determining the point at which a unit can be considered a case of a condition and, contrariwise, when it is not such a case or some fuzzy version thereof. Calibration processes help to assign membership scores within sets to such empirical information (Schneider and Wagemann 2012: 32).

As mentioned earlier, set relations methodology rests on a Boolean logic that can take on values between 0 and 1, where 0 is equal to being a non-member and 1 being a full member of a set. Calibration is a process that transforms any numerical distribution into scores that fall between the values of 0 and 1,[6] making such scores amenable to Boolean forms of analysis. Calibration is an important step because it sets the boundaries in a set by deciding which values distinguish set membership of a certain condition.[7] Such boundary setting becomes important especially when set memberships are fuzzy, because the concepts can be clear but there is little clarity on how they should correspond with empirical estimates. That is, we may know what goes into and remains out of a concept, but when we have a numerical distribution that instantiates the concept, it is not always clear where to exactly draw the line to distinguish the concept from the non-concept when there is no theoretical justification to draw that line.

Additionally, much of data-driven social science research relies on statistical intuitions related to a central tendency to distribute the data, but such intuitions do not find a place in QCA-based reasoning because relying on statistical measures that are informed by the data itself does not help us to better understand the meanings and distinctions between varying magnitudes of the concept that is meant to be captured.[8] For example, while water boils at 100 degrees Celsius, it does not help us understand what we think or feel is hot, warm, fiery hot, or just "normal" water. We need to think of thresholds associated with these categories so that we can better understand what the hotness of water means and decide which degrees on the Celsius scale we think of water as being very hot, more hot than cold, more cool than hot, and very cool (Ragin 2008: 71–86). For the purposes of this project, I explain in Chapter 5 what it means to be a full populist, "more in than out populist," "more out than in populist," and "not a populist."

Necessary and Sufficient Conditions

Once a dataset is calibrated, it is ready for analysis. The first step in the analysis is to identify which conditions or combinations of conditions are necessary or sufficient, or some other combination that is constitutive of the outcome of interest.

Necessary Conditions

A necessary condition can be formally stated as "X ← Y", where Y is the outcome and X is the necessary condition and which translates as "Y only if X". That is, the outcome Y can only be present if X is present. It is not always the case that if X is present, Y should also be present. For example, we can say that those who take the final exam can only do so if they have attended classes. Attendance then becomes a necessary condition for taking the final exam.[9]

In set relations, X condition would then be considered a superset, and Y outcome would be the subset, as shown in Figure 3.1.

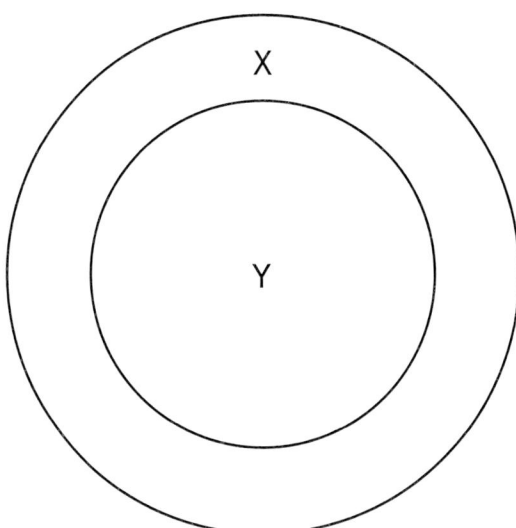

Figure 3.1 Necessary Condition

This illustration is easy to understand when membership can be organized into a crisp set, but necessary and sufficient conditions can also be understood as a 2 × 2 table, which is intuitively important to appreciate when data is fuzzy and can be plotted on an XY chart. For now, a necessity condition can also be understood as crisp set (taking on values of only 0 and 1), for example, through the 2 × 2 table and its four quadrants, described in Table 3.1.

The four quadrants in this table are labeled as A, B, C, and D. Condition X is on the *x* axis, and outcome Y is on the *y* axis and take on values of either 0 or 1. Cases should be in quadrants A, B, and C, and the more the cases in Quadrant A, the more the condition can be identified as being necessary for the outcome. Quadrant A has values where X = 1 and Y = 1. Quadrant B has values where X = 1 and Y = 0. Quadrant C has values where both are 0, and quadrant D has values where X = 0 and Y equals 1. We do know that for X to be a necessary condition of Y, it must be a superset of Y, and so will have cases where the outcome set is smaller than or, at the maximum, equal to the condition set.

Table 3.1 Necessary Conditions

	1	Quadrant D No Cases	Quadrant A Many Cases
Outcome Y	0	Quadrant C Not Important Cases	Quadrant B Some Cases
		0	1
		Condition X	

In quadrant A whenever Y the outcome is present, X the condition is also present. Cases in quadrant B would be where X is 1 and Y is 0. Such cases are inside the superset X but outside the subset Y, that is, X is present but Y is absent. It is fine to have such cases where the condition is present and the outcome is absent, and they can be labeled as negative cases and can be included in the analysis. Quadrant C follows a similar logic (both condition and outcome are absent, being equal to 0), and it is fine to have them in the sets though they are not important and not relevant. Quadrant D has cases where Y equals 1 and X equals 0, which indicates that there could be cases where Y is present and X is absent, and visually, therefore, some part of Y would be outside X. It is better that there are no cases in this quadrant, but if there are any, they will have an impact on the condition being identified as a necessary condition. Having no cases in quadrant D and all cases in quadrant A would be the clearest representation that X is a necessary condition for Y.

But it is also possible to understand the relationship (Y occurs only if X occurs) when membership scores are fuzzy scores. XY plots as in Figure 3.2 help us to visualize relationships between fuzzy sets.

Figure 3.2 is an XY plot with the condition on the x and the outcome on the y axes, and the black dots are the various cases. This figure reflects a perfectly necessary condition because in all the cases Y is less than X as they all are below the diagonal where X = Y. In a real-world setting, there may of course be cases that are above the diagonal, but recalling the 2 × 2 chart described earlier, they cannot be on the top left corner of the chart, which would indicate that Y > X.[10]

However, it must be noted that necessary conditions are rarely relevant by themselves—one would be hard-pressed to make an empirical claim that an outcome is present only when a single condition is present. When conditions are necessary conditions, they are considered so usually in conjunction with

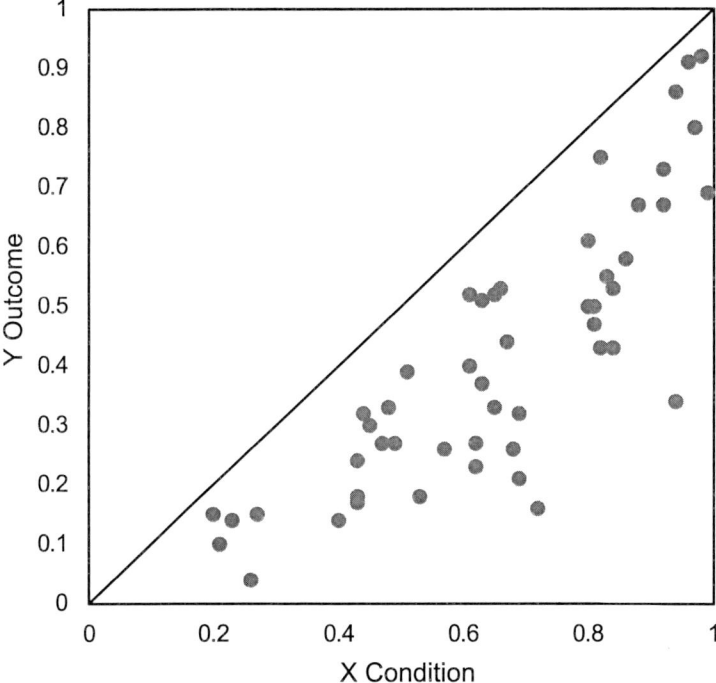

Figure 3.2 XY Plot for a Necessary Condition

other conditions, and such a condition is referred to as an SUIN condition—that is, a condition which is "sufficient but unnecessary part of a factor that is insufficient but necessary for an outcome" (Mahoney 2018). For our purposes, SUIN conditions can be understood as a conjunction of conditions that are related by the "or" function. That is, an SUIN condition is considered necessary when A or B or C are in conjunction considered necessary (Oana, Schneider, and Thomann 2021).

In addition to the aforementioned, it is also important to know whether a condition is considered a necessary relevant condition or a trivial necessary condition. Conditions could be considered necessary, but they are so trivial to consider that perhaps one is better off not considering them at all. For example, to argue that water is a necessary condition for ships to float is so obvious that it adds little value to understand what makes ships float. In set theory, they could be seen where X is such a large superset that makes Y look small, or Y is such a small subset that X would almost seem irrelevant to the analysis. This can be seen in Figure 3.3. Triviality is calculated as the relevance of necessity score, or RoN score, as part of the analysis of the necessary conditions test, in which

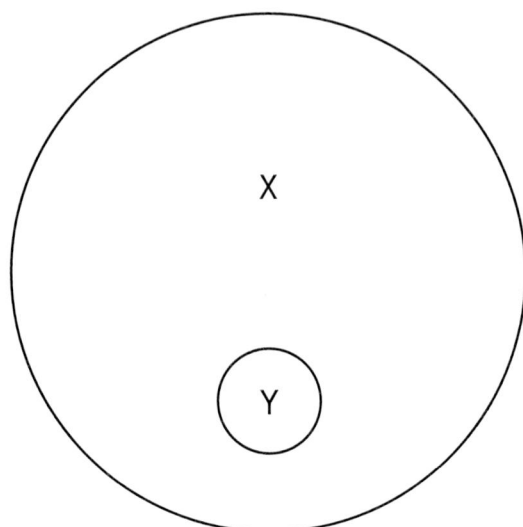

Figure 3.3   Relevance of Necessity Condition (RoN)

a score below 0.5 is usually considered to be a trivial necessary condition. The third section of the chapter interprets these tests.

Sufficient Conditions

A sufficient condition can be formally written as "X → Y", which means "if X then Y". Y can be present of course without X, but if X is present, Y will be present. Y could arguably be present because of other reasons, but if X is present, Y will be present. Additionally, a condition can be considered an INUS condition, that is, a condition which is "an insufficient but necessary part of a condition that is itself unnecessary but sufficient for the outcome" (Mackie 1965). Again, this could be understood as a conjunction of several sufficient conditions that by themselves are not sufficient. INUS conditions are usually intersected sets, as can be seen in Figure 3.4. A and B intersect to create an INUS condition for the outcome Y, and C is a sufficient condition for Y. Technically, the INUS condition is the intersection between A and B, and the remaining crescent shapes of A and B are the remaining conjuncts for the INUS condition.[11]

Again, like necessary conditions, sufficiency conditions can also be understood on a 2 × 2 table (Table 3.2), which provides the basis to better understand fuzzy set memberships on XY plots.

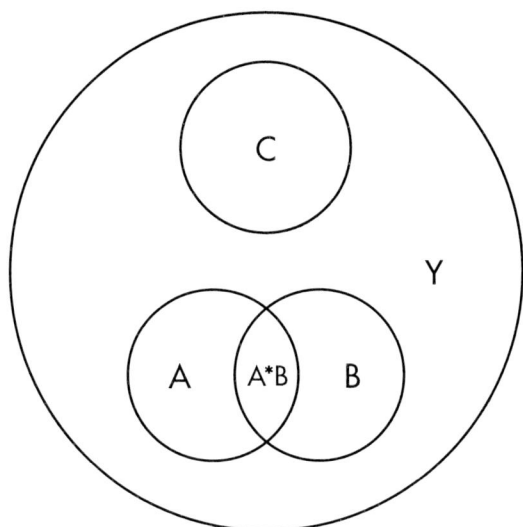

Figure 3.4 Sufficient Conditions

Table 3.2 Sufficient Conditions

Outcome Y	1	Quadrant D Some Cases	Quadrant A Cases
	0	Quadrant C Not Important Cases	Quadrant B Some Cases
		0	1
		Condition X	

In the case of sufficiency conditions, it is important that X is less than or equal to Y, and so if there are cases where X is present but Y is not (in this case, Quadrant B), these would be cases that could potentially falsify the claim that X is a sufficient condition for Y. Quadrants C and D are not directly relevant because Y can be equal to or greater than X, whereby X cannot completely explain why. But clearly, if we have cases where X exists but Y does not, it does have implications upon our claims and the strength of our arguments. In other words, idiosyncratic cases can be present and will be considered deviant cases in the 2 x 2 here.

Figure 3.5 provides an XY plot of a sufficiency condition. It is a mirror image of the necessary condition as shown in Figure 3.2 earlier, with all

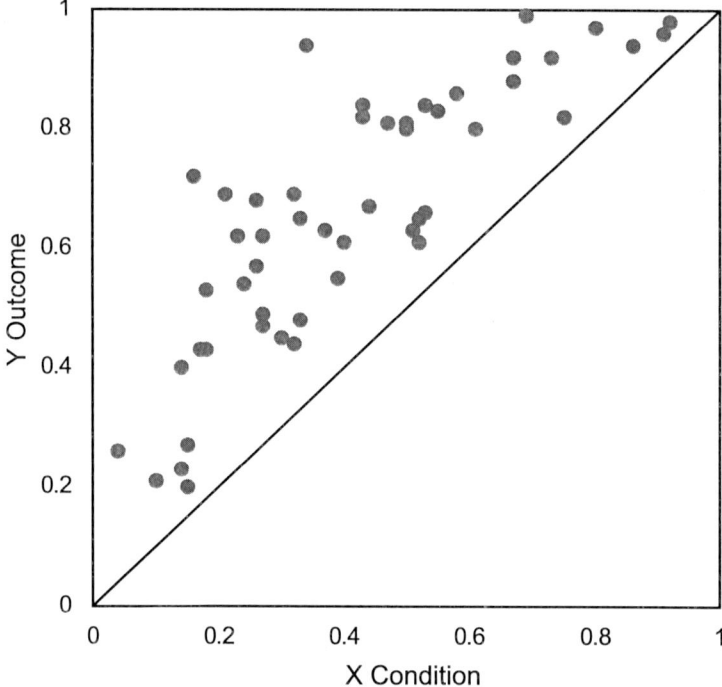

Figure 3.5   XY Plot for a Sufficiency Condition

the cases above the diagonal. Being above the diagonal shows that when X is present Y is also present, but also that Y is greater than or equal to X, accounting for a sufficiency condition.

There may, however, be cases that can be found in the bottom right corner, or below the diagonal. Such a situation is not uncommon. As explained below, consistency and coverage measures provide us precisely the tests to assess such situations.

Parameters of Fit for Necessary and Sufficiency Conditions: Consistency and Coverage

The parameters of fit, that is, how well these conditions fit with the outcome, are based on two tests that measure consistency and coverage.

Consistency Tests

A consistency parameter of fit tests the extent to which the condition is located along with the outcome, that is, how completely is the condition set aligned to the outcome of the interest set. Do the membership sets fully align with each other such that the condition is fully located within the outcome (and therefore is consistent with the outcome) or is much of the condition outside the outcome set? Put another way, does the condition set equally eclipse the outcome set or does it partially eclipse the outcome set? Figures 3.6 and 3.7 illustrate high and low consistency, depending on how far "in" is the condition X to the outcome Y.

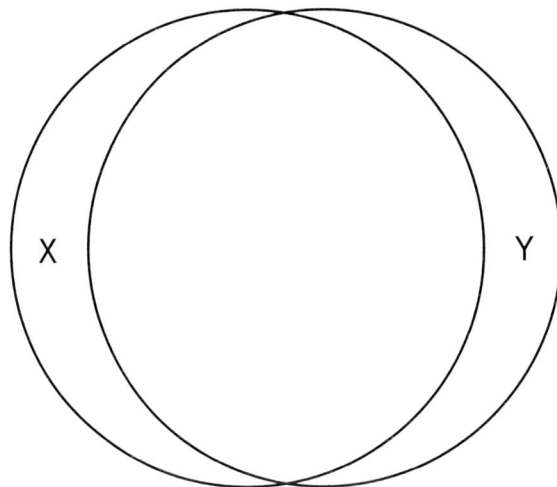

Figure 3.6 High Consistency

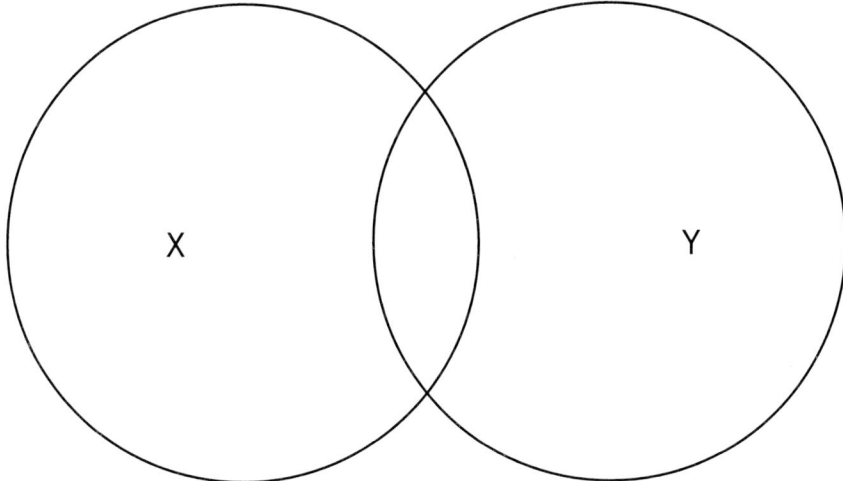

Figure 3.7 Low Consistency

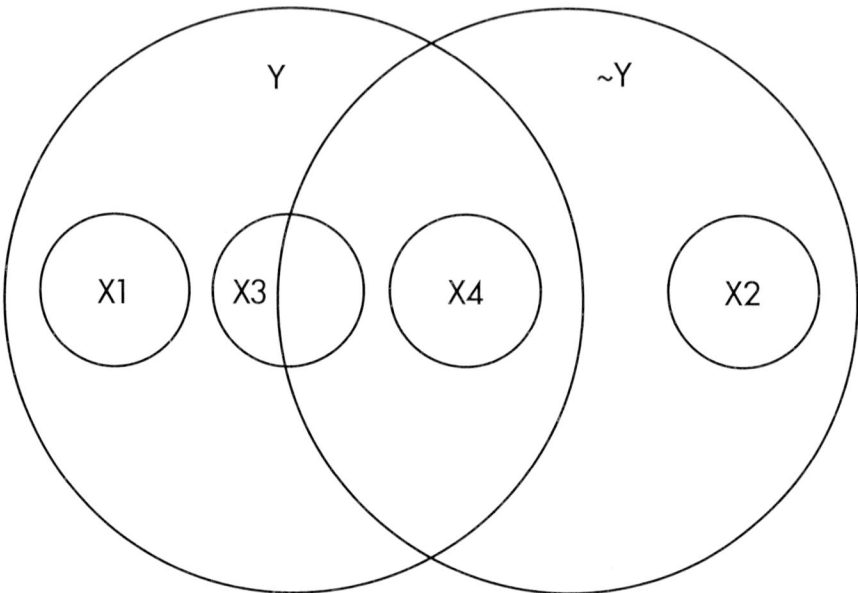

Figure 3.8 Simultaneous Consistent Sub-Set Relations

Additionally, there may be sufficient conditions that are simultaneous sub-relations—that is, these conditions can be sufficient for the outcome and the non-outcome at the same time, especially if the outcome score is determined on a fuzzy relationship. For instance, the resource levels can perhaps influence the level of both conflict and democracy in a country (if we were to calibrate resources on a fuzzy scale); high levels of resources can provide the foundations for economic development, but can also be a "resource curse" that creates conflict between groups to control the resources. These kinds of simultaneous sub-relations of consistency are illustrated in Figure 3.8.

Let us assume that there is an outcome Y with a non-outcome ~Y. Because the outcome is a fuzzy set, the intersection between the two would not be an empty set, because the intersection would have members that belong to both the outcome and non-outcome sets. Such membership, that is, membership in both sets, is ambivalent. For example, what a median income level really implies in terms of happiness (Y) or unhappiness (~Y) can be ambivalent. And so in Figure 3.8 such a member (X4) should be placed fully in the intersection between the two sets..

In Figure 3.8, X1 is clearly a sufficient condition for Y and X2 for ~Y. But X3 and X4 are problematic because both overlap with different levels of consistency with Y and ~Y. Thus, X3 and X4 are considered sufficient conditions that display simultaneous sub-relations of consistency. This kind of relation of consistency, simultaneous sub-relation, is measured through an indicator called the proportional reduction in inconsistency (PRI), whereby the higher the PRI score, the more relevant is the condition at explaining the outcome to the non-outcome. For instance, a PRI score of 0.75 means the condition or configuration is better at explaining the outcome than a PRI score of 0.25 for some other condition or configuration.

Coverage Tests

Coverage tests for sufficient conditions explain the extent to which the cases that make up the membership in the condition set cover the outcome set. This could be visually understood as the relative sizes of the condition and outcome sets. They may not be aligned, but are the condition sets as big as the outcome sets or are they smaller?

The RoN measure explained earlier is a coverage test for a necessity condition because, depending on the proportionate sizes of the condition and the outcome, one can ascertain whether the condition is a relevant necessary condition or a trivially necessary condition.

Coverage tests for sufficiency rely on a more visual understanding of coverage based on indicators labeled as solution, unique, and raw coverage of conditions for outcomes, as seen in Figure 3.9.

In Figure 3.9, conditions X, A, and B*C make up the sufficient conditions for Y. But the extent of the coverage of these conditions requires a closer analysis. Let us assume that the coverage of X is 0.2—that is, the X condition covers 0.2 of all cases sufficient for the outcome. Similarly, the coverage of condition A is 0.5 (because it looks larger) and of condition B*C is 0.3. Let us also assume that the intersection of X*A is 0.1.

Coverage tests describe three kinds of coverage—solution, unique, and raw coverage. Raw coverage is simply the addition of the raw values of all the sufficient condition sets, which in this case would imply adding up the coverages of X, A, and B*C, which would come to 0.2 + 0.5 + 0.3 = 1. Solution coverage subtracts the intersection between conditions, such as X and A (0.1) from the raw coverage, and so the solution coverage in this example will be 0.9. Solution coverage will either be equal to or more oftentimes would be lower than raw coverage if the membership sets overlap, as it removes the intersections to avoid duplication. Finally, unique coverage is the coverage

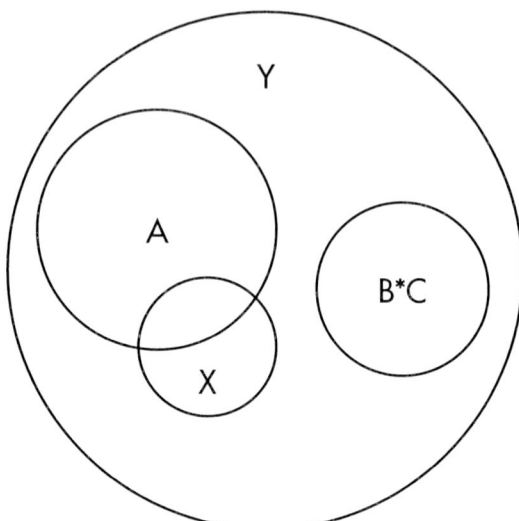

Figure 3.9   Coverage of Sufficient Conditions

that is unique to each of the membership sets. In this example, the unique coverage of X would be 0.1, and of A would be 0.4 and of B*C would be 0.3 (because it has no further intersections). Since most analysis is usually based on identifying configurations, interpretations usually rely on solution and unique coverages rather than raw coverage.

The Analytic Moment: Truth Table Analysis

Once we have understood the consistency and coverage scores of the necessary and sufficient conditions, we further understand the sufficient conditions through truth table analysis.

Truth table analysis provides a visual description of the various combinations of set memberships. A truth table is essentially a data matrix, but what it has in columns and rows is very different from a standard data matrix. A standard table of data would usually have variables as columns and cases as rows. The truth table has conditions (or better, membership sets) as columns, and each row represents the logically possible various "and" conditions between the conditions. Each row represents a distinct combination of conditions. Since each condition can occur either in its presence or in its absence to be sufficient for the outcome, the number of rows or combinations of conditions is calculated by the expression 2^k, where k represents the number of conditions[12] and 2 represents the two different states (presence or absence) in which they can occur (Schneider and Wagemann 2012: 92).

The truth table can be understood somewhat as a dashboard that maps the status of the conditions for sufficiency analysis. Below is a truth table that can be used for illustrative purposes. It points out the various configurations that can lead to a democratic outcome. In the truth table, Table 3.3, A, B, C, and D are the conditions for the outcome (OUT).[13] The combinations of conditions are numbered under the first column[14] and are described in descending order in terms of the outcomes. The combinations are of three kinds: (*a*) combinations of conditions that have cases and are sufficient for the outcome (outcome = 1), (*b*) combinations that have cases but they are not sufficient for the outcome (outcome = 0), and (*c*) combinations that are

Table 3.3 Truth Table

OUT: output value
n: number of cases in configuration
incl: sufficiency inclusion score
PRI: proportional reduction in inconsistency
Truth Table for Democracy

Row	A	B	C	D	OUT	n	incl	PRI	Cases
7	0	1	1	0	1	2	0.906	0.743	5,13
15	1	1	1	0	0	18	0.512	0.334	1,2,3,4,9,10,11,12,13,14, 15,16,23,24,25,26,27,29
5	0	1	0	0	0	1	0.493	0.140	33
13	1	1	0	0	0	1	0.487	0.218	34
3	0	0	1	0	0	2	0.448	0.176	6,30
9	1	0	0	0	0	3	0.407	0.237	8,20,32
1	0	0	0	0	0	5	0.380	0.170	19,22,2831,35
11	1	0	1	0	0	3	0.365	0.182	7,18,21
2	0	0	0	1	?	0	–		–
4	0	0	1	1	?	0	–		–
6	0	1	0	1	?	0	–		–
8	0	1	1	1	?	0	–		–
10	1	0	0	1	?	0	–		–
12	1	0	1	1	?	0	–		–
14	1	1	0	1	?	0	–		–
16	1	1	1	1	?	0	–		–

logically possible but do not have cases and are therefore described as logical remainders (where the outcome would be indicated as a "?" or a "-").

Apart from the conditions, the truth table also provides the consistency scores (incl) and the PRI scores, and the cases that follow that combination of conditions. For example, in Row 1, configuration 7 has cases 5 and 13 that are sufficient for the outcome where B and C intersect, but others are absent and can be written as ~A.B*C.~D -> Y. This configuration in Row 1 has a consistency score of 0.906 and a PRI score of 0.743. A consistency score below 0.85 is usually considered not consistent, and a PRI score less than 0.5 implies that the configuration cannot explain the outcome and can explain the non-outcome. Except for configuration 7, none of the other configurations in the table have an outcome score of 1 and obviously will not provide us with solutions for further interpretation. If we do have outcomes that are positive and are above the consistency and PRI thresholds, the analysis will move to the next step, which is logical minimization.

Empirical Limited Diversity and Logical Minimization for Solution Terms

Once we have derived the truth table, the next step is to identify the solution terms that provide us with set theory-based configurations that indicate the pathways to the outcome.[15] A solution term would look like the following statement: A.B*C.~X → Y, which translates as A and (B intersection C) and not X would be sufficient for Y. This should be read as a full statement as it indicates the complete configuration that can lead to Y. In plainer language, this pathway indicates that when A is present, along with a condition where B and C intersect, in the absence of X, it leads to a solution that is sufficient for the outcome Y. A solution term will have multiple such configurations or pathways that lead to the outcome, with the sign "+" (OR) between the pathways, indicating the multiple pathways to the outcome.

To identify solution terms, however, we need to first undertake logical minimization procedures so that our solution terms can overcome limitations due to the number and kinds of cases,[16] which could potentially have had an impact upon consistency and coverage tests of our necessary and sufficient conditions. We need to ensure that the cases that we have arrived at are not just empirically relevant, but also that there could be cases that we could not account for if there is conceptually the possibility of such logical combinations.

In other words, the truth table comprises logical remainders (combinations with no cases) that one would like to account for (or delete) to understand the possibility of what are and could be possible solution pathways if we had additional or different cases that could be identified with such configurations.

Up to this point, the steps outlined are usually considered to be standard analysis. But more recently, scholars who use QCA have faced comments and questions relative to the validity of the methods when measured against more evolved and dominant benchmarks attributed to quantitative analysis. Once logical minimization procedures are followed, one can derive solution terms such as standard analysis.

However, additional research has also shown that it is not uncommon that these logical remainders or even the researchers themselves can make some untenable assumptions that are logically contradictory or somehow contradict our knowledge of how the world (or our theoretical understanding of the problem at hand) works. We need to remove these easy counterfactuals from the analysis before we arrive at the solution terms. These easy counterfactuals that should be eliminated from the set of logical remainders include (*a*) contradictory simplifying assumptions (CSAs), that is, logical remainders that occur in both the outcome and non-outcome as logical remainders, (*b*) counterfactuals that contradict statements of necessity, and (*c*) basic logic whereby logical remainders are simply not tenable. This intermediate step, which is the conscious removal of the counterfactuals mentioned here, is known as enhanced standard analysis.

The final step in the analysis, whether standard or enhanced standard, is to provide the three kinds of solution terms, depending on the needs of the researcher. The conservative solution is the logically minimized truth table with solution pathways from the logical combinations where the outcomes of cases are "1". The solution terms are derived only from the configurations that display positive outcomes. In the case of the truth table (Table 3.3), a conservative solution can be derived because of configuration 7 in Row 1.

The parsimonious solution is the exact opposite, whereby solution pathways are calculated by including all the logical remainders with the outcome "0". That is, all the configurations where the outcomes are either a "?" or "-" are included in the derivation of the solution terms. By doing so, we can account for all the logical configurational possibilities that are not included in the current truth table simply because there are no cases that describe such configurations in the current dataset. In this truth table, for example, as part of enhanced standard analysis, parsimonious solution terms are derived after removing the easy counterfactuals that are CSAs, contradict statements of necessity, or are simply implausible logical remainders. We would consider including configurations 2 and below, as they are the logical remainders, to derive a parsimonious solution.

Conservative solution terms are usually very complex and can be considered inadequate because they do not account for all logical possible configurations, but only the ones that are derived from the cases in the current dataset. At the other end, parsimonious solution terms are considered the simplest because they account for all possible logical configurations.

The intermediate solution is the in-between solution. This solution term is derived by providing directional expectations (presence or absence of each condition), thereby injecting theoretical knowledge to retain or eliminate the counterfactuals from the analysis (Oana, Schneider, and Thomann 2021b: 127). For example, from the truth table we may argue that configurations 10 and 16 do not make conceptual sense and can deliberately exclude them to derive an intermediate solution. Because this exercise is conceptually informed by excluding configurations that do not make sense in the context of the concept in question, the intermediate solution seems to usually be the preferred solution term to identify pathways to the outcome.

Robustness Checks

Another component of enhanced standard analysis is called robustness checks. It is premature to explain these concepts in this section of the book since these would be confusing to those who are trying to understand the QCA for the first time. I therefore provide only a brief outline of what these robustness checks are and why they can be considered important.

There are multiple discretionary decisions that a researcher takes as part of the QCA analysis—choosing calibration thresholds and sufficiency thresholds, for example. The question then is: how robust are these findings if the researcher is given some discretion to choose thresholds? Moreover, the idea of robustness itself can be defined differently—in terms of stability of solution terms or of parameters of fit and such—and Oana and Schneider have developed several robustness tests in R that make the job of checking for robustness easier (Oana and Schneider 2021; Oana, Schneider, and Thomann 2021b). The three main tests of robustness comprise evaluating sensitivity ranges, fit-oriented robustness, and case-oriented robustness. These tests evaluate how sensitive the results are to the different analytical choices made as part of the analysis, and identify the extent to which the analysis will hold even if alternate analytical choices were made. For instance, if we change the calibration and consistency thresholds, would the solution terms derived from the existing dataset still hold? What would the robust core set of cases be that would be common to alternate hypothetical sets of cases with different thresholds? And finally, what are the robust typical cases that withstand alternate possibilities, and what are the other types of cases (irrelevant, deviant, shaky)[17] even under such alternate scenarios? These questions are best illustrated with the help of a dataset and are answered in this book after the standard analysis is undertaken in later sections.

This chapter is a summary of the distinctive approach and the various steps undertaken as a QCA analyst. The overview should help in understanding the results and their interpretation in the later sections of the book. Having said this, much more remains in terms of understanding the method. QCA takes on different forms (multi-value, two-step, temporal, ideal type) and has many more possibilities (cluster analysis, theory building) that are not covered here, apart from other comparative configurational analytical forms.

In sum, developing configurational and comparative thinking will bring theoretical depth and coherence to our understanding of political modernization, certainly in India. Unpacking labels to understand configurations provides a promise of shared coherence, which seems more fraught than ever before. We will now turn our analysis back to the question of the logic of populism in India.

Notes

1. There is no better place to begin to learn about the QCA method than the resources available on the website https://compasss.org/. More recently, books authored by scholars such as Carsten Schneider (Schneider and Wagemann 2012) for a solid theoretical foundation, Eva Thomann, Ioana-Elena Oana (Oana, Schneider, and Thomann 2021) for understanding QCA functionality with R, Patrick Mello (Mello 2021) for a simple and accessible introduction focusing on the QCA application, Adrian Dusa (Dusa 2019) for an advanced understanding of R, and Claude Rubinson (Rutten and Rubinson 2022), among many other scholars, are key to learning QCA. While this chapter is an attempt to help the reader understand the method

rudimentarily and to help read this book, the mentioned books are essential to learn and apply the method.

2. This observation was made at "Set Theory, Constructivism and Social Science: A Symposium on James Mahoney's The Logic of Social Science," May 25, 2023, Central European University, available at https://www.youtube.com/watch?v=hANikUOX_Zc (accessed December 13, 2024).

3. These relations are first founded upon the ideas that make up the algebra named after the nineteenth-century British mathematician and logician George Boole, whereby variables can have only two possible values of 0 or 1. Fuzzy set logic is an extension of the same Boolean logic where variables can take on values between 0 and 1 (Vis 2010: 33).

4. The container-like entity description has been given by George Lakoff and Rafael Nunez in their book *Where Does Mathematics Come From?* James Mahoney provides us with the description of sets based on setting boundaries (Mello 2021: 45).

5. This section will not cover R-related aspects of doing the QCA. If one is keen to learn QCA using R, refer to the books by Oana, Thomann, and Schneider (2021a) and Mello (2021), and to Dusa (2019) for a more technical understanding useful for those with an advanced knowledge of R.

6. The process is a log transformation of scores that R computes very conveniently. But more than the mechanics, it is really important to know why calibration is important.

7. Calibration is an attempt to overcome the question posed by the Sorites paradox, which can be described using the following example. Imagine a heap of sand comprising 100,000 grains of sand. If one grain is removed, the 99,999 grains will still be considered to be a heap of sand. If we remove one more grain, the 98,998 grains of sand will still be considered a heap. If we keep removing grains of sand one by one, it will never be clear when the heap of sand no longer constitutes a heap. Such fuzziness is prevalent everywhere in the real world: no clear line, for example, divides bald men from those who are not. The paradox is, no matter how empirical the measurement, the concept remains indifferent to precision and yields a falsehood. Calibration is a conscious effort to draw that clear line. I would like to thank Patrick Mello (2021) for bringing attention to this philosophical reference.

8. To reinforce this point, consider the difference between probabilistic reasoning and fuzzy set reasoning. Mello (2021: 49) provides a useful example. Imagine two chillis A and B that look exactly the same. Chilli

A has a probability of 0.01, that is a 1 percent chance, of being spicy. Chilli B has a fuzzy set membership of 0.01 of being spicy. You want to make a dish that is mildly spicy, so which chilli would you choose? At first glance, it would look like there is no difference in spiciness between the chillis. But on a closer look, they are substantively different. Chilli A has a 1 percent chance of being spciy, but you can never be sure if you have picked the right chilli in the set of chillis. On the other hand, Chill B, having a membership of 0.01, would certainly be spicy, however mild, in a set of chillis. One would choose Chilli B for this dish.

9. It does not necessarily mean that the condition is always prior to the outcome, and if so, one could perhaps make a causal argument if there a theory that explains why X can cause Y. All that is being said, literally, is that Y occurs only if X occurs.

10. Cases that do occur on the top left corner are known as deviant consistency in kind (DCK) cases, and their presence in that corner implies that the necessary claim can be falsified. However, if there are very few and, based on case knowledge, are considered significant, albeit idiosyncratic, one should mention so in the analysis.

11. This INUS condition would be written as $(A{\sim}B) * (A^*B) * ({\sim}AB) \to Y$.

12. It is misleadingly understood to denote the number of cases. It actually denotes the number of conditions whereby one could logically have an equal number of cases for the condition.

13. This outcome is not the outcome in the dataset but is the sufficiency outcome. The latter obviously derives from the former, but one should note that they are not the same.

14. There are four conditions in this project; hence there were a total of 2^k conditions, that is, 16 possible combinations of conditions.

15. This step can be difficult to understand beyond a point without sufficient detail and explanation. While I hope to repeat some of these concepts in the results section to clarify these concepts further, it is advisable to refer to the basic texts mentioned in the beginning of the chapter for a more elaborate explanation of the steps involved in QCA analysis after deriving the truth tables.

16. This problem is referred to as a problem of limited empirical diversity. It would, in fact, be quite surprising if a QCA does not have this issue. Intuitively, one would rarely find an equal distribution of cases across all logical combinations of conditions. Instead, one would find some combinations

having more cases, and certainly some combinations of conditions with no cases. Because what is logically possible does not make it empirically possible as well; it can remain as an ideal type with no empirical cases.

17. Irrelevant and deviant cases are those cases in the current dataset that are not covered under alternative scenarios and so can be deemed irrelevant or deviant for robustness. Shaky cases are those that are currently robust but can become deviant if alternate analytical decisions are taken. Finally, typical cases are those that withstand alternate analytical decisions.

4

The Cases

Fully In, Fully Out, and In Between

Over the past 75 years, there have been at least 800 state government terms ruled by around 375 political leaders as chief ministers and counting. Populist leaders are a small but pivotal subset among these leaders. Scholarship on such leaders has necessarily been long on descriptive accounts because of their exceptional rise to and stay in political office. Such accounts are the basis upon which this comparative account is built.

The unit of analysis in this study is not a populist personality over a period of time, but a personality in a particular year that corresponds with either an assembly or a national election year. For example, a single case would not be "Kejriwal," but would instead be cases like "Kejriwal 2015" or "Kejriwal 2020." This chapter, therefore, does not aim to provide elaborate accounts of the leaders, but tries to strike a balance with the details and their relevance and, in doing so, provide a narrative of each that is tenable for comparative analysis.

This "case by year" approach seems justified for a couple of reasons. First, while almost all populist leaders come to power riding a wave, they inevitably routinize into the mainstream over successive elections. The fever breaks. Second, it may appear that the period of such long-term leaders is linear, that is, from the heights of riding a wave to come to power, and subsequently routinizing into a banal steady but sustained popularity over time. Breaking this narrative into multiple periods provides space for curvilinear possibilities because it allows for a closer look into the ups and downs of political life in that declining trajectory. And third, instead of only just looking at the same case over time or multiple cases at a time, extending both the temporal and spatial dimensions of our cases helps to maximize homogeneity (which gives us better explanatory terms by removing contextual distortions) and heterogeneity, which makes the findings robust (Vis 2010: 23).

Cases were selected from among the 375 political leaders who contested assembly elections as chief ministerial candidates till the middle of 2024. Narendra Modi and Indira Gandhi were the only two prime ministerial candidates who have been considered.[1] First, literature was reviewed to see which candidates were identified as populists in the literature and were able to eventually identify around 23 candidates where the word 'populism' was used in reference to these leaders in multiple sources.[2] To reduce the bias that can come from deriving scores for the conditions and the outcome from the literature because conditions can be "cooked" to suit the outcome, public opinion data and electoral results were subsequently included in the dataset.[3] However, since public opinion data was not available for the crucial period between 1980 and 1996,[4] the number of leaders shrunk to 16,[5] which created the subsequent problem of having too few cases for too many conditions. Eventually, I split these leaders by term and have finally arrived at a dataset of 16 leaders spread over 37 legislative terms with 5 conditions. In sum, we have 37 cases and 5 conditions. Further, to enhance robustness, populist outcomes have been calculated independently of the electoral data, understood as an unprecedented vote share to the candidate that can be attributed to the candidate alone (details in Chapter 5).

Thresholds

Before we understand the scores associated with the cases, we need to understand the thresholds upon which these scores have been benchmarked. Thresholds in set theory are the boundaries that differentiate whether cases are in or out of the sets. In Chapter 1, the concept of populism was described by both understanding its key attributes and distinguishing the concept from what it is not (its negative pole). This chapter is an extension of the same concept-building exercise by understanding the positive and negative poles of the attributes (Goertz 2006), the continuum in between the two, and the threshold that draws the line between the concept and its opposite.

In this book, the five attributes—invocations to the people, boundary setting, leadership, populist attitudes, and future anxiety—are the sets, and their various thresholds are discussed later. A case can be "fully in," "fully out," "more in than out," and "more out than in" and the threshold decides whether a case is "in" or "out."

In the case of invocations to the people, "people" would refer to the widest notion of a community such that there are no clear referents (empty signifiers), and they are connected to the populist through the chain of equivalent experiences. At the extremes, one end would refer to people in a universal sense, and the other end would refer to people that are closest to the social group that the populist is identified with; the wider the group, the more it is associated with populism. Akin to the notions of bonding and bridging social capital (Narayan 2002), socially inclusive invocations to the people would be inside the populist group, and vice versa. Outside the set invocations would be people who are exclusively like each other (they share common bonds), and inside the set invocations would refer to people who are inclusively unlike each other, whereby the invocation is to bridge differences between them and connect as "people." Thus, in this vein, any mobilization based on small groups, such as a single caste or a group of castes (Other Backward Classes, or OBCs), would fall outside the populism set. On the other side, arguably, the label "Hindu" could possibly represent a group inside the set because it is an inclusive social group (majoritarian, but inclusive nonetheless) but has enough diversity comprising vertically and horizontally organized social groups within the Hindu fold, yet it is still not the widest possible populist grouping. In recent times, I would identify a slogan like the "Aam Admi" (common man) as the prime example of a populist invocation to the people because it refers to everyone and has no clear identifiable referents.

Thus, as scores on the indicator, electoral invocations to the people as Hindus would get a 0.6 and above on the fuzzy score membership within Set P (The People) and references to caste clusters or some subset thereof would get a fuzzy score of 0.4 or below. References to more than just Hindus, such as references to terms that speak to wider notions of a community, such as 'Bahujan Samaj' (0.8) or 'Aam Aadmi' (1.0), would get scores higher than 0.6 depending on, and arguably, the scope of the term being used as an invocation to the people.

The threshold for the second attribute—boundary setting—can be understood as a type of breach of liberal pluralist democratic politics. Contestations and competition among groups divided by various cleavages are usually resolved through accommodation in liberal democratic societies and, at worst, through the capture of state institutions by rotation through regular and fair elections. These kinds of politics are within the possibilities of electoral democratic competition when the sanctity of the general rules of public institutional order is presumed to be maintained, because of which everyone is assured that they may get an equal chance at political office through elections. Populists, however, connect to the people based on the alternate anxiety, a disenchantment that the establishment promotes liberal but undemocratic causes (intellectuals, refugees, minorities) at the cost of democratic interests (natives, common folk, dominant ethnicities), and so power has to be wrested from their hold and moved toward the popular sector. At one end are the pluralist politics of accommodation and compromise and at the other end are the populist politics of fundamental Manichean incommensurability between dichotomous groups. The crossing of the threshold can possibly be identified when political mobilization is not about competition among equally competing interests, but when the construction of the people is both majoritarian and dominant enough to ensure that the democratic rules are skewed toward the majority. That is, the rules can be broken to cater to the popular sector. And if the other groups are not willing to abide, that is, when groups feel their differences are incommensurable, the non-populist affiliated groups are either expected to go away or the incommensurability takes an extreme turn and matters turn violent.

In the case of fuzzy scores for membership in Set B (Setting of Antagonistic Boundaries), any case where the boundary is drawn as a dominant majority–minority dyad (usually Hindus versus other groups in India, for instance), the fuzzy score would be a 0.6 and above. And any reference to competition as being amongst mostly equal groups (such as castes within the OBC strata) would get a 0.4 or below as they indicate mostly accommodative liberal plural democratic competition. A score above 0.6 (0.8 or 1) would indicate that the populist seeks to undermine institutional fetters (0.8) or, even worse, the antagonistic boundary of the populist justifies turning violent toward the groups on the other side of the boundary line (1.0).

The threshold for populist political leaders is based on whether the political leader is considered a political outsider to the party system or a party insider. As argued earlier, populists usually emerge as orthogonal alternatives within a cartelized party system by articulating a rupture that cannot be addressed among available party or programmatic alternatives. Additionally, Weyland identifies political outsiders, depending on the political bastion of established leadership, as those who win against a dominant faction of an established party, defeat an incumbent party, or provide a regime-level transformation (Weyland 2002: 48). While the threshold to qualify as an outsider (and therefore as a populist) is necessarily imprecise in the Indian context because rank outsiders in the electoral arena can rarely expect to win elections without sufficient financial capacity and established electoral clout, one can nevertheless describe the extremes. A fully in-populist would perhaps be a leader who is singularly responsible for articulating who the people are and who they are against, is clearly irreplaceable as a leader, and establishes such a clear antagonistic division that it polarizes the electorate in a way that they, simply put, either love him or hate him. A fully out-leader would be one who is popular but is very much a party insider whose independent views do not undercut the supremacy of the party in the electoral arena.

In Set L (Populist Political Leadership), a fuzzy score membership of 1 in this set would indicate the emergence of a politician in the political arena who is more often than not contesting for the first time, and therefore is not a career politician, nor has a family background in politics, but nevertheless is able to maintain an intense and direct connection with the masses. At the other extreme, 0 or a 0.2 fuzzy score would be a career politician, internally vetted and endorsed by the affiliate party and connects with the people on a party-based platform. A rebel political "insider" would get a 0.4, representing himself as being the tallest political leader of his party from among competing party elites. A rebel political "outsider" would get a 0.6 score if he projects his personality as the basis for connecting with the masses, and a 0.8 score as an outsider who is indispensable to the party concerned, whereby the party is completely subjugated to the leadership of this single leader.

Finally, the two remaining conditions of populist attitudes and anxiety. Lacking clear conceptual thresholds to decide when an attitude or an anxiety is populist or not, I have made an empirical case for the same. That is, empirically the distribution of the scores is clustered and as a result they are not evenly spread across the spectrum. Therefore, I have identified the gaps between clusters that justify themselves as being identified as thresholds for the scores. In other words, I have not relied on statistical measures like a mean or a median, because the conditions are not variables, and instead identified thresholds within gaps between clusters that I think are reasonable. These points have been discussed in greater detail in the next chapter.

Having explained the conceptual boundaries to identify thresholds across the conditions, I now turn to the indexation of the scores. Each of the cases was scored as fuzzy scores between 0 and 1 (0, 0.2, 0.4, 0.6, 0.8, and 1) instead of using crisp sets. Fuzzy scores provide me with the necessary latitude to index the cases for the following reasons. It is important to clarify that the word "fuzzy" does not mean "wishy washy," as it tends to be interpreted in everyday language, but in fact has its origins in mathematics dating back to the 1960s (Schneider and Wagemann 2012: 27). First, fuzziness helps us to clarify that conceptually the concepts have imprecise boundaries, but they can be precisely measured. It cannot be exactly established when a politician can be termed "a populist," but we can precisely provide empirical information about the case by identifying a score to that case. Second, the precision in empirical information allows for partial membership, thereby providing some latitude to qualitatively distinguish leaders from each other and argue whether a leader is not just fully in, but more importantly whether such a leader is mostly in, mostly out, and so on. Third, this latitude becomes important because, while these scores can be disputed by experts in the cases, in a comparative sense, these scores are defensible so long as there is agreement about the difference in kind, even if there is disagreement in degree. That is, it is important to know the space in which the specific conditions lie (in or out of the set), even if the differences in degree are debatable (more in or vice versa). This is because the analysis is a comparison that hinges on avoiding maximum ambiguity (the closer the cases are indistinguishable, the greater the ambiguity that cases explain the outcome and non-outcome). So fuzzy sets accommodate possible disagreements without giving up on the substantive membership of the case (Schneider and Wagemann 2012).

In the following sections, I explain only the fuzzy scores of the conditions attributable to each leader at each time period, but it must be clarified that one will not get an overall assessment of whether a leader is a populist yet from this table. That is, it is not a summary that can help us identify who is a populist or not because the other two conditions (populist opinion and populist anxiety) and the measurement of populist outcomes have not been presented in Table 4.1. These have not been included because these scores were not based on the interpretation of the literature; they were collected independently, and so the scoring is based primarily on empirics and not conceptual differences, which is the primary emphasis in this chapter.

Understanding the Attributes across Cases

Table 4.1 provides the fuzzy scores across the three conditions—invocations to the people, boundary setting, and leadership—of all the 37 cases in the dataset. Each case is coded as 0, 0.2, 0.4, 0.6, 0.8, and 1 on all three conditions.

Scores of 0 and 0.2 are fully and mostly out cases, and scores of 0.8 and 1 are mostly and fully in cases respectively. Cases with 0.4 are considered more out than in cases, and cases with 0.6 are considered more in than out cases.[6] And the boxes in the table have been labeled to get a sense of what that particular range interval indicates in terms of the scoring. For example, in 2018 Chandrasekhar Rao would have a score of 0.8, which means that in 2018, Chandrasekhar Rao seemed to invoke notions of popular sovereignty that suggested ideas of bridging people across divides. Likewise, Indira Gandhi in 1971 was clearly a polarizing figure and so fits a "1" on the polarization score. Arvind Kejriwal was arguably very much an orthogonal political outsider in the 2013 and 2015 elections and hence also gets a "1" on the leadership score, and so on.

Presented next are very short biographies of the leaders to understand the context and basis of the scores in Table 4.1.[7] I present these biographies as extreme and intermediate cases—fully and mostly in cases, fully and mostly out cases, and then as more in than out (and vice versa) cases. Three caveats are necessary before the section. First, summing up the scores of these cases as adequate to label them as populist leaders (of whatever degree) is not conclusive because the dataset has other conditions, and the outcome has been measured independent of these fuzzy scores. And so, one can only conclusively state who are the populist leaders and the pathways for their emergence after accounting for all the conditions. Second, the data only includes the cases where data was available across all conditions at the time of writing. Therefore, while I have had to exclude many leaders because public opinion survey data was not available between 1980 and 1996, I have, additionally, also had to exclude some periods of the leaders being considered here for the same reason. And third, the specific scores may vary across the conditions even though the leaders are described within the extreme or intermediate categories. For example, Mamata Banerjee (2016) scores a 1 on two conditions and is described as a populist case in this chapter, even though her score on the third condition is lower at 0.6.

Fully In Cases

The fully in populist cases are those that have mostly scored a 1 across the three conditions. Such populist cases would invoke the broadest notions of the people that can be best described as abstract images of a community

Table 4.1 Fuzzy Scores on Conditions of Populism

	Popular Sovereignty	Polarization	Leadership
Fully In	"All" People	Cannot Live as One	Orthogonal Outsider
1	Indira Gandhi (1971)	Indira Gandhi (1971)	Indira Gandhi (1971)
	Narendra Modi (2012, 2019)	Narendra Modi (2002, 2012, 2019,2024)	Narendra Modi (2012, 2019)
	Arvind Kejriwal (2015)	Arvind Kejriwal (2013, 2015)	Arvind Kejriwal (2013, 2015)
	Mamata Banerjee (2016)	Mamata Banerjee (2021)	Mamata Banerjee (2011, 2016)
	J. Jayalalithaa (2016)	J. Jayalalithaa (2001)	Chandrababu Naidu (1999)
	M. Karunanidhi (2006)	M. Karunanidhi (1996)	Bal Thackeray (1995)
		Lalu Prasad Yadav (1995)	
		Bal Thackeray (1995)	
More In than Out	"Bridging" People	On Majoritarian Terms	Rebel Party Outsider
0.8	Narendra Modi (2007, 2014)	Raman Singh (2008)	Naveen Patnaik (2009)
	Arvind Kejriwal (2020)	Chandrababu Naidu (1999)	K. Chandrasekhar Rao (2014)
	Mamata Banerjee (2021)	Indira Gandhi (1980)	Narendra Modi (2007,2024)
	Digvijay Singh (1998)	Mamata Banerjee (2011)	M. Karunanidhi (1996)
	Pawan Kumar Chamling (2009)	Narendra Modi (2014)	Lalu Prasad Yadav (1995)
	Nitish Kumar (2010, 2015)		J. Jayalalitha (2001)
	Raman Singh (2008)		Mamata Banerjee (2021)
	Chandrasekhar Rao (2018)		
	Naveen Patnaik (2009)		
	J. Jayalalithaa (2001)		

(*Contd.*)

Table 4.1 (*Contd.*)

	Popular Sovereignty	Polarization	Leadership
0.6	J. Jayalalithaa (2011) Lalu Prasad Yadav (1995) Naveen Patnaik (2004) Indira Gandhi (1980) Narendra Modi (2002, 2024) Mamata Banerjee (2011) Arvind Kejriwal (2013) Bal Thackeray (1995)	Raman Singh (2003, 2008) J. Jayalalithaa (2011, 2016) Arvind Kejriwal (2020) Narendra Modi (2007) Naveen Patnaik (2009) Mamata Banerjee (2016)	Nitish Kumar (2015) Naveen Patnaik (2014) M. Karunanidhi (2006) K. Chandrasekhar Rao (2018) J. Jayalalithaa (2011, 2016) Arvind Kejriwal (2020) Indira Gandhi (1980) Narendra Modi (2002, 2014)
More Out Than In	"Bonding" People	Equal Competition	First Among Equals Insider
0.4	Chandrababu Naidu (1999) M. Karunanidhi (1996) K. Chandrasekhar Rao (2014) Nitish Kumar (2005)	M. Karunanidhi (2006) K. Chandrasekhar Rao (2018) Pawan Kumar Chamling (2009) Naveen Patnaik (2004)	Raman Singh (2008) Naveen Patnaik (2004) Nitish Kumar (2010)
0.2	Naveen Patnaik (2014)	Naveen Patnaik (2014) K. Chandrasekhar Rao (2014) Digvijay Singh (1998)	Pawan Kumar Chamling (2009)
Fully Out	Local/Narrow "People"	Interest Accommodation	Dissenting Party Insider
0	Naveen Patnaik (2019) Raman Singh (2003, 2013) Nitish Kumar (2020)	Nitish Kumar (2005, 2010, 2015, 2020) Naveen Patnaik (2019) Raman Singh (2013)	Digvijay Singh (1998) Nitish Kumar (2005, 2020) Naveen Patnaik (2019) Raman Singh (2003, 2013)

with little reference to social characteristics. They would also concurrently polarize the electoral arena by clearly identifying groups or actors across a Manichean divide who are construed as being opposed to the people. And lastly, such populists would also be typically political outsiders who mobilize orthogonally or at the least against the status quoist establishment. In this category, I include Arvind Kejriwal, Narendra Modi, and Indira Gandhi as the clearest cases, followed by Mamata Banerjee, J. Jayalalithaa, M. Karunanidhi, Lalu Prasad Yadav, and Bal Thackeray as the mostly in cases.

Arvind Kejriwal

Kejriwal is a straightforward example of a populist leader from India in recent times (Jayal 2016; Lama-Rewal 2019). He first emerged as a crusader (as part of an organization he founded—Parivartan) against crony-capitalism-based market reforms in and around Delhi (Bhaduri and Kejriwal 2005), and subsequently gained national popularity for spearheading, along with Anna Hazare, the India Against Corruption campaign in 2010–11. After Hazare left and the campaign fizzled out, Kejriwal launched the Aam Aadmi Party with many associates from the campaign around 2012 (EPW Editorial Desk 2014). This study is focused on three Delhi assembly elections (2013, 2015, and 2020), where Kejriwal was the quintessential populist in the 2015 elections. After the 2013 elections, whereby Kejriwal had to seek the support of the Congress because of the hung assembly results (EPW Editorial Desk 2014), he continued to come across as a crusader focused on corruption and against party elites rather than trying to deepen and broaden his connection with the people.[8] But apologizing to the people of Delhi for resigning from the chief minister position after 49 days of being hamstrung by the power politics of the establishment (both the national government and the Congress coalition partner), his breathtaking majority of 67 out of 70 seats with a vote share that practically doubled to 54.3 percent in 2015 enabled the fullest expression of his reforms for governance. His party launched several innovative programs in Delhi that have received national attention (alternate days of even- and odd-numbered vehicles to ply so as to moderate air pollution, revision of school-level curriculum focusing on mental well-being, home delivery of many basic services, neighborhood-level participatory committees, and other reforms). By 2020, Kejriwal and the Aam Admi Party acquired a niche in the party system and expanded their electoral reach to other states such as Punjab and Goa; their populism seems to have been routinized. Over the past 10 years,

Kejriwal has proven to be resilient as the quintessential political outsider in the face of challenges thrown at him that include electoral competition, court cases, financial investigations, and so on.

Kejriwal clearly would get a 1 on the leadership score for the first two elections because he was a political outsider, emerging in the political arena with no background based on political privilege. But by 2020, one could give him a score of 0.6 on the leadership score because he is now tolerated within the political establishment and possibly is connected to the median more than the disaffected voter. While Kejriwal is clearly for popular direct democracy, one saw more attention given to his anti-elitism in 2013, perhaps because he was preoccupied with fighting for his space within the political system. Kejriwal was emphatic in a public speech when, responding to allegations from elites who claimed that he was spending too much time exposing the corrupt instead of governing, he said, "Come on, acting against the corrupt is true governance" (Lama-Rewal 2019: 181). And so, in 2013, he would get a 1 on boundary setting and 0.6 on invocations to the people score, but in 2015 he would get a 1 on both. In 2020, one could argue that he would get a 0.8 on invocations to the people (as he continues to expand his coverage through various service delivery programs) and a 0.6 on his boundary setting.

Narendra Modi in Gujarat

Modi in Gujarat is very much a precursor to the Modi that became the prime minister. Modi was elected the chief minister of Gujarat three times before he became the prime minister. He was perhaps one of the first high-tech populists, being able to reach out to masses using holograms and other digital media, bankrolled by local industrialists and stage managed by corporate American public relations (PR) agencies that had run similar campaigns for other autocrats like Nursultan Nazarbayev and billionaires like Mikhail Khodorkovsky. His target audience was primarily the middle castes and urban middle classes. Dalits, Muslims, and the rural population were peripheral to his concerns (Jaffrelot 2013, 2024).

In terms of the scores, Modi could be indexed as a full populist by the end of his term in Gujarat, initially emerging as a polarizing figure, then widening his appeal with the people, and strategically rising above party leaders and affiliates to build a populist persona before he became the prime minister. In his early years, Modi would get a 0.6 on the popular sovereignty index because he was mainly interested in consolidating the Hindu middle class and dominant caste (Kshatriya, Patels, and the upper castes) vote. I would argue that his strategy was at that time to mobilize Hindus across hierarchical cleavages, by, however, referring to the people as those who shared social capital that bonded with each other rather than by bridging differences among them. Hindus were being united, notwithstanding internal hierarchies, by paying attention to their shared affinities, and not by trying to accommodate the differences that keep them apart. By the 2007 election, the polarization rhetoric was toned down, and he tried to project himself as a "Vikas Purush," embodying the idea of development, ostensibly for all (Jaffrelot 2008). By 2012, his appeal had widened by invoking a depoliticized ideal, Gujarati Asmita, a self-assured sense of identity based on forward-looking pragmatism but so depoliticized that it could appeal across cleavages (Suhrud 2008; Chandhoke 2012), and so he should get a 1 on this score.

On the second index, the extent of setting boundaries, there has perhaps been no other chief minister who polarized Hindus and Muslims under their watch as much as Modi did, as is well known from the post-Godhra riots of 2002 and thereafter. On this particular attribute Modi will get a clear 1. While this was perhaps diminished in his middle years, it has become a stable polarity in Gujarat politics toward the end of his term in 2012.

Modi has always remained a loyal BJP party member and has never rebelled or sought to carve an identity for himself outside the party. However, in becoming the first among equals, Modi spared no effort in removing all his detractors within the BJP—Keshubhai Patel, Shankersinh Vaghela, Pravin Togadia—and Ahmed Patel and Sohrabuddin Sheikh, among others, within Gujarat (Jose 2012). Thus, on the leadership score he would get 0.6 initially, but he has since acquired a persona that is larger than the party and the regional leaders in the state and should get a 1 by 2012.

Narendra Modi as Prime Minister

Narendra Modi as prime minister has been labeled as a populist by many global scholars, similar to the rise of populist figures in Hungary, Russia, Brazil, and the US. However, in Indian scholarship, his politics is also mixed with the ethnic nationalist mobilization of the BJP, and so I would argue that it is not a clear case of populism unless we label it as right-wing populism (Varshney 2019b) or an Indian version of competitive authoritarianism (Jaffrelot 2021). Survey evidence also seems to show that populism and nationalism, while concurrent, appear to be distinct political phenomena on the demand side of mobilization, and so perhaps one would have to explore this distinction further.

For the purposes here, I would argue that Modi's populism as prime minister is not as stark as that of Indira Gandhi. For one, he has remained a party insider and in fact fits the description quite neatly because he has certainly emerged as the tallest leader of the party, having been able to sideline or purge other powerful leaders and voices within the party before becoming the prime minister. And he has not sought to sideline his Hindu nationalist bearings even though he projects himself as an inclusive leader. On the leadership dimension then Modi would get a 0.6. On the invocations to the people dimension, even though Modi has initiated several programs for economic inclusion, I would argue that they are mostly targeted toward consolidating his base of supporters within the Hindu fold, and not really aimed at bridging the gap with other religious groups. That is, consolidating the divided Hindu vote (Varshney 2017) has been his electoral imperative more than pursuing a stark nationalist project but the net that has been cast for that divided Hindu vote is so broad that its edges seem undefined. On this invocation to the people dimension, therefore, he also gets a 0.8 since his focus has essentially been to tighten the bonds within the Hindu community very broadly defined. And finally, if in consolidating the vote, if it takes an inherent turn toward an anti-Muslim mobilization, so be it. That is, while Modi has projected himself as one consolidating the Hindu vote, other affiliates with his party have turned that mobilization as a signal to mobilize against Muslims as well, to which he seems to have either turned or not been emphatic enough in condemning or repealing such actions. Certainly, the massive widespread mobilization against the amendments to the Citizenship Amendment Act was one of the largest polarization initiatives in recent times, but Modi's position on this has been mostly to avoid confronting the mobilizers or avoid condemning the lower state-level authoritarian tactics that have inflicted all sorts of hardships upon the critics of this majoritarian nationalism. On this boundary-setting dimension, which has been polarizing, Modi would get a 0.8 and not a 1 because, while he does not directly advocate such violence, he is criticized for not calling out such incidents explicitly enough.

In the Lok Sabha elections in 2024, surveys seem to show that Narendra Modi's image seems to have stagnated over the preceding decade, perhaps because his strategy of populism had run its course (Shastri 2024). He was certainly not an orthogonal political outsider anymore or even invincible considering that the Rashtriya Swayamsevak Sangh (RSS) also sought to indirectly chasten him (Pandey 2024), and hence a 0.8 on the leadership score. What was, however, very marked in this election was the extent to which they sought to set the boundaries by ramping up Hindu nationalist rhetoric, weaken the opposition by freezing opposition party funds, incarcerating political opposition leaders, muzzling the media into submission, and so on (Devasahayam 2024). He also tried to invoke and mobilize the Hindu people, mostly by inaugurating the Ram Temple at Ayodhya, though the spectacle proved to eventually be tangential to the OBC and Dalit communities, who felt that their constitutionally guaranteed rights, especially affirmative action policies, were under threat (Lakshman 2024), and to a sizeable section of the population who continued to feel financially impoverished with the bulk of the contractual opportunities going to other castes (Alam 2024). Thus, Modi will get a 1 on the boundary-setting score and a 0.6 on the invocations to the people.

Indira Gandhi

Indira Gandhi is well known as a populist of the classical tradition wherein political control is highly centralized and redistributive projects are targeted at a multi-class coalition that is stitched together through this direct connection, thereby bypassing power contestations that come from within the political party or system as institutional checks to counterbalance executive power. Like the Latin American leaders of her time, she followed a bureaucratic authoritarian model of governance that centralized all political, legislative, federal, and administrative control. However, unlike them, her support did not come from the support of the armed forces but from her connection with the people, ensuring successive electoral mandates and sustained targeted programs directly to the people (Kaviraj 1986; Kenny 2021; Guha 2017).

After Nehru, Indira Gandhi was the undisputed leader of the Congress Party. She was initially brought in by the regional leaders as a young, pliable political outsider whose strings could ostensibly be pulled by the establishment party men. But she overcame their grip by breaking up the party and by raising the rallying cry of *garibi hatao* (remove poverty) to directly connect with the people and came back with a resounding mandate in 1971.

I would consider her a party outsider who started a splinter faction that ended up becoming the restructured Congress Party eventually. And so, on the leadership score, she would get a 1. On the invocation to the people score too I would score her at 1. This is because there was probably no contemporary leader who not only centralized power in the office of the prime minister but also in the name of the people threatened all checks to power through various constitutional amendments and the unprecedented and arbitrary use of Emergency powers. Of course, consequently she polarized opinion, which eventually led to her downfall, but there is no denying that she was able to follow through on such radical measures because she had the populist connection.

On the polarization dimension, Indira Gandhi demonstrated her willingness to impose an Emergency and postpone elections on the one hand and on the other stepped back from condoning bloodshed upon those she violently opposed otherwise and so would possibly get a 1 on this score. She imprisoned many opposition members, removed potential threats or internal challengers, deposed governments until they aligned with her, and used state power against regional separatists and others who resisted her rule.

In the 1980 election, while Indira Gandhi got a two-thirds majority with around a 42 percent vote share, it was the opposition that altogether secured the majority popular vote share. Her victory was mostly because there simply was no other alternative, as the opposition was in disarray, segmented by internal contradictions of ideological differences and political ambitions (Gould 1980). By this time, Indira Gandhi's popularity and leadership seemed routinized with the exception of Operation Blue Star initiated against the secessionist movement in Punjab that was polarizing, and so she would get a 0.6 on popular sovereignty and leadership but a 0.8 on polarization.

Mostly In Cases

J. Jayalalithaa

Jayalalithaa Jayaram was among the second generation of populist leaders along with M. Karunanidhi and M. G. Ramachandran (MGR). Jayalalitha emerged in the political arena after MGR's death, fighting her way up as a virtuous political outsider[9] who was bequeathed the sole responsibility to fulfill MGR's legacy by MGR himself (Pandian and Geetha 1989). Having grabbed the reins of the All India Anna Dravida Munnetra Kazhagam (AIADMK), she was unassailable in the party, and became the chief minister of Tamil Nadu first in 1991 and then several times over the next two decades. She lost power in 1996 primarily because of her unabashed display of power and privilege and then regained her position after rounds of imprisonment on corruption charges and subsequent release in 2002 (M. T. 2001; Wyatt 2002). Thereafter, and despite intervening prison terms and failing health, she won again in 2011. Jayalalitha can be considered a populist because of the intense loyalty she got from the masses despite the corruption within her own party, her autocratic and distant behavior with her voters and party colleagues, and her vindictiveness for her "enemies" (Vaasanthi 2019).

Looking back over successive electoral cycles, Jayalalitha soon became a routinized politician, retaining her direct connection with the masses even though she governed her party and the state like an autocrat. In 1991, she had to fight her way, akin to a classic political outsider, and was mostly concerned with finding her space amongst her various adversaries and legitimizing her claim by appealing to the masses as the rightful heir to MGR's legacy but without much substance except for her image on and off screen. Till 1996 she continued in the same vein, making plebiscitarian appeals to the masses, but the corruption and vindictiveness against the Dravida Munnetra Kazhagam (DMK) did cost her the election in 1996. In the early 2000s, she went to jail because of the mounting corruption cases against her and had to drop her economic reforms. She was most unassailable between 2011 and 2016, during which time she made the unprecedented move of arresting Karunanidhi in the middle of the night (she was meted the same treatment later on), confronting and out-maneuvering institutions and coalition allies that sought to rein her in, and certainly polarizing the electorate in an attempt to establish her presence by projecting herself as a victimized woman who had finally emerged out of the shadows as MGR's legatee. In 2001, I would argue that her score would be 0.8 on leadership and popular sovereignty, but she was at the heights of wielding power and antagonizing her political adversaries and so would get a 1 on the polarization score. Thereafter, Jayalalitha became even more routinized, dealing with her share of litigation and failing health and certainly kept out of the spotlight between 2006 and 2011. Weaknesses in the DMK led to her election as the feasible alternative in 2011. By 2011, I would argue that she was essentially the only viable mainstream alternative in a context of anti-incumbency against the DMK, with a miniscule difference of 1 percent between their respective state-level electoral coalitions that fought the 2011 elections (EPW Editorial Desk 2011a). For 2011, one could arguably give Jayalalitha a 0.6 on all three counts. Post-2011 elections, Jayalalitha outcompeted the preceding governments by expanding the public distribution system of rations and including with two-wheelers and laptops.

The only difference then in the 2016 elections would be a 1 on the popular sovereignty score and retaining 0.6 on the other two counts because while the rest of her populist politics remained the same, her focus that time round was mostly to deepen and widen her patronage and thereby, yet again, outcompete the DMK.

M. Karunanidhi

M. Karunanidhi has been the longest-serving politician at the state level[10] and was well known as the backstage brain behind Dravidian politics, being cut from the same cloth as the original Dravidian leaders. He was the primary scriptwriter for MGR during their heydays of film production and was well known for his erudition in Tamil culture. He came across as a Tamil chauvinist, especially to those outside Tamil Nadu, because of his ostensibly maverick ideas on Hindu mythology and Sanskritic culture. However, as the tallest leader in the DMK, he remained committed to the welfare of the backward castes and classes (Wyatt 2002). As a mastermind of the use of all forms of media, he was able to retain the connection of the party with the masses, his hold over the reins of power despite the internal feuds within his immediate and extended family, and strategically wield power at the national level as a key coalition partner to the ruling dispensation in Delhi (Jose 2011).

Karunanidhi emerged as first the replacement for C. N. Annadurai in 1969 after the latter's untimely death but was mostly overshadowed by MGR between 1977 and 1987. While he was a highly respected figure by 1969, his rise as a populist political leader was yet to take shape. It is only after MGR's death that we witness Karunanidhi establishing his supremacy in Tamil Nadu and emerging as a key player in the national arena. His reign over the party remained mostly unchallenged through the 1990s, purging dissenters like Vaiko, keeping his family under his control while providing them with leadership opportunities within the party, the state, and the national governments, and keeping the Dravidian ethos alive at a time when the political arena had come to be characterized by personalistic politics and caste cleavages.

And so, being the tallest and mainstream populist leader of the DMK, Karunanidhi would get a 0.8 on the leadership score, with a drop to 0.6 from 2006 after he began to rely on his chosen son, Stalin, though it was contested briefly at the time. The delegitimization of his espousal of the Eelam cause because of Rajiv Gandhi's death muted his ethnic chauvinist appeals in the early 1990s, and his policies were more progressive and innovative than populist as he sought to consolidate well-established welfare programs (Wyatt 2013b). It was in post-2006 that we see the enhancement of populist welfarist schemes. And so, I argue that he would get a 1 on the boundary-setting score for 1996 because he was battling the central government antagonistic to the Eelam cause and deriding the political ascendancy of Jayalalitha at home. By 2006 though, his polarization score would fall to 0.4 as his party itself was delegitimized by allegations of corruption against his party men at the national level. On the invocation to the people score, his appeals to the people were mostly through progressive schemes that were already well-established programs and so would get a 0.4 in 1996, and from 2006, we see a dramatic escalation of populist welfare, giving him a 1 on the popular sovereignty score.

Mamata Banerjee

Mamata Banerjee rose to prominence because she was singlehandedly able to overthrow the Communist bastion in West Bengal after 34 years in 2011. More recently, in 2021, she also emerged victorious from the onslaught of the intimidatory power of the BJP juggernaut. Initially known as more of a rabble rouser who connected with the public and a thorn in the flesh of the ruling establishments at the center and the state, she is now perhaps better understood as a politician who represented the antagonisms of the rural and the urban against prevalent orthodoxies in the state (Howladar 2014).

Banerjee has been described as a populist[11] not just because she was at the helm of an antagonistic popular sector, but also because she combined her politically ascetic style with Hindu iconography, is considered a chaste woman, and has been able to sustain an undifferentiated construction of the "people" (Ray Chaudhury 2022). She has always been a political outsider, even though she has been a part of mainstream national and regional politics, as a parliamentarian, central government cabinet minister, coalition ally, and opposition leader since the early to mid-1990s. Within West Bengal, she is an orthogonal alternative to the Left, Right, and the Congress Party, occupying a certain pragmatic non-ideological space that is characterized by encompassing empty signifiers such as "Ma, Mati, Manush" (Mother, Soil, and People) and "Poribartan" (Change) (Howladar 2016).

Her first breakthrough in Bengal was when she electorally displaced the 34-year-old Leftist regime in the 2011 assembly elections, but arguably her victory was because of the Communist government more than anything else, wherein the inept handling of the Nandigram protests was the proverbial last straw. One would argue that her 2016 victory would be the highest point of her populism because one got the full picture of her redistributive intent (through the various welfare schemes) (Chakrabarty 2016), her intensified connection with the popular sector,[12] and her centralized control over the government (Samaddar 2016; Guha 2016).

Mamata would score a 1 on the leadership dimension but became more mainstream by 2021, and so this score can be reduced to a 0.8. One could argue that while she connected with the people as a rebel outsider in the 2011 elections, she was able to broaden and deepen her connection with all groups except perhaps the middle classes and the "bhadralok" elite by the time of the 2016 elections. So, on the people index, she should initially get a 0.6 in 2011 and 1 for the 2016 elections, with a drop to 0.8 in the 2021 elections because the BJP had also gained entry into the politics of West Bengal for the first time.[13] On the boundary-setting dimension, one could think of her as more polarizing than not. This is not just because of her adversarial hostility and violence toward competing parties, especially by her party members, but because she has traditionally been the underdog contesting the establishment and therefore has to constantly challenge the hierarchy to electorally compete against them and overthrow them from office. By the 2021 elections, while she continued her redistributive projects, her popularity had become both mainstream and somewhat diminished because of the malpractices of her party men, including corruption and nepotism. But 2021 was a huge success because she defeated the BJP despite defections, sabotage, money, and media pressure. Thus, for 2021, she would get a 0.8 on leadership, a 0.8 on invocation to the people, and a 1 on boundary setting.

Bal Thackeray

Bal Thackeray was a contemporary of the populist leaders of Tamil Nadu but arguably could not have been more different than the Tamil populists. His politics was ethnically chauvinist, exclusivist, and based on a militant approach to other ethnicities in Maharashtra, particularly in Mumbai. Second, his claims for Maratha empowerment were secondary to Indian nationalism; they were not juxtaposed as a claim against nationalist domination, especially since the 1980s. Third, Bal Thackeray publicly stated that he did not believe in "democracy," though it is unclear what he precisely meant because the Shiv Sena has continued to compete and win elections over the past few decades.

There is possibly little disagreement among scholars that Bal Thackeray was a populist, by which they mean that he was the leader who articulated a nativist appeal for empowerment (Gupta 1980a, 1980b, 1980c) as an expression of cultural populism (Palshikar 2004; Heuzé 2000), and wherein his party members adopted performative strategies that were locally relevant and had a dashing appeal (Bedi 2007). Bal Thackeray was the first in Maharashtra who articulated the need for mobilizing the masses into what was till then an acceptable condition of non-Marathi-speaking migrants occupying stable professional positions in Mumbai in the government and in businesses. What began as an irreverent, lighthearted satirical weekend publication, the *Marmik* soon began to publish weekly rosters that articulated the extent to which Maharashtrians were being excluded from key economic opportunities under the weekly column head "Vacha ani Utha" (Read and rise). Thackeray continued to be necessary as the populist leader for the party even several decades later. When confronted by a rebellion of senior party leaders in 1992, Thackeray feigned resignation that led to a backlash from the public and thereby reconfirmed the emotional bond with his followers and showed the senior party members who was the boss (Palshikar 2004).

At the time of his emergence, he was certainly an orthogonal alternative, unfettered, irreplaceable, and constantly adapting to the exigencies of the times, and so would get a 1 on the leadership score.[14] On the invocation to the people score, Bal Thackeray would get a 0.6 because he advocated for an ethnic identity essentially whereby other intersectional identities would have to subsume and conform to the same, and so he was more rather than less on this score because his barriers to membership were more open than closed. For example, south Indians could be included within the Shiv Sena so long as they were willing to abide by Marathi language and culture. Thus, the idea of popular sovereignty was not pluralistic but clearly based on a dominant and homogenous ethnos. And to protect the ethnos, it was important for the Shiv Sena to show an avowedly action-based virulence against "others" such as Muslims, Communists, and corrupt elites, be it through murders, damage of public property, or riots. Thackeray was certainly more polarizing than pluralistic and so gets a 1 on the polarization score.

Lalu Prasad Yadav

Lalu Yadav was the chief minister of Bihar from the early 1990s till around 1998 and then by proxy when his wife, Rabri Devi, was chief minister till around 2005. Lalu's son is a dominant voice in Bihar's politics today despite charges of corruption and a violent past that have led to the current imprisonments in jail, which speaks of the deep imprint he has upon the politics of the state (Ankit 2018). Lalu's rule was important for Bihar for several reasons. First, he was possibly the most avowed secularist in the state and in national politics because for a long time he was able to not just stem the aggressive mobilization of Hindu nationalists in the state, but in doing so effectively became the protector of minority interests and the idea of a secular India. Second, no other state has perhaps seen such levels of institutional self-destruction and corruption under the rule of a politician who has nevertheless remained popular. Witsoe (2011: 79) describes this apparent contradiction not as a capture of state institutions by lower castes, but as the systematic weakening of upper-caste-dominant formal institutions by the concomitant strengthening of informal sources of power that used criminality, corruption, and caste networks to govern the people. Lalu's popularity lay precisely in weakening the formal institutions of power by strengthening the more proximate and accessible, but nevertheless informal, sources of power.

Lalu's populism has been described as a political struggle for social justice in caste terms, where his party argued that "vikaas nahin, sammaan chahiye" (we need dignity, not development), and the Janta Dal (JD) raised the slogan of "Bhurabal Hatao" (Destroy the Bhu-ra-ba-l, which comprises the Bhumihars, Rajputs, Brahmins, and Lala castes) (Nigam 2010). The other aspect of his populism was the cultural repertoire he deployed to powerful effect that won him both the hearts of his people and the mirth of the urbane, and together ensured his visibility in national politics. For example, in a conversation with Witsoe, Lalu asks him to notice that he is missing a toenail, and after a bewildering pause, he says that he lost the toenail when herding buffaloes as a child, but now he is sitting on the tallest chair as chief minister! He was alluding to democracy's radical potential to level radical social inequalities, such as bringing this buffalo herder to the "throne" (Witsoe 2011: 78). He has been seen conducting interviews on some serious national political issues whilst sitting on his haunches and milking his cows who lived in his official residence. There are many such instances, but suffice it to say that such theatrics did entertain the genteel middle classes but were deliberately deployed to taunt them of their naivete and actually signal that the rustic had arrived.

Lalu became the chief minister in 1990 after the JD won the assembly elections and then again in 1995, till around 1998, and ruled by proxy through his wife, Rabri Devi, till 2005. Arguably, Lalu's populist dimensions peaked in his second term as a leader who could take on the BJP; this period also coincided with the height of his corruption, criminalization of politics, and other forms of anti-institutionalization. He remained popular during that time because such forms of mobilization were seen as retributive entitlements by backward ascendant castes from state institutions that were historically dominated by upper-caste elites.

In terms of the populist score, Lalu would probably get a 0.6 on the people score because, while his appeal continued to be caste-centered and limited to the Yadavs, he is also known to have included and deepened reservations for other groups, such as Muslims. This vote base and his appeal mostly remained stable through his terms as chief minister. On the polarization front, Lalu justifies getting a 1. He was initially not seen as a polarizing figure because he felt that the backward caste groups and minorities should compete on equal terms. Corruption was clearly a problem during his terms in office; he either turned a blind eye to or justified it as recompense for past elitist domination. But after coming to power in 1990 and following the demolition of the Babri Masjid in 1992, his anti-institutional, anti-Hindutva stance was so deeply polarizing that other castes (lower and upper) were intimidated and threatened by intermediate caste ascendance. Finally, as a leader, he flaunted his rural peasant persona and used it to connect with the masses, even if it gave much mirth to the establishment, and to that extent, he was possibly a political outsider who charted a path of his own. And therefore, on the leadership score, he should possibly get a 0.8, notwithstanding that he started his own party, the Rashtriya Janata Dal (RJD), in 1997.

Fully Out Cases

Fully out cases are party insiders who tend to pursue accommodative (as opposed to Manichean confrontational) politics and are comfortable within the consolidated electoral constituency that they connect with. While they are also charismatic and reformist, and hence part of this dataset, they do not come across as populists because their connections are routinized, stable, and tend to abide by liberal democratic norms and practices. Nitish Kumar and Naveen Patnaik certainly fit this mold, while Raman Singh is in this category mostly because of the scale of his welfarist policies.

Nitish Kumar

Along with Lalu, Nitish Kumar also emerged initially as a socialist politician in the 1970s and belonged to the other dominant but backward caste of Kurmis. He has been the chief minister of Bihar since 2005, withstanding the National Democratic Alliance (NDA), the Modi wave, and several other such challenges since then. He is most known—and perhaps the reason behind his successive victories—for his reputation as a reformer. He ushered in several administrative reforms related to law and order, crime, reporting, and the right to information, and redistributive reforms related to service delivery, flood management, and industrial development, among others, and all this notwithstanding the concurrent growth of unbridled consumerism boosted by the "mall/parlour" culture (Anup Kumar 2011: 110–11).

Nitish's mandate and rise to power are quite different because he was able to avoid the role of musclemen during elections, and reached out to the middle class, women, and the Bihari diaspora. He has consciously avoided cultivating an image akin to that of Lalu Yadav and therefore has maintained a certain reserve. He avoids theatrics and tends to keep the company of intellectuals and other elites. He possibly comes across as a reformist, implementing decisions that are progressive and inclusive (Kumar 2013; Kumar and Ranjan 2009).

Nitish Kumar is respected as a reformist leader. He became the chief minister in 2005 after a fragmentation of not just the party (JD) in Bihar but also the state, when Jharkhand was split from Bihar and made a separate state. The end of Lalu's reign, the tussle between Ram Vilas Paswan and the JD leaders, and the entry of the NDA eventually created the way for Nitish Kumar to emerge. For 2005, therefore, I think he would get a 0.4 on the people score as he was interested in building an inclusive constituency but not necessarily widening its appeal, a 0 on boundary setting because he does not come across as a polarizing figure (and in fact may have made many overtures across the political aisle from time to time to manage elections), and while a reformist, he does not come across as being interested in carving out a niche or legacy for himself; therefore, he will also get a 0 on the leadership score. But by 2010, Nitish Kumar had widened his support by reaching out to the Pasmanda Muslims through various welfare schemes, had stabilized the rule of law, and also managed to bring together backward castes like Kurmis and Koeries and the upper castes under his umbrella. The 2009 election in some sense was a watershed election for Nitish Kumar. And so, on the people score, he should get a 0.8 because he grew in popularity. In an opinion poll cutting across all communities, around 88 percent said they were happy with his governance, which was possibly unprecedented in any other state (Kumar and Ranjan 2009). He should get a score of 0.4 on leadership because he was considered distinct in matters of governance though not quite a populist. By the 2015 elections, one can argue, Nitish Kumar had not only established his credentials as a popular development-oriented reformer but had also emerged out of the shadows of both the RJD and the BJP by breaking the alliance with the latter (Kumar 2013). He should get a slightly higher score on the leadership index at 0.6. By 2020, Nitish Kumar had spent around 15 years in governance and was being challenged by Tejaswi Yadav. His reform agenda seems to have run its course even though he remains politically relevant even in 2024, having become a key coalitional ally for the NDA government. But one cannot attribute any populist dimensions to him, and so on that count he should probably get a 0 on all three dimensions.

Naveen Patnaik

Naveen Patnaik was one of the longest-serving chief ministers of any state in India, having won five successive assembly terms in Odisha ever since he founded the Biju Janata Dal (BJD) in 1997 until his electoral defeat in the 2024 assembly elections. Patnaik would not strike anyone as being a populist. He does not speak Odiya, is of royal lineage, and is the sole inheritor of the dynastic political power wielded by his father, Biju Patnaik. A public intellectual, patron of the fine arts, and generally known to not tolerate corruption, Patnaik would easily fit the label of an elitist modernizer with a liberal heart considering the redistributive magnitude of many of his welfare programs in the context of a fragmented opposition and weak administrative capacity (Manor 2015). While he shares an affinity in terms of his background and disposition toward public affairs with inclusive liberal reformers, he centralized decision-making to avoid corruption and used the administration to deliver instead of devolving power to local democratic institutions.

In his early years in power till 2009, he was in a coalition with the BJP. But he severed his links from the BJP as a response to the communal violence in the state in 2007–08 and was returned to power with a massive majority in 2009 (Misra 2009). Analysts argue that Patnaik remains in power because none of the other competing parties, and internal dissidents, have been able to put forward a strong alternative. Additionally, what keeps him in power is the attention he gives to welfare programs (public distribution system, forest rights, self-help groups, and more recently sports promotion) and his ability to bring in many mining and industrial projects for the state's economic development (Mohanty 2014) though such developments have mostly benefitted the Brahmin and Karan castes in the state.

Patnaik is known as a modernizer, and modernization is fraught with the risks associated with private capital incursions into a resource-rich state, and so the modernizer label does not easily fit the label of a populist. Except for the 2009 elections, where he came into his own electorally, one would probably consider him to be one of the few personalistic leaders who do not fit the label. And so, his scores in the first term as a leader or a polarizing figure would be 0.4 and slightly above the threshold for the popular sovereignty score at 0.6. In 2009, he certainly realigned his vision to become more inclusive and taller than the legacy of his family and his party. So, he would get a 0.8 on leadership and on the people score, and his moving away from the BJP would shift his polarization score to above the threshold at 0.6. But by 2014 and thereafter, his populism scores would drop because his politics and governance strategies remain popular but mostly routinized. In 2024, Patnaik's party lost the majority in the assembly elections and won no Lok Sabha seat in the national elections, paving the way for the BJP to enter Odisha and marking the end of a 24-year-long regime under Patnaik.

Raman Singh

Raman Singh was the chief minister of Chhattisgarh from 2003 to 2018. He was mostly known as the person who fixed the public distribution system (by devolving delivery to village committees and transporting grains to them directly) and won praise from both development economists and the people—they called him the Chawar wala Baba, or the elder who gives us rice—(Dreze and Khera 2015; Puri 2012; Roy 2019). His populism was essentially described as redistributive governance. Also, like other populists who vilify the "other," he organized the Salwa Judum (a counter-terrorist force) to exterminate the Naxalite movement in the state, but subsequently was forced to retract because of a Supreme Court ruling that the force itself was illegal, and he followed a more dialogical path thereafter.

Raman Singh would be better described as a moderate reformist rather than a populist. While the BJP came to power in 2003, mostly because of Congress disarray, Raman Singh was able to maintain his hold over office in 2008 despite the Congress–Nationalist Congress Party (NCP) alliance, attributable to the welfare schemes that he had introduced in the first term (Joshi and Rai 2009). He continues to be a party insider in the BJP and was clearly a public-purpose-driven reformist focused on development to secure legitimacy for the party and not necessarily for his persona.

On the scores though, I would give him 0.6 on the boundary-setting score for his first two terms because he did set up a violent outfit to exterminate the Naxalites, but a 0 on other attributes on his first term because he was essentially brought into the state to govern but was not the face of the party in the 2003 elections. By 2008 though, his reform schemes made him popular and certainly the tallest BJP leader in the state, and so he should get a 0.8 on the people score and a 0.4 on the leadership score. But by 2013, his programs were routinized such that he would get a 0 on all three scores, and not surprisingly, he was replaced in 2018 as he had mostly delivered on what he stood for.

Intermediate Cases: More In than Out and Vice Versa

The in-between categories, the "more in than out" and the "more out than in," are conceptually difficult to parse from each other because they are closer but on either side of the crossover threshold. For instance, it is quite natural to assume that most politicians would try to bridge cleavages, although the core of their constituents would be bonded together. "More in" leaders would conceptually be those who are mostly reformist, relying on their party or programmatic agendas as much as their personalities to drive them, and would invoke notions of popular sovereignty supportive of such reformist claims. "More out" leaders would be less autonomous from their party though they are strong and respected party men, tend to be inclusive in the liberal pluralist sense, and consequently are relatively unenthused to polarize the voters. Chandrababu Naidu and Chandrasekhar Rao fit the former category, and Digvijay Singh and Pawan Chamling fit the latter category.

Chandrababu Naidu

Naidu, son-in-law of N. T. Rama Rao, or NTR, was the quintessential neo-populist, promoting neoliberal reforms and democratic deepening simultaneously, referred to as dual transitions (Ayyangar 2007; Reddy 2002).

With the changed World Bank policy of allowing subnational governments to borrow directly from the bank in the mid-1990s, Naidu was one of the first in India to take on a structural loan and soon became the poster boy for all things related to economic modernization (Kirk 2005)—be it information technology (IT), greenfield investments, infrastructure reforms, market pricing and fiscal austerity, and digital governance. He sought to catapult Andhra Pradesh out of the traditional politics and economic functioning and leapfrog into a world of high economic growth and democratic accountability. However, he was given only five years (1999–2004) to make that happen and had slowly slid into some sort of political obscurity for almost two decades since then, being subject to harassment and humiliation from those politically opposed to him. But what he did and how he conducted himself was iconic enough for other leaders to emulate at the time, and he perhaps became the model for other chief ministers to follow when they began to promote economic reforms in their respective states (Rudolph and Rudolph 2001). Being given a second lease of political life as a key coalition partner in the NDA government and as chief minister since the 2024 elections, much remains to be seen as to how Naidu reinvents himself on the political stage.

I would also think that he was popular among the aspirational classes as a political leader because there really has been no one like him in Andhra politics who was brazenly talking about economic modernization and adopting neoliberal approaches for political and economic development. He was the original articulator of the promise of market reforms (P.V. Narasimha Rao or Manmohan Singh for that matter had not really advocated for liberalization and had framed it mostly as a pragmatic and necessary step to avert a larger economic crisis) and came up with several innovative ideas to promote his state. Therefore, on the leadership score, I would argue that he would get a 1. On the invocation to the people score, Naidu would possibly get a 0.4 because he was primarily interested in deepening the control of extant core groups that voted for the Telugu Desam Party (TDP), and so was more about bonding the groups rather than bridging the gap among different groups. He did not allow the BJP to enter Andhra politics by tying up with them as a coalition partner. He was keen to exclude the Left and the Congress from all reformist ideas, and so one can infer that his aim was to undercut others and promote the traditional TDP affiliated groups. On the boundary-setting score, his polarization was not based on social biases but more driven by his neoliberal reforms. I would argue that he certainly polarized public opinion with his progressive ideas, where those who resisted felt that his reforms were misguided (especially from the rural areas) and others felt that he was the necessary leader to promote the needed reforms (urban voters), and so would get a 0.8. In any case, all these ideas came crashing to the ground with his defeat in 2004 from which he has not been able to recover (he was a chastened version in 2009) and has eventually become historically interesting but politically obscure.[15]

K. Chandrasekhar Rao

K. Chandrasekhar Rao, or KCR as he is known, is the first chief minister of Telangana and was at the forefront of the Telangana statehood movement. Telangana was much like other subregions within other states (Vidarbha in Maharashtra, Bundelkhand in Uttar Pradesh) that felt historically deprived because of uneven development and political representation. The migration from the coastal districts of Andhra, the predominance of the coastal caste networks in various entrepreneurial opportunities (including in the IT sector) and in the political arena that deprived the *mulki*s (locals) of equivalent upward mobility, the domination of Andhra (mostly coastal districts) neo-middle class and business elite in the capital city's (Hyderabad) cultural landscape, and the capture of profitable agrarian tracts that were either well irrigated or close to the intrastate highways, by the nexus between local contractors, politicians, and business elites, were all contributory factors that legitimized the historical claims for a separate state distinct from Andhra Pradesh (Maringanti 2010).

However, Telangana's success at achieving statehood makes it distinctive because it is possibly one of the few subregions to have got this status despite sharing the same language and culture with Andhra Pradesh. One would be overstating the case to attribute KCR's leadership to this movement for statehood, though he was certainly present at the moment that was both historically defined and politically salient at the time. What legitimizes him as a populist was his ability to articulate a political strategy that "othered" the political establishment in Hyderabad. He was able to convince his folks that Andhra neoliberal reformers were essentially adopting draconian tactics to eliminate Telangana's rightfully perceived claims as "militant" and pushing reforms through compensatory payoffs to contractors, politicians, and other Andhra entrepreneurs or any form of opposition (Maringanti 2010).

Thus, on the leadership dimension, in 2014, KCR would get a 0.8 because he was not just a political outsider that launched his own party with the single agenda of Telangana statehood; he dramatized the grievance, with the help of a sensationalist media, as a "crisis," and was able to remain at the forefront despite having broken the "protest fast" midway while his supporters were apparently committing suicide for the same larger cause. On the invocation to the people dimension, KCR would get a 0.4 because he essentially tapped into a long-standing feeling of historical deprivation whose referents were clear but were nevertheless circumscribed by geography, class, and caste. On polarization, KCR would get a 0.2 because his political strategy was primarily aimed at capturing power based on a historically legitimized set of grievances that he had little role to play in articulating, and that the crossover to statehood was based on institutional opportunities and a political mobilization that surpassed his own contributions to it. By the next round of elections in 2018, KCR had consolidated his hold over the state, but as a more routinized political leader. Social re-engineering through caste-based patronage, coopting political competitors into the party fold through political tactics, redistricting and economically decentralizing local provinces with an eye on creating avenues for the dominant caste–class groups, and reaching out to the cosmopolitan and the Andhra elite in Hyderabad were moves that gave the TRS a strategic depth in Telangana (Vaageeshan and Chitrapu 2021). And so, while his leadership score as a populist diminished to 0.6, his scores on popular sovereignty would be 0.8 and polarization would be 0.4. By 2024, his party with a relaunched name (Bharat Rashtra Samithi), ostensibly to widen its appeal beyond Telangana, turned out to be mostly inconsequential; he lost the assembly elections in 2023, and his daughter has been incarcerated based on some serious corruption charges. KCR's larger-than-life image in Telangana politics has mostly been cut to size.

More Out than In Cases

Digvijay Singh

Digvijay Singh brought in a new strategy and a new kind of politics that attempted to displace the old politics of clientelism and patron–client relations (Manor 2010) by empowering people through democratic institutional devolution, and so he would not be considered a populist.

While he won electorally because of his progressive policies, he was not a political party insider who wriggled his way to the top by usurping power to himself. He was possibly chosen as a compromise candidate in 1994, who nevertheless displayed a keen interest in development policy while allowing the regional party bosses above him to establish themselves at the national level and turning a blind eye to their attempts at fortifying their personal networks for self-enrichment. His personality, while shrewd, articulate, and attractive, was also self-effacing, and has since remained a key and important Congress party man even decades after becoming electorally insignificant. So, on the leadership dimension, Singh would get a 0 because he does not fit the label of a populist. His method of working was not to articulate a new discourse, but to act on the advice of key bureaucrats, civil society organizations, and elected *panchayat* representatives. Singh's social base came from a coalition of intermediate castes, some backward castes, and Muslims. In the process, he faced tensions from the upper castes and Dalits. On the popular sovereignty dimension, therefore, he would probably get a 0.8 because he aimed to be pluralistic, but historical cleavages were always a challenge to the coalition that he constructed. On the boundary-setting index, Singh sought to bypass party intermediaries below and above, but that strategy was not polarizing. Instead, he seemed keen to promote a bottom-up development approach by listening to civil society organizations, promoting education, and building a solid representative base for *panchayat* elections. Since his flagship program that guaranteed education was demand based, one could argue that on polarization, Singh would get a 0.2.

Pawan Kumar Chamling

Pawan Kumar Chamling was the chief minister of Sikkim for a decade from 1994 to 2004 and was one of the most respected leaders of the state. He rose against the autocratic and corrupt leadership of his predecessor, Nar Bahadur Bhandari, on the shoulders of the unorganized rural masses and sought to promote both democracy and development in his state (Bora 2004). Referring to contemporary populist scholarship from Latin America and in the context of Thaksin's populist rule, Synagbo finds similarities between Chamling and the former in terms of mass mobilization, personalized leadership, and a challenge to established life (Syangbo 2010).

Chamling came to power on slogans like "Janta Ko Raj Ma Jantai Raja" (In a popular regime, people are sovereign) and "Khali Khutta ko Sarkar" (Government of the barefoot people), and as a pluralistic alternative to his autocratic and corrupt predecessor who had governed the state for a decade (Malu, Rajan, and Jindal 2023). He made a range of promises to the people: political representation for the Nepalis and Tsongs, inclusion of the eight social groups of the Limbo, Tamang, Rai, Gurung, Manger, Bhujel, Chettri, and Sunwar in the list of OBCs, and making Bhuti and Lepcha official languages of India under the Eighth Schedule of the Constitution. He also promised delivery of better health and education, elderly care, political decentralization, and policies to promote agriculture, tourism, investments, and the environment. In many ways, it seems like Chamling ushered in many positive changes by widening democratic participation, redistributing welfare benefits, and promoting economic development in the region. And as is not uncommon, it led his political competitors and successors to further promote the dual transition of democracy and development.

I would give Chamling a 0.8 on the people score precisely because he was a pluralist, where he carefully identified groups and tried to address their needs under a common umbrella. Whether it was political representation, affirmative action, linguistic recognition, or economic development, policy actions were advocated according to the needs of specific groups. On the polarization dimension, I would give Chamling a 0.4 because he does not come across as someone who was polarizing but certainly sought to provide a fresh alternative to the preceding corrupt autocratic rule and did compete with them on a footing that matched the power of the erstwhile political regime. On the leadership dimension, I would give him a 0.2 because while he did start his own party, he was in some ways still a party insider because his hand was forced as he was asked to leave the Sikkim Sangram Parishad. His problem was with the chief minister and not with the party, and therefore I cannot consider him to be a rebel party outsider because he was very much a part of the same party system establishment but was distinctively inclusive and democratic in his approach.

Having completed the survey of the leaders and identified their scores, I will analyze and interpret the scores in the subsequent chapters. These scores will help to identify the various configurations and the pathways that constitute populism in India and its states over a period of time.

Notes

1. It makes no difference to this project if the candidate is competing in assembly or national elections because the scores for the attributes are fuzzy and the outcomes are percentages, and both are on the same respective scales.

2. I would like to thank Vibha Swaminathan for excellent research assistance and to the Azim Premji Foundation for providing the necessary financial support for this part of the project.

3. Results from the initial versions of the dataset (where only the three attributes and the populist outcome were considered) showed that the cases were clustered around a single configuration of conditions wherein all the conditions generated a sufficient outcome. Apart from the clustering, that all conditions mattered in a configuration is basically a result that seemed obvious because that is why they were part of the data frame in the first place. And so, to avoid these results, I added two other conditions (populist attitudes and risk aversion) to make it possible to spread the cases. I would like to thank Patrick Mello for the suggestion.

4. Lokniti CSDS did not conduct state-level survey during this period, and there seems to be no other alternate source that polled public opinion during that time.

5. Certain well-known populists, particularly M. G. Ramachandran, N. T. Rama Rao, Devraj Urs, Sheikh Abdullah, and Karpoori Thakur, who could have been critical to the analysis, have had to be excluded because there are no public opinion survey results during the times they were in power.

6. To avoid maximum ambiguity with fuzzy scores, QCA analysis recommends not coding cases as a 0.5 score because a 0.5 score can explain both the outcome and non-outcome. In a quantitative approach, a 0.5 score indicates a distance from zero, but in a QCA a 0.5 score is a threshold level that distinguishes the outcome from the non-outcome, and hence the need to parse that score into either below or above the threshold if we think the case is 0.5. Adhering to this and to improve the consistency thresholds, I chose a matrix with an even number of thresholds to avoid ambiguity.

7. The scores of the cases are the foundation upon which the rest of the analysis rests, and so, needless to add, is perhaps the first significant step to a QCA analysis. I would like to thank Stephanie Tawa Lama-Rewal, Andrew Wyatt, and Yatindra Singh Sisodia for reviewing some of the cases and providing revisions to the scores when necessary. Many finer details in the narratives may have been omitted, which may not satisfy local experts. Having said so, while the errors of omission are mine, the purpose is primarily to compare across cases that will inevitably compromise levels of in-depth analysis. Being in the correct set (appropriate side of the threshold) is certainly more

important than accurately identifying where they are within their side of the threshold.

8. For example, during his 49-day term as chief minister, his government took on two private electricity companies that sought higher tariffs but refused to allow their accounts to be audited and registered a criminal complaint against India's biggest industrialist, Mukesh Ambani, for allegedly manipulating the price of natural gas (Varadarajan 2014).

9. Being the romantic consort to MGR both on and off screen, she was subject to much ridicule by the legally wedded wife of MGR, internal party elites, and the opposition as well.

10. Even though Karunanidhi was the chief minister of Tamil Nadu intermittently since 1989, the dataset considers only two periods that he was in power (1996, 2006) because public opinion data is not available for the other periods.

11. Many local experts have written papers on her populism as part of a conference under the auspices of the Mahanirban Calcutta Research Group (http://www.mcrg.ac.in/RLS_Populism/RLS_Populism_Home.asp, accessed December 18, 2024).

12. In a popular English daily in Bengal, a respected public intellectual described her connection with the people:

> The lady, reared by street fighting, speaks a language and uses a vocabulary that bewitch them. She has an ample stock of foul abusive words to run down the organized Left. They roar in approval. The lady promises them the moon which, she assures, involves no pain; they just have to stand by her. They believe her because she is so much like them. They have sworn undying allegiance to her. She too is resolute never to disown their company, she is for them; they are for her. The freebies she is distributing are her way of requiting their love and loyalty. (Mitra 2012)

13. For instance, Suvendhu Adhikari, a key functionary within the Trinamool Congress (TMC), joined the BJP and defeated Mamata Banerjee at Nandigram, the ground zero for her political ascendancy, in the 2021 assembly elections, but she became the chief minister after winning the byelection in Bhabanipur a few months later. There were many others who had defected to the BJP but meekly returned to her fold after her party's victory in the 2021 elections.

14. Bal Thackeray had never stood for elections though he has always been the face and the leader of his party. Finding it difficult to exclude this case for the reasons mentioned earlier, I included him in the data by considering the party's chief ministerial candidate's electoral data as the proxy.

15. "Naidu 2024" could not be included as a case because exit poll data for the 2024 assembly elections was not available at the time of writing. Even though he has returned as chief minister of Andhra Pradesh and as a coalition partner to Modi, he has mostly remained outside the media spotlight.

5

The Configurations of Populism in India

In this chapter, I will present the results of the qualitative comparative analysis (QCA) and then interpret them to describe the configurations that constitute populism in India. I will then provide the results of the tests for necessary and sufficient conditions and discuss the parameters of fit in terms of consistency and coverage. Finally, I will cover the various solution terms that indicate the pathways to populism.

The Sets of Data

Table 5.1 presents the data, that is, the sets of data, comprising 37 cases along five conditions and a populist outcome. Describing the worksheet as comprising sets of data instead of a dataset seems more accurate because each of the columns in the sheet is a set and its members are points of data (as fuzzy scores or as percentage scores) along the rows as constituent parts of the unit of analysis. The unit of analysis is an instance of a party candidate contesting elections at the state or at the national level. The cases have been purposively selected by reviewing the scholarship that explicitly indicates that the cases can be identified as instances of populism. And the conditions described earlier—electoral invocation to their people (P), antagonistic boundary setting (B), populist political leadership (L), populist attitude (A), and anxiety about the future (F)—are some of the commonly accepted attributes in the comparative scholarship on populism. In set theoretic terms,

Table 5.1　The Logic of Populism Dataset (Raw Scores)

S. No	Acronym	Name	Year	P	B	L	A	F	Y
				Fuzzy			%	%	Ratio
1	AK1	Arvind Kejriwal	2013	0.6	1	1	6.6	9.27	1.92
2	AK2	Arvind Kejriwal	2015	1	1	1	32.1	15.07	0.79
3	AK3	Arvind Kejriwal	2020	0.8	0.6	0.6	23.8	13.3	0.61
4	BT1	Bal Thackeray	1995	0.6	1	1	11.03	8.37	1.42
5	CN2	Chandrababu Naidu	1999	0.4	0.8	1	23.36	18.6	1.05
6	CSR1	Chandrasekhar Rao	2014	0.4	0.2	0.8	31.1	26.73	0.65
7	CSR2	Chandrasekhar Rao	2018	0.8	0.4	0.6	20.4	26.73	0.87
8	DS2	Digvijaya Singh	1998	0.8	0.2	0	12.02	6.73	1.91
9	IG2	Indira Gandhi	1971	1	1	1	16.9	39.88	0.91
10	IG5	Indira Gandhi	1980	0.6	0.8	0.6	10	26.3	0.88
11	JJ2	J. Jayalalithaa	2001	0.8	1	0.8	44.5	7.35	0.54
12	JJ4	J. Jayalalithaa	2011	0.6	0.6	0.6	19.1	12.87	0.44
13	JJ5	J. Jayalalithaa	2016	1	0.6	0.6	32.6	13.51	1.3
14	MK4	M. Karunanidhi	1996	0.4	1	0.8	15.95	7.35	2.04
15	MK5	M. Karunanidhi	2006	1	0.4	0.6	25.6	10.18	0.44
16	LP2	Lalu Prasad Yadav	1995	0.6	1	0.8	14.7	15.91	1.83
17	MB1	Mamata Banerjee	2011	0.6	0.8	1	13.2	17.83	2.06
18	MB2	Mamata Banerjee	2016	1	0.6	1	15	19.19	0.18
19	MB3	Mamata Banerjee	2021	0.8	1	0.8	11.9	34.5	1.82
20	NMG2	Narendra Modi Gujarat	2002	0.6	1	0.6	40.4	1.69	1
21	NMG3	Narendra Modi Gujarat	2007	0.8	0.6	0.8	28.9	3.62	0.88
22	NMG4	Narendra Modi Gujarat	2012	1	1	1	37.3	9.36	1.16
23	NMP1	Narendra Modi PM	2014	0.8	0.8	0.6	23.7	21.2	1
24	NMP2	Narendra Modi PM	2019	1	1	1	17.1	17.9	1.04
25	NMP3	Narendra Modi PM	2024	.6	1	.8	10.29	18.4	0.71
26	NP2	Naveen Patnaik	2004	0.6	0.4	0.4	10.63	1.29	1.2
27	NP3	Naveen Patnaik	2009	0.8	0.6	0.8	6.17	8.33	1.52
28	NP4	Naveen Patnaik	2014	0.2	0.2	0.6	28.9	15.07	1.41
29	NP5	Naveen Patnaik	2019	0	0	0	12	27.18	1.03
30	NK2	Nitish Kumar	2005	0.4	0	0	11	15.62	1.27

(Contd.)

Table 5.1   (*Contd.*)

S. No	Acronym	Name	Year	P	B	L	A	F	Y
				Fuzzy			%	%	Ratio
31	NK3	Nitish Kumar	2010	0.8	0	0.4	27	9.75	0.24
32	NK4	Nitish Kumar	2015	0.8	0	0.6	25.2	29.98	0.26
33	NK5	Nitish Kumar	2020	0	0	0	31.8	22	0.38
34	PKC4	Pawan Kumar Chamling	2009	0.8	0.4	0.2	3.24	3.9	0.86
35	RS1	Raman Singh	2003	0	0.6	0	33.6	14.9	0.91
36	RS2	Raman Singh	2008	0.8	0.6	0.4	30	2.6	1.28
37	RS3	Raman Singh	2013	0	0	0	6.7	12.5	1.19

we will explore if P, B, L, A, and F are the conditions that constitute the membership of the populist outcome Y.

As explained earlier, conditions P, B, and L are fuzzy scores. A and F are percentage scores, and Y is a ratio. Here, I first explain the measurement of the outcome Y, and then only the conditions A and F, because the measurement of conditions P, B, and L have been explained in Chapter 3. I then explain the choices behind the calibration thresholds of the conditions, and the subsequent sections that follow are related to the QCA analysis.

Concept Measurement

As mentioned earlier, the conditions P, B, and L are coded using fuzzy scores that are based on the literature from the cases and have been reviewed by soliciting comments either from the authors who wrote the cases or otherwise from expert scholars who are familiar with these leaders. In the case of populist attitude (A) and future anxiety (F), there were no clear conceptual precedents followed by a measure, and so the measurement of these concepts is post hoc using the data that is available; therefore, it is necessary that they be explained. For instance, there is no theory that I can think of that can define the exact percentage point as to when a public attitude tips over to become electorally significant in India, never mind a populist attitude leading to a populist outcome. In this section, I try to explain the rationale behind the measures and their concepts (of Y, A, and F),[1] dealing with the populist outcome first and then the conditions A and F.

First, how can one measure a populist outcome? While those that follow the ideational approach have adopted various ways of measuring populist outcomes, they seem to broadly follow either a survey-based approach or a coded analysis of the speeches of various political leaders (Hawkins et al. 2019). Except for two national surveys in 1967 and 1971 for parliamentary elections, Lokniti began the surveys again in 1995, and responses to their survey questions till June 2024 have been included in this study to construct the conditions for populist attitudes and anxiety about the future. Even if the data were available, identifying a survey question as an outcome measure that indicated populism seemed misplaced unless the question was developed with the intent of understanding populism and was a part of the design of the survey instrument. And coding speeches across subnational leaders over the past 25 years at least did not seem to be a practical option to follow through on, considering the unavailability of such speeches in a systematically organized archive or suchlike.

Electoral data is easily available,[2] does not provide cause to misinterpret a survey question as a post hoc measure of populism, and certainly speaks to the idea of public opinion. However, the data had to be reflective of the two contrasting approaches to populism. On one side, the ideational approach points toward a public opinion-based mandate and, on the other side, the leadership approach distinguishes the populist from other victorious leaders by highlighting the intense personal connection the populist shares with the masses. Electorally, this implied that populists should not just emerge victorious, but their victory should be to a great extent attributable to their personal connection. Considering these benchmarks (a clear endorsement and the distinct personal connection), it is conceivable that the mandate that a populist should get must be more than what his party gets in the same period (thereby establishing that his connection is salient as it is more than party affiliation), but also that such a higher share should be proportionately larger than all preceding mandates that a politician has got compared to his party (thereby establishing that such a connection is indeed a populist connection).

This idea translated into electoral numbers means that a populist outcome can be measured if the vote share of a political leader in his constituency is more than the average vote share of the party concerned, and that proportion is greater than a similar proportion of all such preceding party leaders and their parties from all earlier elections. Hence, a populist outcome is essentially the level to which the concerned candidate got an unprecedented vote share that not only surpassed his party's popularity but also surpassed all similar proportions from preceding elections.[3]

Next is the measurement of populist attitudes and the measurement of the condition on future anxieties.

Since the references underlying populist attitudes can be multiple (anti-elitism, invoking popular sovereignty, personal connection, Manichean divide, and so on), there were many corresponding questions to choose from even within the same survey questionnaires. The questions included candidate versus party preference, whether the people felt cared for by the government, whether they felt that some groups were blocking their progress, whether the will of the majority should prevail, strong leadership versus institutions, and so on. Post hoc, it was difficult to choose among the pool of questions because all these themes reflect populist attitudes, and so it eventually became a decision to choose the question with the lowest percentage response if there were competing options, to err on the side of conservative estimates.[4] In most cases (24 out of the 37) responses to the question on whether the candidate mattered more than the party were the ones that got included because they got the lowest scores among the competing options.

On recording scores related to future anxiety, I was interested in getting an answer that was prospective, that is, how they feel about their future. With two or three exceptions, the question that was used the most (21 out of the 37 cases) was whether the respondent felt that their financial situation would improve, deteriorate, or remain the same in the next few years. Getting the scores relevant for this condition proved easier, because this question was often the only one (concerns about their prospective economic situation) that was closest to the condition and was being asked over successive National Election Studies (NES) surveys.[5]

I now turn to the analytical sections of the research. I will first discuss the calibration thresholds and then present the results of the QCA analysis.

Calibration

Calibration thresholds are crucial because they define the precise points at which boundaries are set to establish whether the datapoints are members within the set or outside it. Three thresholds—the crossover threshold, the fully in threshold and the fully out threshold—have been identified and explained here for the five conditions and the outcome. The thresholds for

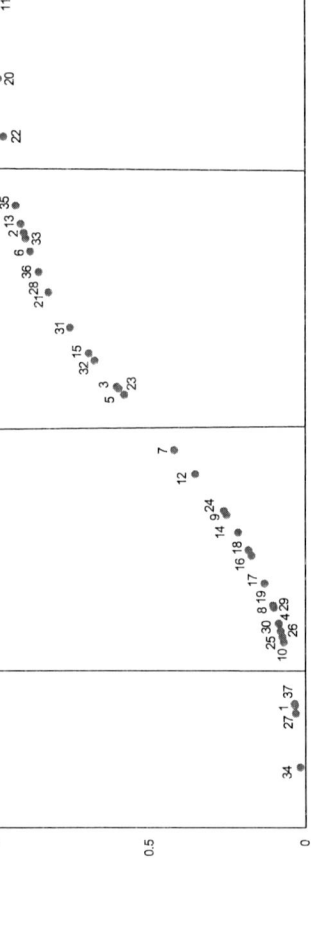

Figure 5.1 Calibration Thresholds for Populist Attitude (A)

Note: The numbers above the dots are the case numbers in the dataset. The vertical lines between the data points are the threshold points.

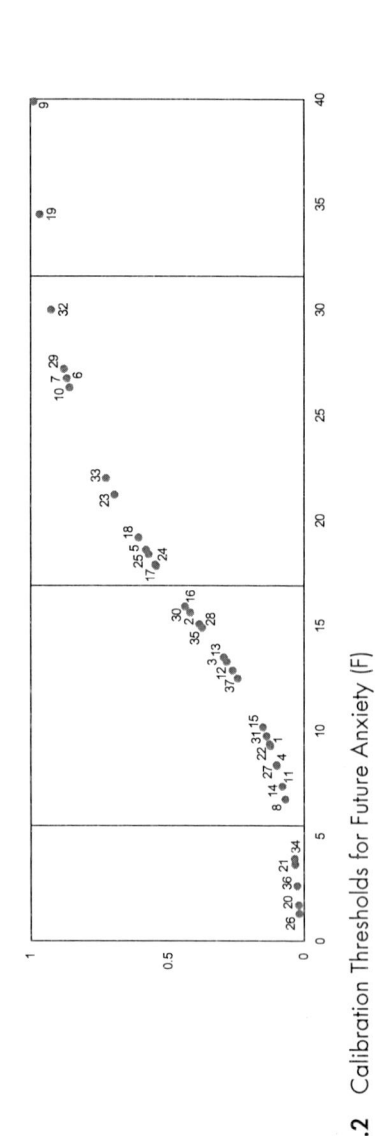

Figure 5.2 Calibration Thresholds for Future Anxiety (F)

Note: The numbers next to the dots are the case numbers in the dataset. The vertical lines are the threshold points.

the three conditions whose scores are fuzzy are relatively simple to establish because the scores are indexed within 0 and 1 and therefore the crossover will be 0.5 and the fully in and fully out thresholds will be 0.75 and above and 0.25 and below respectively.

The thresholds for the remaining conditions (populist attitude and anxiety about the future) and the outcome were not that obvious. Clear correspondent empirical referents for the conceptual distinctions within each condition are not available, that is, there really is no theory that can inform at what percent score does a public opinion become a populist attitude or when does an anxiety about the future translate into a mandate for a populist. In any case, it is not advisable for this project to go down the path of quantitative reasoning by mechanically identifying central tendencies and associated thresholds because that contradicts the reasoning behind the research design itself.

Thresholds for the remaining measures were defined by identifying the gaps between the data points and choosing those gaps that seemed empirically justifiable. For instance, in the conditions populist attitude (A) and anxiety about the future (F), the cases (that is, the data points of the cases for the respective conditions) were clustered with clearly visible four or five gaps between them. I identified the cases that were adjacent on either side of the gaps to see if the concerned adjacent cases indicated a substantial difference between them that hence justified inserting a threshold at the point between them.

To set the calibration parameters, some conditions were straightforward, such as the P, B, and L conditions because they were fuzzy scores between 0 and 1. For the remaining conditions and the outcome, while five breaks in the conditions were identified, thresholds were anchored only in those gaps where the adjacent cases on either side of the threshold were clearly distinct.

For instance, from Figure 5.1, one can see that the data (percentage scores) on populist attitude has gaps at 8.35 percent, 13.95 percent, 21.88 percent, 27.95 percent, and 35.45 percent points.

First, I discuss the point, the fully in threshold, at which fully in cases reflecting a populist attitude was chosen. To choose the cases that were fully in, I had to decide between the 27.95 percent point and the 35.45 percent point as possible threshold points. Both percentage scores were reasonably high (above 25 percent) to assume that such cases can be considered fully in cases. Cases adjacent and on either side of the 27.95 threshold were Case 31 (slightly less than 27.95) and Case 28 (slightly more than 27.95) which were Nitish Kumar in 2010 and Naveen Patnaik in 2014 respectively. Cases adjacent to and on either side of the 35.45 threshold were Case 35 (slightly less than 35.45) and Case 22 (more than 35.45) which were Raman Singh in 2003 and Narendra Modi in 2012. Clearly, the distinctions between Nitish Kumar and Naveen Patnaik in the considered time periods is less compared to the distinctions between Narendra Modi and Raman Singh. Narendra Modi would more clearly fit the bill of a populist by 2012 (a more well-known, populist potential prime ministerial candidate) than would Raman Singh in 2003 (a fresher chief ministerial and party candidate), and so it made sense to anchor the inclusion threshold at 35.45.

At the other end, the percentage point at which cases can be considered fully out, or the exclusion threshold, was a choice between the 8.35 and 13.95 percentage points. The cases on either side of 8.35 percentage point were Raman Singh in 2013 (Case 37 and slightly less) and Indira Gandhi in 1980 (Case 10 and slightly more). At the 13.95 percentage point, the cases were Mamata Banerjee in 2011 (Case 17 and slightly less) and Lalu Prasad Yadav in 1995 (Case 16 and slightly more). Again, the distinctions between Raman Singh and Indira Gandhi were much larger than between Mamata Banerjee and Lalu Yadav, and so the exclusion threshold was chosen at the 8.35. The mid-point or the crossover threshold was set at 21.88. It seemed self-justifying because it was in the middle, and the two adjacent cases, Chandrasekhar Rao in 2018 (Case 7) and Chandrababu Naidu in 1999 (Case 5), were clearly also distinctive where, as the case descriptions have shown in the earlier chapter, the latter was the more well known as a populist compared to the former.

A similar exercise was done for the future anxiety condition. Again, the thresholds were chosen at the extremes because the cases were more distinctive than the cases in the gaps that were closer to the middle. From Figure 5.2 one can see that at the inclusion end of the future condition, Nitish Kumar 2020 (Case 33) and Indira Gandhi 1980 (Case 10) were at either end of the 24.15 mark, and Nitish Kumar 2015 (Case 32) and Mamata Banerjee 2021 (Case 19) were at the 32.23 mark. Mamata Banerjee in 2021 (a cornered

Table 5.2 Calibration Thresholds

	Fully Out/Exclusion Threshold	Crossover Threshold	Fully In/Inclusion Threshold
P, B, L	Less than 0.25	Above 0.5	Above 0.75
F	5.31	16.87	32.23
A	8.35	21.88	35.45
Y (Outcome)	0.49	0.71	1.1

but firebrand anti-BJP leader) seemed far more distinct when compared to Nitish Kumar in 2015, relative to Indira Gandhi in 1980 and Nitish Kumar in 2020. The latter two seemed to have mellowed into the mainstream at their respective time periods. At the exclusion end, the choices did not seem all that stark. Karunanidhi 2006 (Case 15) and Raman Singh 2013 (Case 37) were at the 11.33 threshold and Chamling 2009 (Case 34) and Digvijaya Singh 1998 (Case 8) were at the 5.31 percentage point. Digvijaya Singh was an outlier in 1998 considering his developmental politics and so I chose the 5.31 data point as the exclusion threshold. The crossover point was identified at 16.87 with the case of Laloo Prasad in 1995 (Case 16) to the left of the line and Narendra Modi in 2019 (Case 24) to the right. To identify this point as the crossover with absolute clarity was difficult because the case of Mamata Banerjee in 2001 (Case 17) was adjacent and overlapping with Case 24. But clearly the distinction between Narendra Modi in 2019 (as the full instantiation of a populist) and Laloo in 1995 justified the crossover threshold at this point.

Calibrating the outcome was fairly straightforward. Because the outcome was an odds ratio, the fully in threshold would be anything at or above 1. The data indicated that 1.1 was a gap and that could be easily understood to be the fully in threshold. However, to decide the crossover threshold was a bit challenging as there was no gap in the data at 0.9 or anything closer to 1. There was a gap at 0.71 and so I chose this as the crossover threshold instead of 0.9 because it reflected how the data was clustered. 0.49 was the lowest gap and so naturally fit the exclusion (or the fully out) threshold.

The raw calibration scores are given in Table 5.2 with the exclusion (e), crossover (c), and inclusion (i) thresholds.[6]

With these calibration thresholds explained, I now turn to the parameters of fit to analyze whether the conditions are necessary or sufficient, and the extent of consistency and coverage that they represent.

Parameters of Fit: Necessary and Sufficient Conditions

Necessary Conditions

Table 5.3 explains whether the various conditions are necessary and whether they meet consistency and coverage requirements. The table also has a relevance of necessity score as the last column, which indicates the extent to which the condition is trivially necessary or otherwise (lower score means higher triviality).

Table 5.3   Necessary Conditions

	Consistency	Coverage	Relevance of Necessity
P	0.67	0.731	0.674
B	0.697	0.815	0.783
L	0.655	0.746	0.71
F	0.425	0.743	0.853
A	0.417	0.65	0.777
~P	0.414	0.814	0.907
~B	0.371	0.652	0.812
~L	0.417	0.763	0.871
~F	0.663	0.778	0.752
~A	0.653	0.834	0.832

The threshold for a condition to be necessary would require that the condition meet the consistency threshold of 0.90. None of the conditions cross this threshold with the highest consistency score at 0.697. All coverage scores are above 0.50 and even the relevance of necessity (RoN) scores are above 0.5 (ranging between 0.67 to 0.907), which indicates that the conditions provide good coverage and are not trivially necessary, but in the end are not necessary for the outcome because they do not cross over the consistency threshold. One must add that there were also no necessary conditions for the non-outcome, and so they are not presented here. Hence, conditions of necessity for both the outcome and non-outcome were not present in this study.

Conceptually, two points can be concluded from the table. First, even though there is an argument that can be made that leadership is a necessary condition for populism as outlined in Chapter 2 earlier, the results indicate otherwise; that populist leadership cannot be considered a condition of necessity. In fact, further results below will show that leadership is an important condition but as an INUS condition. Second, the necessary results show that the condition "invocations to the people" is also not a necessary condition. These results confirm the argument in Chapter 2 justifying why this condition should not be considered a necessary condition.

Sufficient Conditions

Table 5.4, which is the truth table, provides us with a comprehensive understanding of whether the conditions are sufficient or otherwise, along with the relevant cases that represent those sufficient conditions. Before the discussion of the results, some basic ideas to understand the truth table before the analysis.

The truth table is a dashboard that tabulates all the possible configurations (including individual conditions) that are sufficient for the outcome primarily, with some additional information. It tells us the conditions that make up the said configuration, whether the configuration is sufficient for the outcome (0 or 1) and with what level of consistency (incl) and coverage (PRI), and which are the cases that represent the said configuration. In Table 5.4, the configurations are mentioned in the first column, followed by the five columns of the conditions (P, B, L, F, A) and then the outcome (column labeled Y). The column labeled N indicates the number of cases that are related to the configurations that lead to the outcome (or non-outcome) followed by the consistency and PRI scores and eventually the list of the actual cases that are associated with the configuration.

For instance, in Table 5.4, the first row is configuration 13 which comprises the presence of conditions B and L (indicated as 1) with the other conditions P, L, F, and A being absent (indicated with a 0) in the configuration. Configuration 13 shows that conditions B and L combine and prove sufficient for the outcome, having one case, identified as Case 14. Specifically, configuration 13 is an INUS condition[7] that is sufficient for the outcome (out = 1) with a consistency of 0.927 and with the number of cases (n) equal to 1 which in this configuration is Case 14 (Karunanidhi in 1996).

The total number of possible configurations is 32 ($2^{k=5}$; k = number of conditions) because each condition can either be present or absent (hence $2k$), and there are 5 conditions in all. As good practice, it is worthwhile to have as many cases as there are possible configurations so that we allow for the possibility to have a representative case for each configuration. Such a situation, where every configuration has a case that represents it, rarely ever happens, but it is nevertheless provided for. And since this is not the case in the current dataset as well, the configurations are sorted according to the outcome, with the positive outcomes first, then negative outcomes, and finally the inconclusive outcomes, labeled as "logical remainders."

Configurations 13 and below, up to configuration 30, are sufficient configurations for the outcome based on a consistency threshold of 75 percent. For instance, Configuration 30, comprising the conditions (P·B·L·A· $\sim$F[8]), has a consistency of 0.765 and so is sufficient for the outcome. The PRI score is 0.701, which means that this configuration is a valid condition for the outcome because a PRI score of 0.5 and below would imply simultaneous subset relations (the configuration could explain both the outcome and the non-outcome). Configurations below 30, that is, from configurations 8 to 18, are configurations that are not sufficient for the outcome (out = 0). Configurations below 18, that is, from 2 to 28, have no cases (out = ?) and are known as logical remainders because while such configurations seem logically possible, their relationship with the outcome remains inconclusive because there are no cases available in the dataset.

Truth Table Results

What are the few results that can be derived from the truth table?

First, there are 12 configurations (13, 16, 10, 32, 31, 1, 29, 3, 6, 26, 17, and 30) that are sufficient for the outcome. That is, when any among these 12 configurations are present, the outcome will also be present, or these 12 configurations each points to specific pathways that can lead to the outcome because when these configurations are present the outcome will also be present. Further, there are a total of 31 cases that represent these 12 configurations, and there are 6 cases that are not sufficient for the outcome. Finally, there are 14 configurations (from 2 to 28) that do not reflect any outcomes, nor are there cases in them, and are labeled logical remainders as they remain inconclusive even though they are logically possible configurations (possible according to Boolean logic, not necessarily conceptual logic).

Second, all the configurations are combinations of the various conditions. There is no configuration that operates on a single condition, and so we can argue that isolating a single condition as a factor that matters to populism seems misplaced. Each of these conditions appears to work only in conjunction with the other conditions. And therefore, conceptually, one would have to articulate the significance of these conditions that constitute populism in a manner that reflects the conjunctive—and not the isolative—character of these conditions. In any case, neither the point behind the design nor real circumstances would validate the possibility of a single condition being sufficient for the outcome even if the Boolean logic would indicate so.

Third, among these conditions, the boundary-setting condition seems to be the most salient, as it is a part of 8 configurations out of the total of 12 that

Table 5.4 Truth Table: The Logic of Populism in India

Configuration	Conditions P	B	L	F	A	Outcome Y	Cases N	Consistency incl.	PRI	Cases
13	0	1	1	0	0	1	1	0.933	0.905	14
16	0	1	1	1	1	1	1	0.915	0.858	5
10	0	1	0	0	1	1	1	0.88	0.807	35
32	1	1	1	1	1	1	1	0.875	0.801	23
31	1	1	1	1	0	1	7	0.857	0.807	9, 10, 17, 18, 19, 24, 25
1	0	0	0	0	0	1	2	0.84	0.773	30, 37
29	1	1	1	0	0	1	5	0.827	0.774	1, 4, 12, 16, 27
3	0	0	0	1	0	1	1	0.82	0.738	29
6	0	0	1	0	1	1	1	0.788	0.672	28
26	1	1	0	0	1	1	1	0.78	0.696	36
17	1	0	0	0	0	1	3	0.777	0.707	8, 26, 34
30	1	1	1	0	1	1	7	0.765	0.701	2, 3, 11, 13, 20, 21, 22
8	0	0	1	1	1	0	1	0.676	0.471	6
23	1	0	1	1	0	0	1	0.633	0.466	7
4	0	0	0	1	1	0	1	0.619	0.41	33
22	1	0	1	0	1	0	1	0.604	0.477	15
24	1	0	1	1	1	0	1	0.601	0.422	32
18	1	0	0	0	1	0	1	0.598	0.461	31
2	0	0	0	0	1	?	0	–	–	
5	0	0	1	0	0	?	0	–	–	
7	0	0	1	1	0	?	0	–	–	
9	0	1	0	0	0	?	0	–	–	
11	0	1	0	1	0	?	0	–	–	
12	0	1	0	1	1	?	0	–	–	
14	0	1	1	0	1	?	0	–	–	
15	0	1	1	1	0	?	0	–	–	
19	1	0	0	1	0	?	0	–	–	
20	1	0	0	1	1	?	0	–	–	
21	1	0	1	0	0	?	0	–	–	
25	1	1	0	0	0	?	0	–	–	
27	1	1	0	1	0	?	0	–	–	
28	1	1	0	1	1	?	0	–	–	

are sufficient for populism. Leadership is the next most important condition, present in 7 of the 12 conditions, followed by invocations to the people, populist attitude (in six conditions), and, finally, future anxiety in 5 conditions.

Fourth, invocation to the people is not the primary condition relative to the other conditions in India. Going by the predominance of this concept in the literature, one would have assumed that it would matter and would reflect in all the configurations with a positive outcome. But it reflects in half the number of configurations, where one of the configurations (configuration 32) reflects a conjunction of all the conditions. Such a configuration does not seem to contribute to theory building because the idea that all these conditions matter was the premise upon which they were brought into the dataset in the first place.

Lastly, the purpose of the truth table is to eventually be able to identify, and abstract out of them, the constitutive elements of the cases and the pathways taken up by these cases that help us better understand populism. To arrive at the underlying logic that constitutes these pathways, one has to formulate the solution terms that summarize these various configurations that can lead to the outcome.

Solution Terms

Solution terms summarize the information from the truth table by simplifying the configurations to pathways that are sufficient for the outcome. Summarizing and thereby understanding the pathways makes the information amenable to building the theory that we are eventually interested in explaining, by identifying the combinations of attributes that can lead to the outcome. The analysis provides us with three kinds of solution terms, and it eventually is at the discretion of the researcher to choose the right solution term to his research problem and explain the thinking behind the choice, and the same will be done here.

The three kinds of solution terms are conservative, parsimonious, and intermediate solution terms. It is important to describe what they capture and what is left out and why. As mentioned earlier in Chapter 3, summarizing the information requires following the logical minimization procedure, which is the process by which all configurations are logically minimized to their prime implicants so as to identify the solution terms and their coverage that apply across the configurations accounted for. A conservative solution term accounts for only the configurations that are sufficient for the outcome and therefore is the most conservative estimate because the solution term is comprehensive only to the extent of the cases selected in the dataset. At the other end, it is true that the label "parsimonious" solution term can be misleading, but this solution term incorporates all configurations, including the logical remainders, and comes up with a solution term that is arguably the "best case" scenario (because it assumes that there are cases for all configurations) as it is the most expansive version of the problem because it includes all possible scenarios. The intermediate solution is the solution term in between the two because the researcher uses his discretion to remove a few configurations that he thinks are simply not theoretically plausible. Which solution term is the best one to identify pathways is a question that really depends on the data and the explanatory power of the solution terms and their parameters of fit.

In the discussion below, the intermediate solution term seems to offer the clearest possible pathways to understand the logic of populism in India. However, I first provide the conservative solution term and the parsimonious solution term, discuss their limitations for this project, and then discuss the intermediate solution term.

The solution term in Table 5.5 is the conservative solution term. It is understood as a conservative term because it accounts for only those

Table 5.5 Conservative Solution Term

M1: P*B*L + ~P*~B*~L*~A + ~B*~L*~F*~A + B*~L*~F*A + B*L*~F*~A + B*L*F*A + ~P*~B*L*~F*A -> Y

	Configurations	Consistency	PRI	Solution Coverage	Unique Coverage	Cases
1	P*B*L	0.801	0.760	0.524	0.165	1,4,12,16,27; 2,3,11,13,20,21,22; 9,10,17,18,19,24,25; 23
2	~P*~B*~L*~A	0.853	0.803	0.192	0.039	30,37; 29
3	~B*~L*~F*~A	0.806	0.749	0.200	0.046	30,37; 8,26,34
4	B*~L*~F*A	0.805	0.731	0.158	0.028	35; 36
5	B*L*~F*~A	0.845	0.804	0.301	0.037	14; 1,4,12,16,27
6	B*L*F*A	0.879	0.812	0.175	0.006	5; 23
7	~P*~B*L*~F*A	0.788	0.672	0.085	0.015	28
	Model	0.835	0.809	0.763		

Note: The commas in the last column indicate that the cases belong to the same truth table row; the semicolons indicate that the cases belong to different truth table rows.

configurations, 12 configurations in this study, that have proven sufficient, and these configurations can be derived based only on the cases that are available in the dataset.

The challenge with this solution term is its complexity—it is just not simple enough to understand and articulate conceptually because it has seven pathways and with both positive and not positive attributes (indicated with '~' next to the specific condition) in six of the pathways. There are five different conditions that are either present or absent, and they configure in different configurations, resulting in seven different pathways. Even though the overall model is consistent at 0.835 threshold, and the PRI score is high at 0.809 and the coverage is also quite high at 0.763, the bewildering complexity of the seven pathways makes it difficult to interpret and perhaps even runs the risk of overinterpretation.

At the other end, the parsimonious solution provides the simplest solution. If one were to include all the logical remainders (all the configurations with "out = ?") along with the positive outcomes to encapsulate all possible logical configurations (irrespective of whether the assumptions for such remainders are tenable or contradictory), one would arrive at the parsimonious solution.

The parsimonious solution in this dataset is three possible pathways (B + ~P*~F + ~L*~A -> Y) with overall model consistency of 0.819, PRI of 0.795, and coverage of 0.869. On the face of it, it would seem obvious to consider this solution term as final because both the model consistency and coverage are quite high. But looking at the solution closer, one realizes that the parsimonious solution term is almost redundant considering the nature of the pathways. The first pathway is a single condition (B), and the remaining two other pathways are configurations that are based on the negative poles of the conditions (~P * ~F, or ~L* ~A).

My hesitation in adopting this model stems from three reasons. First, having a single condition (B in this case) as a single condition pathway is simply not plausible. Second, the other two conditions indicate that the negative poles of the concept (~) provide the pathways to the populist outcome. This does look contradictory because it is normal to assume that the positive poles of a concept are associated with the outcome, and therefore the negative poles would be contravening. However, I consider these not as much contravening conditions but more as underspecified conditions. It is clear what these attributes are, but what they are not, while specified in Chapter 4, I do feel would require much greater clarity before I can use the negative poles as having explanatory power. What does, for example, ~L, the absence of a populist leader, mean in the context of a populist outcome? Does it, for example, indicate that political parties matter more than the leader? This seems unclear to me, and at this point a risky post hoc explanation. Third, the solution term includes some logical remainders that do not seem theoretically possible. For example, there were some configurations that do not seem theoretically plausible because they consider the presence of only single conditions. For instance, configurations 2, 5, and 9 each (as seen in the truth table) considers a single condition with inconclusive relations with the outcome and are hence considered logical remainders. There really seems little value in considering these logical remainders, and so I exclude them from the analysis to arrive at the intermediate solution term.

The argument in this book relies ultimately on the intermediate solution. To recall, the intermediate solution is a solution that excludes logical remainders that are not theoretically tenable. The intermediate solution term arrived at is depicted in Table 5.6.

The intermediate solution term[9] seems much clearer than the other two solution terms and best explains the logic of populism. The model is also not ambiguous and is consistent at 0.825 and with a PRI score of 0.800 and has a high coverage of 0.820. Thus, this intermediate solution term seems to be the best to identify pathways to a populist outcome.

In terms of pathways, the solution provides us with 4 pathways. However, pathways 3 (~B·~L·~A) and 4 (~P·L·~F·A) seem theoretically

Table 5.6 Intermediate Solution Term

M1: B*L + B*A + ~B*~L*~A + ~P*L*~F*A -> Y

Configuration	Consistency	PRI	Coverage Solution	Coverage Unique	Cases
1 B*L	0.813	0.780	0.601	0.274	14; 5; 1,4,12,16,27; 2,3,11,13,20,21, 22;9,10,17,18,19,24,25; 23
2 B*A	0.781	0.724	0.342	0.157	35; 5; 36; 2,3,11,13,20,21,22; 23
3 ~B*~L*~A	0.820	0.777	0.263	0.157	30,37; 29; 8,26,34
4 ~P*L*~F*A	0.835	0.765	0.137	0.015	28
Model 1	0.825	0.800	0.820		

Note: The commas in the last column indicate that the cases belong to the same truth table row; the semicolons indicate that the cases belong to different truth table rows.

untenable or at least theoretically unclear. Pathway 3 states that the negative poles of conditions B, L, and A are sufficient for the outcome. What these negative poles are, are substantively difficult to fully specify and hence the untenability. For instance, the condition ~B indicates that not setting boundaries in combination with other conditions is sufficient for the outcome. Not setting boundaries in this project indicates a pluralist democratic electoral system. But party systems and political contestation as functional democratic electoral systems within the states in India comprise quite a wide range of characteristics, which the condition ~B cannot fully capture. And therefore, it is an underspecified conceptual space. Understood in terms of fuzzy scores, ~B certainly is a fuzzy score between 0 and 0.5, but it could conceptually also be indicative of the space between 0 and −1, which is not specified in this project. Also, ~B does not indicate the absence or irrelevance of the condition, because if it were so, it would not even have been mentioned in the solution term. It is indicating that the non-boundary-setting space, in combination with other conditions, is sufficient for the solution. To my mind, this kind of a conceptual space is not completely specifiable because of the scope of meanings that can be attributed to such a space (0.5 to −1 is a very large conceptual space). A similar argument can be made of the remaining conditions in pathways 3 and 4. For instance, P is only present as an irrelevant condition in pathway 4 but is otherwise absent in the other pathways. If the condition was simply absent, then this particular decision of considering or not would not have been necessary. Further, it seems justifiable to exclude them in this instance of the intermediate solution term because their contribution to the solution coverage is not as high as the first two pathways as most of the cases are covered by combinations of B, L, and A. And therefore, I would like to use my discretion and exclude pathways 3 and 4 from further analysis in this solution term.

In sum, the set theoretic argument can be identified from pathways 1 and 2 of the intermediate solution term, as shown earlier. And therefore, the logic of populism in India can be written as:

$$B \, (L + A) \rightarrow Y$$

Some preliminary observations can be made based on the logic outlined here. Boundary setting is clearly the condition that matters more than any other condition because it is sufficient for the outcome, but only in combination with populist leadership or with populist attitudes. Invocations to the people and anxieties about the future are present but not to the same degree as the conditions mentioned earlier. Translating this into a study of comparative politics, this result shows that boundary setting is what translates into populism in India either when there is a leader who is able to articulate such a boundary or when there is a latent attitude that is tapped into to realign cleavages that constitute populism.

This formulation, prioritizing boundary setting over leadership or populist attitudes, contributes something new to contemporary approaches to populism. To recall, studies that follow the ideational approach are increasingly being drawn toward understanding populist attitudes, understood as latent attitudinal dispositions that are triggered into a political attitude (such as electoral voting) according to the programmatic content that they are exposed to. This demand-side approach is driven by anxieties about the future (condition F in this study). Those who follow the strategic approach tend to focus on the supply side, by identifying the connections (including cultural repertoires that the cultural approach theorists highlight) and the strategies that political leaders deploy to link with the masses (condition L in this study).

This study shows that it is the setting of the boundary, in conjunction with either how or who triggers it, which is the logic of populism, at least in India. The demand and supply side dimensions help to activate and articulate this condition, but it is the condition of boundary setting that is prior to its activation by anxieties or its articulation by a leader. Anxieties, and aspirations, can trigger the boundary, or the political leaders articulate the boundary to connect with the people but the setting of the boundary comes first. This study shows that the supply-side and the demand-side approaches are relevant to India, but only as conjunctive dimensions to the boundary-setting characteristic of populism. It is the boundary setting that comes first, and the approaches follow next.

The logic of populism in India can also be understood visually through a Venn diagram, such as the one in Figure 5.3.

Figure 5.3 is a Venn diagram with the five conditions as pear-shaped sets respectively. The shaded portions that are part of the intersections in the Venn are the INUS conditions that are present and with which the populist outcome is also present when the conditions occur. The shaded portions outside the pear-shaped sets are of a slightly lighter shade, indicating that these sections are absent (not a part of the analysis). Interestingly, this also includes parts of the sets (F) and (P), which indicates that, as argued earlier, F and P could be absent. The white sections are the irrelevant sections and seem

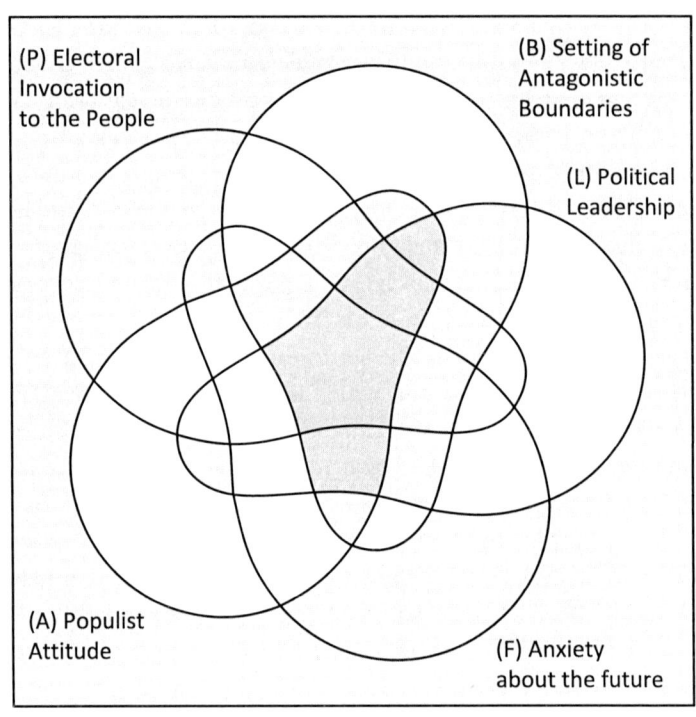

Figure 5.3 Venn Diagram of the Logic of Populism

Source: Author.

to be found in the conditions where the sets are single conditions or some combinations of conditions.

A few things can be inferred from this diagram. Boundary setting is the set that has the most overlap with all the other sets and so clearly is a sufficient condition when in conjunction with other conditions. It seems to share the highest overlap with populist attitudes, and that conjunction becomes more intense in conjunction with leadership.

Finally, there are two questions that require additional clarifications.

First, with high levels of consistency and coverage, can one definitively say that an argument for the conditions that are constitutive of the outcome can be made, or are there any deviant cases that require clarification to remain in the dataset? Second, is this logic, where boundary setting is in conjunction with other conditions, an externally valid argument? Will this argument remain valid beyond this dataset because the dataset is purposively selected? In other words, will this argument remain valid if we increase the coverage of the dataset by considering more cases? The first question on coverage can be understood from the XY plot in Figure 5.4. The second is a question of robustness, which is covered in the section that follows.

The sufficiency plot (Figure 5.4) illustrates where the cases are spread. Most of the cases are above the diagonal and in the top-right quadrant, which accounts for the high consistency and coverage of the conditions (because most of the cases are in the quadrants where $Y > X$). The deviant cases are of two kinds—deviant cases in degree and deviant cases in kind (or DCK cases).

The deviant cases are in the bottom-right quadrant and below the diagonal such that the condition is greater than the outcome ($X > Y$). The deviant cases are important to clarify because, as contradictory elements in the dataset, they impact the parameters of fit and coverage, and therefore one must justify retaining them on in the dataset on the merits of their theoretical relevance.

The deviant cases are 25, 3, 11, 12, and 18. Case 25 is a deviant case of degree because it is close to the diagonal, and a similar observation can be made of Case 3 as well—both are off the diagonal but not so off that they seem to question the idea that $X > Y$. However, cases 11, 12, and 18 are clearly cases of deviant kinds and require clarification.

Case 18, though, is a case of deviant consistency in kind because X is greater than 0.5, and Y is very close to 0. That is, X is 0.6 or so and Y is closer

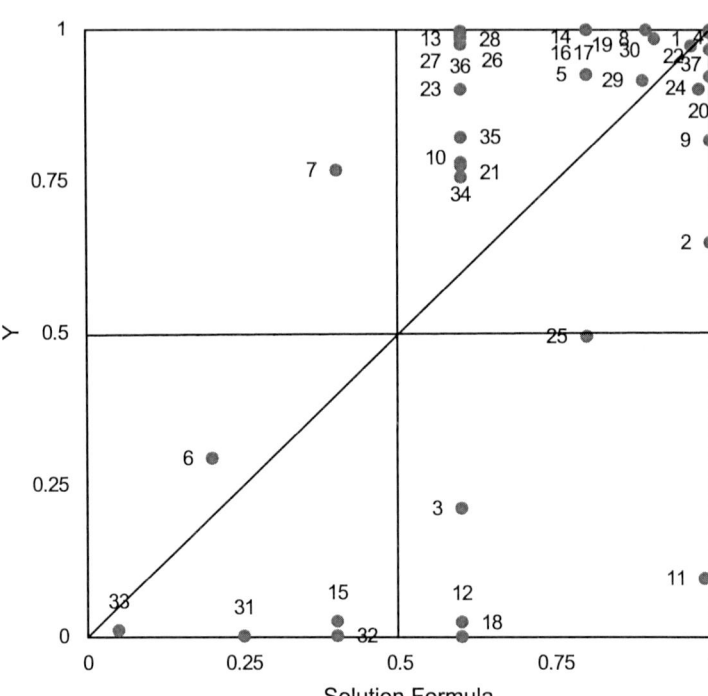

Figure 5.4 XY Sufficiency Plot

to 0 in this case, which means that X actually seems to have little connection with Y, so why is it being included in the dataset given that it seems a deviant case in kind? Case 12 is in a situation that is similar to Case 18, and so what applies to Case 18 also applies to Case 12. Case 11, though, is a different kind of case because X is close to 1 while Y is very low at almost half of 0.25.

Case 18 is Mamata Banerjee in 2016, and Cases 11 and 12 are Jayalalitha in 2001 and 2011 respectively. While the literature would label Mamata Banerjee as a populist and her fuzzy scores reflect that, her electoral outcomes are problematic. This was the only election that she won as part of the regular election cycle,[10] and so it seemed important to not exclude. But the proportion of her personal vote share relative to the party is not unprecedented relative to her predecessors, and so her populist outcome was in fact the lowest in the whole dataset which is reflected on the Y axis. Removing her from the dataset will improve the consistency and coverage scores,[11] but it is important to retain this case for a few reasons. First, this was the cleanest reflection of the outcome since she won this seat without a byelection and, even if her populist outcome is low, it still is a legitimate measure. Second, the real signifier is that the scholarship does consider her a populist, and no one would contest the claim that her persona is almost coterminous with the party, and so it would not be surprising that the personal and party vote shares are similar. All things considered, it seems preferable to retain this case in the data, albeit at the cost of some coverage, because this case is theoretically not a DCK. Similarly, Jayalalitha is well known in the scholarship as a populist and what makes her a DCK here is that her vote shares do not reflect unprecedented vote shares of other incumbent chief ministers. It would not be difficult to argue why she had low electoral personal vote shares because of a variety of factors (for instance, very close electoral contests because of bipartisan electoral fragmentation), but her direct connection with the people and centralized fealty to herself within the party were clear indicators that she has always been a populist and should be retained in the dataset.

Robustness

All said and done, the question to conclude the analysis is usually to understand how robust the results of the analysis are. Robustness, in the case of QCA, can be understood as to whether the chosen solution term remains the same even when alternative plausible analytical decisions are taken. That is, if we can consider alternate plausible scenarios (other calibration thresholds, consistency thresholds, outcome parameters, and suchlike), will the solution term still hold? QCA experts identify robustness of three kinds. First, how sensitive is the solution term to changes in parameters that are currently used in the dataset? Second, how robust are the cases in a context of alternative plausible scenarios that are created by simulating alternative datasets? And finally, which are the specific cases that remain robust under these altered circumstances, and which cases could have been included under such latter circumstances?

Section A.5 in the Appendix provides the technical reports and the inferences that can be drawn from them. One can say in summary that the solution term remains robust even when the parameters in terms of inclusion and exclusion thresholds are taken to the extreme, and it is sensitive to changes in the crossover threshold.

The real challenge posed for this dataset is related to coverage. And so, it became important to test whether the solution remains unchanged when alternative scenarios are created that enhance the coverage of the cases. One can say that 6 out of the 37 cases are robust under all other plausible alternative analytical choices, with a large number being possible cases and some shaky cases (this terminology is used technically and explained in the Appendix).

While robustness can improve, and notions of robustness themselves are contingent upon the researcher's plausible choices, of substantive interest to us are the identification of logical pathways to populism and the cases that robustly typify the same. Such cases and their pathways are summarized next.

Pathways to Populism

In conclusion, I describe the two chosen pathways to populism in India and the ideal typical cases that represent these pathways. These ideal typical cases were derived from the results of the case-based robustness tests, and I explore these cases in some detail in the next chapter.

The results in Table 5.7, also known as a Fiss Chart, show that there are, substantively, two pathways to populism. Both pathways comprise configurations where the setting of antagonistic boundaries as to who is a member of a set and who is not is common. Pathway 1 describes a populist path where boundaries are set in configuration with a leader. Pathway 2 describes a setting of boundaries that aligns with populist attitudes.

Boundary setting is central to populism. Thus, populists in India primarily set or reset boundaries of political alignment, and they seem to emerge especially as those who are able to articulate them in a manner that connects with the people and about the future (most cases in this dataset are in Pathway 1). What is also clear is that populism in India does not necessarily invoke notions of the people or popular sovereignty as the flag around which people mobilize. It seems to work in the opposite direction. Populists realign boundaries where the members outside the set—those who are "not of the people," if you will—are clearly defined causing those who belong to the set "of the people," especially those who are anxious about the future or share a latent populist attitude, to mobilize, and thereby creating the circumstances

Table 5.7 Pathways to Populism

	Path 1	Path 2
	B· L -> Y	B·A-> Y
Invocations to the People	X	X
Boundary Setting	•	•
Leadership	•	X
Future Anxiety	X	X
Populist Attitude	X	•
Consistency	0.813	0.781
PRI	0.780	0.724
Raw Coverage	0.601	0.342
Unique Coverage	0.274	0.040
Covered Case Numbers	1,2, 3, 4, **5**, 9, **10**, 11, 12, 13, 14, 16, **17**, 18, **19**, 20, 21, 22, **23**, 24, 25	2, 3, **5**, 11, 13 20, 21, 22, **23** 35
Solution Consistency	0.825	
Solution PRI	0.800	
Solution Coverage	0.820	

Note: Black dots indicate presence of a condition. The X indicates absence. Cases in bold are the robust typical cases that are discussed further in Chapter 6.

for the populist to emerge at that point in time. Perhaps one could say that populists divide, and so people in such democracies collide.

Notes

1. Further details related to the measuring of these concepts can be found separately in sections A.1.1 and A.2 in the Appendix.
2. I must qualify this statement because the easy availability of electoral data did not always perfectly correspond with the populist outcomes. See section A.1.2 of the Appendix on the dataset for more details on the populist outcome and the electoral data.
3. A more detailed explanation of the outcome is in the Appendix.
4. The percent scores were calculated as a share of the total number of valid responses. The scores did not include NA responses but included "Don't Know" and "Can't Say" responses.

5. The exceptions were the following: The question in 1980 for Indira Gandhi was about how much concern the respondent had for the community. The 2014 NES survey asked respondents to assess their current situation in the light of the past. And the 2019 NES survey asked whether they could fulfil their needs and also save some money.

6. I also noted that shifting the thresholds inward toward the crossover, or outward toward the extremes, with the crossover thresholds constant, made no difference to the solution terms (intermediate solution term) except that I would have gained two cases and one more outcome if the thresholds were set closer to the middle. But on the claim that the cases at the extremes were more distinctive and therefore the gap between these cases is more real than the gap between the middle cases, I chose the extremes as thresholds. In other words, I traded case-level distinctions over better sufficient outcomes in the truth table. I would like to thank Adrian Dusa for pointing me toward this approach to choosing calibration thresholds. The calibrated dataset is available in the Appendix.

7. B and L are not sufficient by themselves, but they are necessary (in that they have to be there) in combination to create a condition that is not necessary but sufficient for the outcome.

8. The configuration should be read as "Invocation and Boundary Setting and Leadership and Populist Attitude and Not Future Anxiety."

9. Since there were no configurations that explained the non-outcome and no untenable assumptions that required to be removed from the logical remainders, identifying solution terms after conducting the enhanced standard analysis did not seem necessary. Hence, the solution term proposed here is based on the standard analysis alone.

10. Her populist outcomes in 2011 and 2021 make the picture murkier because she got her seat during byeelections (and in fact lost her Nandigram seat in 2021 but was reelected from Bhabanipur in a byelection).

11. The consistency increases to 0.91 and coverage to 0.531.

6

Conclusion

The Logic of Populism

Micro-populism

As part of my dissertation research many summers ago, I lived for a couple of months in a few villages that straddled the borders of Karnataka, Tamil Nadu, and Andhra Pradesh. I was initiated into the political economy of this region by Mr Krishne Gowda of Bathlahalli village, an elderly patron of the region, who lived with his married sons and their families. Armed with a law degree from decades ago and a towel over the armpit (Manor 2004) now, Mr Gowda was the quintessential mover-and-shaker politician. On one post-lunch afternoon in the early days, he asked me what subject I was studying, and I told him "Political Science." He looked at me, and then, in his earnestness to educate me, he said what I remember as the following:

> Look, you are studying politics but let me tell you that we villagers know a lot about politics and data because we vote on many things. We vote in the panchayat elections, Assembly elections, and Lok Sabha of course. But we also have votes for cooperative bank elections, committees within panchayats, and so on.
>
> We also know how to deal with the government. When they come and ask us how many members there are in my household, I decide the answer according to who is asking. If it is the forest official who asks, I will say one household. If it is for rations, I will say multiple households. If it is for elections, I will say three households. If it is for census, I will say one household and so on … it really depends on what the benefit is.

[After a brief pause] The fact of the matter is, the number of households in our culture depends on the number of kitchens that are running in the house. [His house had only one kitchen where his wife and their daughters-in-law cooked together.]

In hindsight, recalling this insight, I now understand Mr Krishne Gowda as a micro-populist politician, constantly redrawing boundaries of who was in and who was out of his household by redrawing the boundaries of membership of various sets and thereby changing the course of representation and redistribution in his household and in his village.

I have argued here that populists redraw boundaries of political alignment, thereby reshaping status-quoist notions of representation and redistribution in Indian politics. Such populists draw lines that connect with the people because of their lived experiences that get refracted as attitudes toward politics turning populist (as opposed to being pluralistic or programmatic). And they seem to do so in India not by invoking notions of the people, but by articulating a distinction that questions the status quo.

The Robust Cases

The data, after being exposed to plausible alternative analytical choices through the robustness checks, provides us with a few typical robust cases that instantiate this argument—Indira Gandhi (in the 1971 and 1980 Lok Sabha elections), Chandrababu Naidu of (undivided) Andhra Pradesh (in the 1999 assembly elections), Mamata Banerjee of West Bengal (in the 2011 and 2021 assembly elections), and Narendra Modi as prime minister (in the 2014 and 2019 Lok Sabha elections).[1] All these populists are cases under Pathway 1 (P·L), which means that they are the kind of populists who set boundaries for contestation that resonate with people who are anxious about their prospects in the future. Further, these cases are reflective of moments that can be considered pivotal elections, and it is perhaps worth discussing here to appreciate why these cases can be considered typical and robust.

Chandrababu Naidu was the poster boy of market-oriented reforms in the 1990s. Andhra Pradesh was the first state in India to directly borrow money from the World Bank. Perhaps Naidu came to power because there was no alternative available at the time: Congress was in disarray, rival factions within Naidu's party had been sidelined, and the BJP was kept outside the state by strategically striking a coalition alliance with the party. Naidu consciously created an image of a technocrat, neoliberal, and reformist, and while he was certainly admired by the modernizing middle classes who benefitted from the IT boom, he also unsettled government employees, those belonging to Leftist strongholds, and perhaps even traditional politicians who were used to conventional forms of political mobilization. It was quite apparent that he was drawing a boundary, or "plain-speaking," as he titled his authorized biography (Naidu and Ninan 2000), wherein the established statist and political interests were on the side that were holding Andhra Pradesh back and, as a consequence, the aspirational backward castes, middle classes, and women were on the other side (Mooij 2007). Perhaps the boundary that Naidu sought to draw was between those who were aspirational, which was nevertheless a modernizing anxiety that Naidu was willing to shoulder as a corrective, and those who were ensconced in the all-too-familiar status-quoist past.

Indira Gandhi was the first reformist in the country in the 1970s, and of a completely different vintage from the kind of neo-populists typified by Naidu. Her populism was of the classical populist kind, which sought to extend the dirigiste state into all matters of political economy and under her absolute control as the patron. Her appeal with the people partly rested on the fact that she had the gumption to take on the dominant regional party brokers and party old guard, the royalty, and the intermediate and business classes, and she took that message to the poor people of India, packaged as various redistributive programs. To the public that had just gone through the tumult of the late 1960s and early 1970s that included two wars, a famine, and the passing of Nehru, Indira Gandhi's populism (or some form of populist authoritarian solution) seemed inevitable. As Kenny (2021) states, had Indira Gandhi not existed, it would have been necessary to invent her. Such a solution emerged to redraw the boundaries of political affiliation by projecting to the people a sharpened critique of a dominant but effete political elite.

So was her return to power in the 1980s, though not that pivotal. She returned chastened by the backlash of the socialist activist opposition against her autocratic anti-institutional attempts to usurp power, but she nevertheless seemed to be the only available alternative to the fragmented opposition. If anything, it probably reinforced her point about an impotent opposition and consequently her primary anti-establishment platform.

Ever the thorn in the flesh of the establishment, Mamata became the politically ascendant leader in 2011, becoming the chief minister of West Bengal after more than three and a half decades of Left rule. Everyone seems to agree that her victory was commendable, though they also suggest that the implosion of the Left was a matter of time, especially after the violent conflicts at Nandigram and Singur villages, caused by the government's acquisition of land for industry. While the implosion was probably inevitable, it was perhaps only Mamata who could tear away the Left's popular support—the only leader who faced them frontally and relentlessly on the streets of Kolkata in the decades prior to her victory. It was always clear whom she stood against, though who or what she stands for remains underarticulated—and perhaps this justifies her place among these cases. Having convincingly defeated the Left, she was confronted with the BJP and Modi in the 2021 assembly elections, and that tested her true populist mettle because no other opposition politician had been able to convincingly reverse the momentum of Modi following the 2014 Lok Sabha elections. In both 2011 and 2021, while it was clear that Mamata sets the boundaries of who is outside her set (the Communists and BJP for now), it was not clear who was inside, which seems to be those generally appreciative of "paribartan" (change) and connect with her image of an "elder sister" (*didi*) and a soldier of the masses—perhaps because she connects across multiple groups.

A similar logic can be attributed to the continued ascendance of Modi since 2014, and especially the 2019 elections. One could argue that 2014 was also an anti-incumbent election, and that the corruption and indecisiveness of the UPA regime, along with Modi's popularity, paved the way for the result. The election was also pivotal in that Modi was able to break the mold of coalition politics that had been cast over Indian national elections for the preceding 20 odd years, by establishing an intense direct connection with people across India (not just Gujarat) and in a fashion that was aspirational and overshadowed the Hindu-nationalist antecedents of his party. The 2019 election was not quite the same. Modi came back with a bigger mandate than 2014, something that no other prime minister except Indira Gandhi had achieved. It was also an unprecedented victory because no other party (except the Janata Party and the Congress) had won a parliamentary election on its own thus far (Varshney 2019a). While it is true that Modi draws on support from multiple classes including the poor because of the various redistributive programs that provided subsidized cooking gas cylinders, bank accounts, and toilets to the poor (Jaffrelot 2019), his populist popularity is conceived and designed to be disruptive of the status quo, promoting a logic of difference that articulates who he is against. His anti-elitism, validated by his humble origins and status as a political outsider to privilege, demonstrated through provocations like *andolan jeevi* (career protestors), urban Naxals (left-leaning intellectuals), the Khan Market gang (cosmopolitan anglicized Indian elites), and so on, are broadly against the liberal democratic ethos that seeks to be pluralist and is seen to be incapable of providing exceptional, honest, and patriotic leadership (Vittorini 2022). The 2024 elections did not emerge as an ideal typical case of populism; in fact, one could argue that his image lost some of the sheen precisely because of the paradox of populism that he found himself in. Having set himself up as a political leader with exalted status and capacity, he possibly felt impelled to push that image further to consolidate his hold over the political system that paradoxically worked against him. Reinforcing that exalted image by constructing the Ram Temple in Ayodhya and consecrating the same as a global spectacle and making incredulous claims about himself, other minority groups, and the electoral power of his party did not wash over the anti-institutional undemocratic strategies that scaffolded such claims and seemed to have brought Modi back to power but with a diminished majority.

Boundary Setting

In all the aforementioned cases, there is inevitably an interpretation of populism that relies on a description of who the people are that are supportive of such populists. There is naturally a curiosity about what makes these leaders popular and one could say, almost ineluctably, to understand who they derive their support from. The background of the voters, according to most scholarship, will help us understand the constituency from where the populists derive their support. Indeed, most scholarship on populists in India will follow this trail of analysis and it is also from within this kind of commentary that the cases in this dataset have been interpreted and selected. Yet this kind of commentary does not, post hoc, fully elaborate the conceptual argument of populism derived from the analysis because the attempt here is to argue that the point of departure for populists in India is not going to the people by invoking the notion of popular sovereignty. In fact, the point of departure to rupture the status quo for populists in India is to invoke the notion of the "enemy" instead. We need to pivot our attention away from understanding populists in India as invokers of people, and instead towards understanding populists as invokers of those groups that are culpable of being against the people.

Besides their association with the people, what is also crucial for a populist leader is their performance of difference. While all politicians will try to show that they are of the people, populists have to additionally show that they are not the enemy of the people and are untainted by the murky world of politics (Vittorini 2022: 283). And this reflection of being untainted in turn creates the connection among the voters and constructs their political identities that affiliate with such populist parties. The emergence of anti-establishment political identity is related to the capacity of political entrepreneurs to criticize elites in power for their alleged misbehavior and blame them for the citizens' woes. Without populist agency, it is unlikely that voters will automatically develop an anti-establishment political identity (Melendez and Kaltwasser 2019: 522).

Put another way, my understanding of the conventional model to understand the mobilization of the masses by democratic leaders, including that of the populists, to upend the status quo is as follows. A political leader emerges from the stock of the common masses, shares the sense of difficulties and aspirations that such people feel, and stakes a claim to political power and office on their behalf to seek redistribution, capture or representation, or similar political goals. The trajectory is somewhat linear and from the bottom to the top, where the in-group is created first and then distinguished from the out-group.

I am suggesting that this mobilization trajectory cannot be applied to the populists. I would like to propose that the populist trajectory is not linear and, in fact, is from the top to the bottom and then to the top again. I am arguing that a populist perceives a problem—a gap between how the world is and how it should be—and identifies what or who he thinks is the cause of the problem. The instinct, when one looks at a problem, is to identify who is behind the mess. Thus, the boundary is set as to who is the cause of the problem. The out-group is created first. This articulation of what is the problem and who is behind it connects with the lived experience of the masses, especially those who have a latent populist attitude and are anxious about the future, and that connection sets off the chain of equivalences and   creates the populist affiliation. The in-group is thus created. Such an affiliation is contingent upon the articulation and the boundary set by the leader. Once the boundary is set with a clearly defined out-group, and a relatively capacious in-group, the populist then stakes a claim to political power and office to seek the same goals akin to other pluralist politicians. Therefore, unlike the conventional model, the trajectory here is V shaped, top to bottom and then to the top again, wherein the out-group is created first and only thereafter is the in-group formed.

The populist identifies the rascal first. All are then invited to throw them out.

Therefore, I would describe the logic of populism in India and its states as the articulation of a political leader to rupture the status quo against the elites and for the people. Such a description brings together the various sets used in this study—boundary setting (rupturing of the status quo), elites, people, and the leader.

In a first-ever survey conducted of populist attitudes in India, 48.37 percent of the respondents across 12 major states felt that the elites blocked the progress of people like them. Anti-elitism is more than twice the proportion of any other social category. Only 21.62 percent of the respondents felt that the upper castes were blocking the progress of people like them, and the perception of other groups from above or below (lower castes, minorities, migrants) was less than 15 percent on an average (Varshney, Ayyangar, and Swaminathan 2021). We found some demographic attributes (caste, gender, rural–urban, and so on), but there was no appreciable difference among the categories in these groups that were starkly populist (compared to those that were nationalist) and were also preoccupied at the time with whether populism could be understood as distinguishable from nationalism and did not really understand populism from the starting point of anti-elitism. This book goes beyond understanding populism from the standpoint of the people and their constituents or from the standpoint of its distinction from other concepts, such as nationalism, to get to understand what is behind the label of populism. And it argues that the logic of populism is the setting of boundaries to redraw political alignments, using the language of difference, that connects and, consequently, constructs the people.

Arguing that populists are essentially boundary setters can also help us reexamine the somewhat compulsive predilection to characterize populists as belonging to the supply side or demand side of political mobilization. I do think this argument can be both a supply-side and a demand-side explanation because it tries to make the point that populists are in fact the intercept that decides the relation between the condition and the outcome. While it is the common standard to put arguments of populism either in the bucket of the "people" (such as the ideational approach) or in the bucket of the "leader" (such as the strategic approach), is it possible to consider a third bucket where arguments would fall in the bucket of the "boundary" where both the people and leader can be considered INUS conditions?

Why Now?

It is fair to ask why we need another theoretical formulation of populism. This question is important considering that there has been a profusion of such formulations that do not relate to each other and therefore have obstructed the building of knowledge around populism, and there seems to be a growing consensus on the definition of populism adhering to the ideational approach where populism is defined as a Manichean divide between the people and the elite and the defense of popular sovereignty at any cost (Melendez and Kaltwasser 2019). I argue that it is necessary to keep this consensus open ended to address several alternate scenarios that complicate this consensus.

For instance, what is really at the core of populism in this project is fundamentally different from both the ideational and the strategic approaches. The strategic approach has argued that the leader and the plebiscitarian strategy that he or she adopts are at the core of populism. And the ideational approach proponents disagree that leadership is at the core and instead argue that popular sovereignty is at the core. The question is: how can one define populism where the defense of popular sovereignty is not at the core in postcolonial democracies such as India and perhaps other countries as well, but one aspect among others that constitute the dimensions of populism?

What is fundamentally distinctive about the approach in this book, and drawing from set theory, is that populism does not have a single concept at its core. What it has instead are configurations, configurations of concepts. I argue that the logic of populism in India is the setting of boundaries (commonly by a leader) configured either with a people anxious about the future or having a latent populist attitude or with a leader who sets these boundaries and garners extraordinary intense support for goals that he or she determines on their own.

Second, can we think of populism where popular sovereignty is an invocation not to the people but against the anti-people around whom the people then get constructed? That is, when the boundaries are set is that it seems almost natural to first look at who is inside the set or behind the line that, in this case, constitutes the people. The argument being proposed for populism here, when boundaries are set, is to look at who is outside the set first or beyond the line, as knowing that out-group first helps us understand how the in-group is constituted. Can populism then, when understood as an anti-elite strategy instead of a strategy that relies on people at its core, merit a different approach to explore what constitutes such a strategy?

Third, who defines who the people are and who the elite are? Is it not important to think of the person who draws that line and thereby defines the boundaries between the two groups? The in-group and out-group are constituted around the labels of the people and the other, and hence is it not fair to bring in the leader, even their performative styles, as another attribute in the consensus around populism because without such a leader these groups might remain immanent but not constituted? One should clarify that the argument in this book is not to bring the strategic approach back in because the approach adopted here is configurational and not classical wherein this contested concept has leadership at the core (Weyland 2001), but to make the case that leadership is an important but nevertheless a sufficient (INUS) condition in what characterizes populism.

Fourth, the ideational approach does absorb much populist-case-level divergence because of its elegance, but it is also agnostic to programmatic content, and that becomes problematic when one has to address questions of political modernization. For instance, an illiberal populist at the national level can cause democratic backsliding, but there are instances in India when such populists at the helm have been one of the causes for the emergence or presence of inclusive populists—such as a Kejriwal or a Mamata—at the subnational level. Are such moments—for instance, when we have illiberal populists at the national level and liberal populists at the subnational level in India's democracy—inconsequential, pivotal, or routine? It is unclear how the prevailing consensus can respond to this empirical complication. This book attempts such a response by articulating what is common to the three cases and what are the configurations of these common elements that help us better understand the divergence.

Fifth, early on in this book I describe the boundary setting as antagonistic boundary setting. To be fair, I do think that the boundaries that the populist draws in first outlining the out-group inevitably create an antagonism. The boundary is antagonistic in its very nature because it is holding some group culpable for the current situation. Such an antagonism has moved nations both forward and backward (depending on where one stands ideologically of course), but the point is that there is movement beyond the momentum of normal politics.

By way of conclusion, one must also respond to the end of the day question, which is whether the logic of populism as entailed here has made India more or less democratic. After all, disentangling populism from democracy conceptually was to understand its place in political modernization in India, which can also be understood as a question about whether populism has been a threat or a corrective to Indian democracy.

From Periyar to Modi, populism is not just episodic and recurrent over the past century in India but also indisputably pivotal. Populists in India have been both celebrated for deepening democratic participation and reviled for being exclusionist and revisionist—and, therefore, as mentioned earlier, the conundrum that comes with its emergence. For those schooled in democracy, populism threatens liberal democracies because of its authoritarian and illiberal approach to governance (Levitsky and Ziblatt 2019). And for those schooled in populism, contemporary liberal democratic systems threaten popular aspirations because venal elites have captured and made institutions effete, thereby forsaking the original promise of our republics (Mounk 2018a, 2018b). For instance, there seems little to add to the established commentary for and against Modi's illiberal approach to democracy. The motivation here is to take a step back and recognize the more significant consequence of the conundrum—we seem to be at a conceptual quandary, where our register of meanings around democracy is divided, and we have no fresh approaches to cohere out of this polarized space.

Once disentangled, I have argued, based on the experience from India and its states, populism is an articulation of a political condition, and it is democracy that provides the context and indeed the political color for such mobilization. Populism should be seen as a distinct form of mobilization and not as a deviant incongruity of democracy. Liberal democrats accommodate and unite and populists parse and divide for the greater common good. The former is a centripetal and the latter a centrifugal force within democratic systems. The contestation is not at the core of political concepts but the boundaries where they intersect to cohere, and therein lies the promise of a republic.

Notes

1. See Table A.4 (Robustness Case Ratio) in the Appendix to note that there are an additional 19 cases that are labeled as "shaky typical." That is, these are cases in the current dataset and reflect the two pathways, but they are not robust under the alternate scenarios indicated in the test sets. Shaky typical cases are cases that are in the current dataset and are not robust but could become so under alternate plausible analytical decisions.

Appendix

Below are some clarificatory notes related to the dataset.

A.1 Populist Outcome Related

A.1.1 *Clarifications on Electoral Data*

A few additional clarifications, as background information, are necessary to understand some of the measures related to the electoral data.

1. Bal Thackeray had never contested an election. But it seemed unjustifiable to ignore him, as he was clearly a populist leader of some measure in Maharashtra. Thus, I took the first electoral victory of the Shiv Sena in the assembly elections of 1995 as the populist instance, because Bal Thackeray reigned supreme for many years prior to and after this victory. And I took the electoral statistics of the incumbent chief minister and loyalist, Manohar Joshi, as the proxy for Bal Thackeray, assuming that the party chief that has got the assembly majority for the first time in its history would have its most trusted loyalist as the chief minister.

2. Jayalalitha's elections in 2001, 2011, and 2016 also need clarifications. In 2001, Jayalalitha was disqualified from competing in the election in May 2001 but was acquitted in December 2001 and thereafter won the byelections from Andipatti in 2002. In 2011, even though Jayalalitha won from the Srirangam constituency (which was the

constituency included in the dataset), she was convicted by the Karnataka High Court soon thereafter and acquitted subsequently. She then contested from the RK Nagar constituency and resumed her chief ministership and contested from RK Nagar again in 2016.

3. In 1990, Laloo Prasad Yadav was an MP and was brought in as chief minister after the Janata Dal won the Bihar assembly elections. Since he had not contested, I used his well-known close confidante Jagadanand Singh's election statistics as a proxy for Lalu (Tiwary 2020).

4. Similarly, in West Bengal elections in 2011, once the TMC came to power for the first time, Mamata Banerjee resigned as an MP and fought a byelection from Bhabanipur to become the chief minister. In the only instance in this dataset, Mamata Banerjee actually lost her seat by a narrow margin of 1,000 votes in Nandigram in 2021, even though her party won the assembly majority. She has moved court for a recount and subsequently won a byelection from Bhabanipur, which is the data point in this dataset.

5. Nitish Kumar, the chief minister of Bihar for almost the past two decades, has never contested assembly elections but has been a CM by being a member of the State Legislative Council. And so, for all elections I had to choose his confidants as proxies—that is, the vote shares of Jitan Ram Manjhi in 2010 as the first loyalist who fell out of favor and also Shrawon Kumar, who has remained a part of the inner circle, for the 2005, 2015, and 2020 elections (Rai 2015).

6. Lastly, I had to take the byelections of Raman Singh in 2004 as the data unit for the Chhattisgarh assembly elections in 2003 as Raman Singh was an MP at the time of the assembly elections and was brought in by the BJP to take on the role of the CM after the party won the assembly elections.

A.1.2   Calculation of Populist Outcome

The calculation for the populist outcome is:

$$\left[\left\{ \left(\frac{a}{b} \right) \div \left(\frac{c}{d} \right) \right\} = y \right]$$

a = Percent vote share of populist candidate in constituency in election X

b = Percent vote share of populist party in assembly elections in election X

c = Average percent vote share of all CM candidates in respective constituencies in all preceding elections[1]

d = Average percent vote share of CM-affiliated party in all preceding assembly elections

y = populist outcome

A.2 Populist Attitude

Lokniti has been conducting pre- and post-poll surveys since 1967, concurrent with national and state-level electoral cycles. The surveys have questions covering issues such as voter choice, governance, topical issues, service delivery, and so on, and are easily the most comprehensive repository of survey responses related to elections in India and across its states since 1967 (except between 1980 and 1996, when surveys were not undertaken as mentioned earlier). Under the circumstances, wherein populist attitude studies are still nascent and there have been no such studies undertaken in India so far, I identified questions post hoc which best reflect a populist attitude(s) over the various survey years. To be on the conservative side, the question with the lowest percentage score was chosen if there were multiple questions in the same questionnaire.

The most common question (25 out of the 37 cases) or versions of the same that were used was along the following lines[2]:

Question: People have different considerations while deciding whom to vote for. What mattered to you more while deciding whom to vote for in this election?

	N	%
A. Party		
B. Candidate		
C. Chief Ministerial Candidate		
D. Don't Know/Can't Say		
Total		

Percentage responses to C (when available in the questionnaire) were the main response that was recorded, or B (when C was not available in the questionnaire) or in some cases when the choice was between the various candidates whose names were mentioned (3 cases in this subset) was recorded in the dataset.

The second set of responses (answer B) that were recorded were for the following question, and was indicative of an anti-establishment sentiment amongst the respondents (7 out of the 37 cases)

Question: Do you think that the government in this country can be run better if there were no parties, assemblies, and elections?

	N	%
A. No		
B. Yes		
C. Don't Know/Can't Say		
Total		

The third set of responses (4 out of the 37 cases) were to two other questions focused on the people or on the majority:

1. Question: Would you say that people we elect by voting generally care about what people like you think or that they don't care? (2 cases)
2. Question: In a democracy, is it appropriate that the opinions of the majority community should prevail? (2 cases)

The last set of responses that were recorded in the dataset attempted to capture an anti-other attitude (1 out of the 37 cases):

3. Question: Do you think that the people of some other classes come in the way of the welfare and progress of the people in your class, or do you think this is not the case?

A.3   Anxiety about the Future

A standard question (with slightly different wording across the various NES surveys of 1971, 1996, 2004, 2009, and the Bihar state survey 1995) that was used to record scores related to the anxiety about the future was the following (21/37 cases):

Question: Now looking ahead and thinking about the next few years, do you expect that your financial situation will stay about the way it is now, get better, or get worse?

	N	%
1. Worse		
2. Same		
3. Better		
4. Don't Know/Can't Say		
Total		

This question was prospective because it sought to understand future expectations of the respondent and directly addressed anxieties about the future. However, because a similar question was not asked over all the surveys, I had to use a question related to (*a*) concerns about the community (1/37 from the 1980 NES), (*b*) a retrospective assessment of the current financial situation (10/37 cases based on 2024 and 2014 NES and the Chhattisgarh State Survey of 2003), and (*c*) an assessment of meeting current needs and savings (5/37 cases based on 2019 NES) as an indirect measure of future anxieties. These questions are as follows:

1. Now let us talk about how much concern would you say you have for the condition and problems of your caste/religious group—not at all, some, or lot?
2. As compared to five years ago, how is the economic condition of your household today—would you say it has become much better, better, remained the same, become worse, or much worse?
3. Which of the following statements truly describes your current condition:
   a. We are able to fulfill all our needs and also end up saving some money.
   b. We are able to fulfill all our needs but don't end up saving.
   c. We are not able to fulfill all our needs and face some difficulty.
   d. We are not able to fulfill all our needs and face a lot of difficulty.

A.4   Question Numbers and Survey Year Details

Table A.1 provides the question number and the survey year for the responses for each case.

Table A.1 Question Numbers and Survey Year Details

S. No.	Name	Year	Populist Attitude Question Number	Survey	Future Anxiety Question Number	Survey
1	Arvind Kejriwal	2013	4	Delhi Pre Poll 2013	E 4	NES Post Poll 2009a
2	Arvind Kejriwal	2015	2	Delhi Post Poll 2015	16	NES Post Poll 2014
3	Arvind Kejriwal	2020	4	Delhi Pre Poll 2020	6	NES Pre Poll 2019
4	Bal Thackeray	1995	27	NES 1996 Post Poll	47	NES Post Poll 1996
5	Chandrababu Naidu	1999	27	NES 1996 Post Poll	47	NES Post Poll 1996
6	Chandrasekhar Rao	2014	7	NES 2014 Post Poll	16	NES Post Poll 2014
7	Chandrasekhar Rao	2018	3	Telangana Pre Poll 2018	16	NES Post Poll 2014b
8	Digvijay Singh	1998	27	NES 1996 Post Poll	47	NES Post Poll 1996
9	Indira Gandhi	1971	67f	NES 1971 Post Poll	65b	NES 1971 Post Poll
10	Indira Gandhi	1980	9	NES 1980 Pre Poll	2	NES 1980 Pre Pollc
11	Jayalalitha	2001	9	Tamil Nadu Post Poll 2001	47	NES Post Poll 1996
12	Jayalalitha	2011	8	Tamil Nadu Post Poll 2011	E 4	NES Post Poll 2009
13	Jayalalitha	2016	7	Tamil Nadu Pre Poll 2016	16	NES Post Poll 2014
14	Karunanidhi	1996	27	NES 1996 Post Poll	47	NES Post Poll 1996
15	Karunanidhi	2006	18d	Tamil Nadu Pre Poll 2006	33	NES Post Poll 2004

(*Contd.*)

Table A.1 (*Contd.*)

S. No.	Name	Year	Populist Attitude Question Number	Survey	Future Anxiety Question Number	Survey
16	Lalu Prasad Yadav	1995	17	Bihar Pre Poll 1995	37	Bihar Pre Poll 1995
17	Mamata Banerjee	2011	8	West Bengal Post Poll 2011	E 4	NES Post Poll 2009
18	Mamata Banerjee	2016	5	West Bengal Post Poll 2016	16	NES Post Poll 2014
19	Mamata Banerjee	2021	6	West Bengal Post Poll 2021	6	NES Pre Poll 2019
20	Narendra Modi Gujarat	2002	4	Gujarat Post Poll 2002	47	NES Post Poll 1996d
21	Narendra Modi Gujarat	2007	31b	Gujarat Pre Poll 2007	33	NES Post Poll 2004
22	Narendra Modi Gujarat	2012	2	Gujarat Post Poll 2012	E 4	NES Post Poll 2009
23	Narendra Modi PM	2014	9	NES Post Poll 2014	16	NES Post Poll 2014
24	Narendra Modi PM	2019	13	NES Post Poll 2019	6	NES Pre Poll 2019
25	Narendra Modi PM	2024	3	NES Post Poll 2024	16	NES Post Poll 2024
26	Naveen Patnaik	2004	27	NES Post Poll 2004	33	NES Post Poll 2004
27	Naveen Patnaik	2009	A4	NES Post Poll 2009	E 4	NES Post Poll 2009
28	Naveen Patnaik	2014	7	NES Post Poll 2014	16	NES Post Poll 2014
29	Naveen Patnaik	2019	A4	NES Post Poll 2019	6	NES Pre Poll 2019
30	Nitish Kumar	2005	20	Bihar Post Poll 2005	33	NES Post Poll 2004
31	Nitish Kumar	2010	4	Bihar Post Poll 2010	E 4	NES Post Poll 2009

32	Nitish Kumar	2015	9	Bihar Post Poll 2015	16	NES Post Poll 2014
33	Nitish Kumar	2020	9	Bihar Post Poll 2020	6	NES Pre Poll 2019
34	Pawan Kumar Chamling	2009	D2	NES Post Poll 2009	E 4	NES Post Poll 2009
35	Raman Singh	2003	4	Chhattisgarh Post Poll 2003	22e	Chhattisgarh Post Poll 2003
36	Raman Singh	2008	10	Chhattisgarh Post Poll 2008	33	NES Post Poll 2004
37	Raman Singh	2013	4	Chhattisgarh Pre Poll 2013	E 4	NES Post Poll 2009

Source: Author.

Notes: [a] Almost all state-level responses from NES data were made available by directly requesting Lokniti.

[b] The 2014 survey had to be used for both the 2014 and 2018 years because the question or some version of it was not asked in the state-level prepoll. While the percent score is a repeat on this condition, the scores on the other factors are different.

[c] This question asked how much concern did the respondent have for his caste/community and such. It was not a question based on an assessment of the financial or economic prospects. But the question was used as a proxy because the other question was not available and did anyway ask for a direct response about their concern for their current situation.

[d] I had to use the 1996 poll findings to account for the condition in Gujarat in 2002 because the state-level survey data is not available, and this was the closest time period of relevance.

A.5   Robustness Checks

This section would be of interest to those who are well versed with QCA and can be omitted as a summary, as these results are provided in Chapter 6.

Robustness checks were conducted on the intermediate solution term derived from the standard analysis because the enhanced standard analysis did not show any contradictory simplifying assumptions or any positive outcomes in the non-outcome truth table. The checks were conducted to identify sensitivity ranges, fit-oriented robustness, and case-oriented robustness.

A.5.1   Sensitivity Analysis

Under sensitivity ranges, tests were conducted to understand the robustness of calibration thresholds of the conditions, the consistency threshold to determine sufficiency, and the frequency cut-off. What the tests do is conduct multiple runs of alternate scenarios (that we can specify in the R Code) by changing the number of each parameter to see if the solution term remains the same. For instance, under condition P, one tested whether the solution remains unchanged if the exclusion threshold, currently set at 0.25, were to change to 0.245, 0.24, 0.235, and so on, depending on our specifications. Table 7.2 provides the results of the sensitivity analysis.

Under sensitivity analysis, the tests conducted reveal the range of the conditions within which the solution term remains unchanged. The greater the range, the higher the robustness. For example, under the calibration of condition tests for condition P, the exclusion threshold at 0.25 has a lower bound that is not available (depicted as NA), which indicates that the lower bound stretches to infinity and the range of the exclusion threshold is between infinity and 0.25. This result implies that the exclusion threshold is robust. On the other hand, the crossover threshold at 0.5 is sensitive because there is no range between the lower and upper bounds in this threshold. Similarly, the inclusion threshold is also sensitive. All of these results on the P condition indicate that the condition is sensitive, and it is only robust at the extremes at the lower bound.

Similarly, a few inferences can be derived from these ranges on the calibration conditions. First, all conditions are robust at the lower bound of the exclusion thresholds, which is to say that if one alters this threshold to the extremes of exclusion, the solution term will remain unchanged. Second,

Table A.2 Robustness Checks: Sensitivity Ranges in Practice

Sensitivity to Calibration of Conditions

P

Exclusion: Lower bound NA Threshold 0.25 Upper bound 0.25

Crossover: Lower bound 0.5 Threshold 0.5 Upper bound 0.5

Inclusion: Lower bound 0.75 Threshold 0.75 Upper bound 0.75

B

Exclusion: Lower bound NA Threshold 0.25 Upper bound 0.25

Crossover: Lower bound 0.5 Threshold 0.5 Upper bound 0.5

Inclusion: Lower bound 0.75 Threshold 0.75 Upper bound 0.75

L

Exclusion: Lower bound −4.75 Threshold 0.25 Upper bound 0.25

Crossover: Lower bound 0.5 Threshold 0.5 Upper bound 0.5

Inclusion: Lower bound 0.75 Threshold 0.75 Upper bound 2.75

F

Exclusion: Lower bound 3.31 Threshold 5.31 Upper bound 16.31

Crossover: Lower bound 16.87 Threshold 16.87 Upper bound 31.87

Inclusion: Lower bound 17.23 Threshold 32.23 Upper bound NA

A

Exclusion: Lower bound −23.65 Threshold 8.35 Upper bound 14.35

Crossover: Lower bound 20.88 Threshold 21.88 Upper bound 24.88

Inclusion: Lower bound 31.45 Threshold 35.45 Upper bound NA

Sensitivity to Consistency Threshold

Raw Consistency T.: Lower bound 0.84 Threshold 0.85 Upper bound 0.85

Sensitivity to Frequency cut off

N.Cut: Lower bound 2 Threshold 2 Upper bound 5

conditions L, F, and A seem relatively robust because all the bounds have some range of robustness, with the extremes being very robust. For instance, consider the F condition. The exclusion (3.31–16.31), cross over (16.87–31.87) and inclusion threshold (17.23–NA) bounds show that the solution term will remain unchanged within these threshold ranges. Second, while the two conditions are quite robust (F and A), the remaining conditions derived as fuzzy scores are sensitive except at the extremes (P and B) with the exception of L which is a fuzzy score and robust at the extreme ends. Third, this seems to suggest that the solution terms will remain unchanged so long as we broaden the range of the extreme thresholds outwards and keep the crossover threshold constant.

The results on the consistency threshold and the frequency cut-off show that the solution terms are quite sensitive. The solution terms will change if one changes the consistency threshold to either 0.80 or 0.90 or anything beyond these ranges, because it will remain unchanged only at 0.84. Similarly, the solution term will remain unchanged only up to the frequency cut-off upper bound of 5. Thus, one could say that the solution is sensitive to consistency threshold changes and somewhat robust to changes in the frequency cut-off.

A.5.2   Fit-Oriented Robustness

While this analysis tests the robustness of the solution by assessing plausible alternate choices of the parameters in isolation and is useful in itself, we also want to test whether the solution is robust when such plausible alternate analytic decisions are made simultaneously. However, such plausible alternate analytical choices conducted simultaneously can get out of hand considering the number of choices that can be made. To overcome this problem, Oana and Schneider (2021) suggest that one aggregate all these alternate scenarios into a single test set (*TS*) that represents all the possible alternate scenarios that can be plausibly considered, and whereby the intersection of these sets (*minTS*) and the union of these sets (*maxTS*) can be compared with the set created as part of the project (Initial Set or *IS*). This can be visually seen in Figure A.1.

The intersection of these sets, *MinTS*, *MaxTS*, and *IS*, will reveal the Robust Core, which will represent part of the Initial Solutions (*IS*) that withstands all of the robustness tests performed. For this study, the question that seemed important to ask was whether the solution will remain unchanged if the coverage is enhanced through alternate plausible analytical decisions. And so, it seemed necessary that these alternate scenarios are reflective of decisions that allow for greater inclusion and exclusion—that is, to hollow out the center and accommodate more test cases within the theoretically plausible inclusion and exclusion thresholds. And for that it seemed that lowering the threshold of various parameters would broaden the range and number of alternate cases that can be considered. This meant that I should lower the consistency thresholds and the calibration parameters of at least the

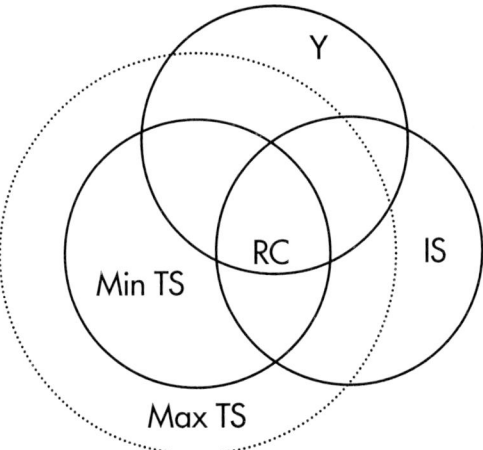

Figure A.1 Robustness Fit: The Initial Set (*IS*), Test Set (*TS*), and the Robust Core (*RC*)

Source: Adapted from Oana, Schneder, Thomann (2021: 147).

Note: *minTS* = Minimal Test Set, *maxTS* = Maximal Test Set, *RC* = Robust Core.

conditions that were based on percentage scores. The calibration ranges were determined by the gaps in the data distributed over the range of cases. The initial set calibration parameters were set at the extremes, with the crossover threshold at a middle range to keep the bar high in terms of membership into the set and considering substantive case-level differences across contiguous cases on either side of the various gaps. For the test sets, I chose the gaps that were at the lower end of the scores for the two scores and chose the third test set by increasing the consistency threshold. Below are the three test sets that were created as part of this exercise:

1. TS 1 = Altering A to lower thresholds (8.34, 13.95, 21.88) from the initial set of (8.34, 21.88 and 35.45)
2. TS 2 = Altering F to lower thresholds (5.30, 11.33, and 16.87) from the initial set of (5.30, 16.87, 32.23)
3. TS 3 = Increasing consistency threshold to 0.85

Table A.3 provides us with the results of fit-oriented robustness. An ideal situation—definitely an ideal abstraction, one should add—is when the *IS* and the *TS* are equal to 1 (*IS* = *minTS* = *maxTS* = 1). Such a perfect overlap would reflect as 1 on all scores in the following table. However, such a result is useful as a point of reference more than anything else. Clearly, the results

Table A.3 Fit-Oriented Robustness

	RF_cov	RF_cons	RF_SC_minTS	RF_SC_maxTS
Robustness_Fit	0.44	0.965	0.415	0.82

show that the Initial Set (*IS*) consistency is robust at 0.965, but coverage remains a challenge at 0.44. Also, interestingly, there is considerable overlap (above 0.5) across the maximum test sets (0.82), but not so much with the minimum test set (0.415). In conclusion, one can say that the solution term is robust but can do better on coverage.

A.5.3   Case-Level Robustness

Table A.4 provides us with case-level robustness results; it tells us which specific cases are robust, possible, shaky, and so on, and that in turn helps to contextualize and better understand the pathways to populism in India. One should, however, bear in mind that these cases are categorized in the context of plausible alternative analytics decisions, and so their location is contingent and reflective of such conditions. In any case, most researchers would develop and consider plausible alternates to see which cases remain robust through all such choices and then choose plausible test sets.

The table shows that the number of robust cases that are considered typical (0.259) and deviant (0.25) indicates that case-oriented robustness is low because the other cases are either mostly shaky or possible. It is important to know, however, that there are zero extreme deviant cases and just two irrelevant cases. In other words, the set of data is very much a plausible dataset but is, however, sensitive to robustness changes. The number of robust cases is 7/37, possible cases are 4, and the highest proportion in shaky cases are in total 22 (19 cases are shaky typical and 3 are shaky deviant). All in all, one can say that case-oriented robustness is low because we have many cases that are not robust and are in the shaky possible section of cases. This reflects in the overall robustness case ratio score at 4, indicating that we have simultaneously cases that are in the possible and shaky quadrants. Ideally, one would prefer to have no possible or shaky cases (rank 1) or possible but not shaky cases (rank 2). Nevertheless, what is of real interest is: which are the cases that are typical and robust? Cases 5, 9, 10, 17, 19, 23, and 24 are the cases that can provide us with substantive ideas as to the logic of populism in India. Chapter 6 deals with these cases in greater detail.

Table A.4   Robustness Case Ratio

RCR_typ RCR_dev RCC_Rank

Robustness_Case_Ratio 0.259 0.25 4

CaseTypes

Robust Typical Cases (IS*MIN_TS and Y > 0.5):

Boolean Expression: A*B*F + B*F*L

Cases in the intersection/Total number of cases: 7 / 37 = 18.92%

Cases in the intersection/Total number of cases Y > 0.5: 7 / 27 = 25.93%

Case Names:

5 9 10 17 19 23 24

Robust Deviant Cases (IS*MIN_TS and Y < 0.5):

Boolean Expression: A*B*F + B*F*L

Cases in the intersection/Total number of cases: 2 / 37 = 5.41%

Cases in the intersection/Total number of cases Y < 0.5: 2 / 10 = 20%

Case Names:

18 25

Shaky Typical Cases (IS*~MIN_TS and Y > 0.5):

Boolean Expression: ~A*~B*~L + A*B*~F + B*~F*L + A*~F*L*~P

Cases in the intersection/Total number of cases: 19 / 37 = 51.35%

Cases in the intersection/Total number of cases Y > 0.5: 19 / 27 = 70.37%

Case Names:

1 2 4 8 13 14 16 20 21 22 26 27 28 29 30 34 35 36 37

Shaky Deviant Cases(IS*~MIN_TS and Y < 0.5):

Boolean Expression: ~A*~B*~L + A*B*~F + B*~F*L + A*~F*L*~P

Cases in the intersection/Total number of cases: 3 / 37 = 8.11%

Cases in the intersection/Total number of cases Y < 0.5: 3 / 10 = 30%

Case Names:

3 11 12

Possible Typical Cases (~IS*MAX_TS and Y > 0.5):

Table A.4   (*Contd.*)

Cases in the intersection/Total number of cases: 1 / 37 = 2.7%

Cases in the intersection/Total number of cases Y > 0.5: 1 / 27 = 3.7%

Case Names:

7

Possible Deviant Cases (~IS*MAX_TS and Y < 0.5):

Boolean Expression: ~A*B*~L + A*~B*F + A*~B*~L + ~A*~B*F*L + ~A*~B*L*~P

Cases in the intersection/Total number of cases: 3 / 37 = 8.11%

Cases in the intersection/Total number of cases Y < 0.5: 3 / 10 = 30%

Case Names:

6 32 33

Extreme Deviant Coverage Cases (~IS*~MAX_TS and Y > 0.5):

Boolean Expression: ~A*~B*~BFLP*L + ~A*B*~BFLP*~L + A*~B*~BFLP*F + A*~B*~BFLP*~L + A*~B*~BFLP*P

Cases in the intersection/Total number of cases: 0 / 37 = 0%

Cases in the intersection/Total number of cases Y > 0.5: 0 / 27 = 0%

Case Names:

No cases in this intersection

Irrelevant Cases (~IS*~MAX_TS and Y < 0.5):

Boolean Expression: ~A*~B*~BFLP*L + ~A*B*~BFLP*~L + A*~B*~BFLP*F + A*~B*~BFLP*~L + A*~B*~BFLP*P

Cases in the intersection/Total number of cases: 2 / 37 = 5.41%

Cases in the intersection/Total number of cases Y < 0.5: 2 / 10 = 20%

Case Names:

15 31

A.6   Calibrated Dataset

Table A.5 shows the calibrated dataset based on which the QCA results were reported in Chapter 5.

Table A.5 Calibrated Dataset

	Abbreviation	Name	Year	P	B	L	F	A	Y
1	AK1	Arvind Kejriwal	2013	0.6	1	1	0.126154	0.034714	0.999892
2	AK2	Arvind Kejriwal	2015	1	1	1	0.387473	0.901815	0.650526
3	AK3	Arvind Kejriwal	2020	0.8	0.6	0.6	0.287141	0.60267	0.212441
4	BT1	Bal Thackeray	1995	0.6	1	1	0.103011	0.086179	0.995337
5	CN2	Chandrababu Naidu	1999	0.4	0.8	1	0.582537	0.5796	0.926163
6	CSR1	Chandrasekhar Rao	2014	0.4	0.2	0.8	0.868871	0.880857	0.294987
7	CSR2	Chandrasekhar Rao	2018	0.8	0.4	0.6	0.868871	0.420168	0.768869
8	DS2	Digvijay Singh	1998	0.8	0.2	0	0.070323	0.104728	0.999882
9	IG2	Indira Gandhi	1971	1	1	1	0.988009	0.252795	0.81816
10	IG5	Indira Gandhi	1980	0.6	0.8	0.6	0.859102	0.070087	0.781497
11	JJ2	Jayalalitha	2001	0.8	1	0.8	0.081274	0.992668	0.096643
12	JJ4	Jayalalitha	2011	0.6	0.6	0.6	0.265214	0.353202	0.025043
13	JJ5	Jayalalitha	2016	1	0.6	0.6	0.297955	0.911011	0.9886
14	MK4	Karunanidhi	1996	0.4	1	0.8	0.081274	0.215767	1
15	MK5	Karunanidhi	2006	1	0.4	0.6	0.153904	0.691506	0.026315
16	LP2	Lalu Prasad Yadav	1995	0.6	1	0.8	0.439324	0.173283	0.999784
17	MB1	Mamata Banerjee	2011	0.6	0.8	1	0.546086	0.131362	1
18	MB2	Mamata Banerjee	2016	1	0.6	1	0.60915	0.182837	0.000868
19	MB3	Mamata Banerjee	2021	0.8	1	0.8	0.96706	0.102304	0.999779
20	NMG2	Narendra Modi Gujarat	2002	0.6	1	0.6	0.020509	0.982338	0.9024

(Contd.)

Table A.5 (Contd.)

	Abbreviation	Name	Year	P	B	L	F	A	Y
21	NMG3	Narendra Modi Gujarat	2007	0.8	0.6	0.8	0.033065	0.821011	0.776297
22	NMG4	Narendra Modi Gujarat	2012	1	1	1	0.128708	0.965969	0.967789
23	NMP1	Narendra Modi PM	2014	0.8	0.8	0.6	0.69667	0.597463	0.901934
24	NMP2	Narendra Modi PM	2019	1	1	1	0.549167	0.261104	0.92322
25	NMP3	Narendra Modi PM	2024	0.6	1	0.8	0.572802	0.074313	0.495316
26	NP2	Naveen Patnaik	2004	0.6	0.4	0.4	0.018536	0.079566	0.976195
27	NP3	Naveen Patnaik	2009	0.8	0.6	0.8	0.102076	0.031711	0.997727
28	NP4	Naveen Patnaik	2014	0.2	0.2	0.6	0.387473	0.821011	0.995096
29	NP5	Naveen Patnaik	2019	0	0	0	0.878347	0.10432	0.916604
30	NK2	Nitish Kumar	2005	0.4	0	0	0.420797	0.085666	0.985248
31	NK3	Nitish Kumar	2010	0.8	0	0.4	0.140164	0.752305	0.001853
32	NK4	Nitish Kumar	2015	0.8	0	0.6	0.92505	0.67269	0.002282
33	NK5	Nitish Kumar	2020	0	0	0	0.727782	0.895898	0.011527
34	PKC4	Pawan Kumar Chamling	2009	0.8	0.4	0.2	0.035415	0.017015	0.757546
35	RS1	Raman Singh	2003	0	0.6	0	0.377039	0.927103	0.82327
36	RS2	Raman Singh	2008	0.8	0.6	0.4	0.025731	0.853446	0.986757
37	RS3	Raman Singh	2013	0	0	0	0.247297	0.035451	0.973553

Notes

1. The earliest election for which this proportion was calculated was 1967 to provide a benchmark for the 1971 Lok Sabha elections. The year 1971 was mostly the starting date considered in this dataset for all state assembly elections and otherwise the start date when the legislative assemblies were first convened, such as Delhi (as the National Capital Territory in 1993), Chhattisgarh (2001), Sikkim (1979), and Telangana (2013). 1971 was arbitrarily chosen as the starting date because most of India was being ruled by the Congress till 1967, but seemed an appropriate choice because it is only after 1971 do we see some populist figures emerge after Indira Gandhi.

2. I refer to the question as being "along the following lines" because the exact wording may differ over the years or across states.

Bibliography

Primary Sources

Asopa, Navya, Shivam Gangwani, Sunaad, and Gilles Verniers. N.d. "TCPD Indian Elections Dataset (TCPD-IED), 1951–1962 Codebook 1.0." Trivedi Centre for Political Data, Ashoka University, India.

Election Commission of India. 1967. "Statistical Report on General Elections to the Lok Sabha – Volume 1." Government of India.

———. 1971a. "Statistical Report on General Election to the Legislative Assembly of Orissa/Odisha." Government of India.

———. 1971b. "Statistical Report on General Election to the Legislative Assembly of Tamil Nadu." Government of India.

———. 1971c. "Statistical Report on General Elections to the Lok Sabha – Volume 1." Government of India.

———. 1972a. "Statistical Report on General Election to the Legislative Assembly of Andhra Pradesh." Government of India.

———. 1972b. "Statistical Report on General Election to the Legislative Assembly of Bihar." Government of India.

———. 1972c. "Statistical Report on General Election to the Legislative Assembly of Gujarat." Government of India.

———. 1972d. "Statistical Report on General Election to the Legislative Assembly of Madhya Pradesh." Government of India.

———. 1972e. "Statistical Report on General Election to the Legislative Assembly of Maharashtra." Government of India.

———. 1972f. "Statistical Report on General Election to the Legislative Assembly of West Bengal." Government of India.

———. 1974. "Statistical Report on General Election to the Legislative Assembly of Orissa/Odisha." Government of India.

———. 1975. "Statistical Report on General Election to the Legislative Assembly of Gujarat." Government of India.

———. 1977a. "Statistical Report on General Election to the Legislative Assembly of Bihar." Government of India.

———. 1977b. "Statistical Report on General Election to the Legislative Assembly of Madhya Pradesh." Government of India.

———. 1977c. "Statistical Report on General Election to the Legislative Assembly of Orissa/Odisha." Government of India.

———. 1977d. "Statistical Report on General Election to the Legislative Assembly of Tamil Nadu." Government of India.

———. 1977e. "Statistical Report on General Election to the Legislative Assembly of West Bengal." Government of India.

———. 1977f. "Statistical Report on General Elections to the Lok Sabha – Volume 1." Government of India.

———. 1978a. "Statistical Report on General Election to the Legislative Assembly of Andhra Pradesh." Government of India.

———. 1978b. "Statistical Report on General Election to the Legislative Assembly of Maharashtra." Government of India.

———. 1979. "Statistical Report on General Election to the Legislative Assembly of Sikkim." Government of India.

———. 1980a. "Statistical Report on General Election to the Legislative Assembly of Bihar." Government of India.

———. 1980b. "Statistical Report on General Election to the Legislative Assembly of Gujarat." Government of India.

———. 1980c. "Statistical Report on General Election to the Legislative Assembly of Madhya Pradesh." Government of India.

———. 1980d. "Statistical Report on General Election to the Legislative Assembly of Maharashtra." Government of India.

———. 1980e. "Statistical Report on General Election to the Legislative Assembly of Orissa/Odisha." Government of India.

———. 1980f. "Statistical Report on General Election to the Legislative Assembly of Tamil Nadu." Government of India.

———. 1980g. "Statistical Report on General Elections to the Lok Sabha – Volume 1." Government of India.

———. 1982. "Statistical Report on General Election to the Legislative Assembly of West Bengal." Government of India.

———. 1983. "Statistical Report on General Election to the Legislative Assembly of Andhra Pradesh." Government of India.

———. 1984a. "Statistical Report on General Election to the Legislative Assembly of Tamil Nadu." Government of India.

———. 1984b. "Statistical Report on General Elections to the Lok Sabha – Volume 1." Government of India.

———. 1985a. "Statistical Report on General Election to the Legislative Assembly of Andhra Pradesh." Government of India.

———. 1985b. "Statistical Report on General Election to the Legislative Assembly of Bihar." Government of India.

———. 1985c. "Statistical Report on General Election to the Legislative Assembly of Gujarat." Government of India.

———. 1985d. "Statistical Report on General Election to the Legislative Assembly of Madhya Pradesh." Government of India.

———. 1985e. "Statistical Report on General Election to the Legislative Assembly of Maharashtra." Government of India.

———. 1985f. "Statistical Report on General Election to the Legislative Assembly of Orissa/Odisha." Government of India.

———. 1985g. "Statistical Report on General Election to the Legislative Assembly of Sikkim." Government of India.

———. 1987. "Statistical Report on General Election to the Legislative Assembly of West Bengal." Government of India.

———. 1989a. "Statistical Report on General Election to the Legislative Assembly of Andhra Pradesh." Government of India.

———. 1989b. "Statistical Report on General Election to the Legislative Assembly of Sikkim." Government of India.

———. 1989c. "Statistical Report on General Election to the Legislative Assembly of Tamil Nadu." Government of India.

———. 1989d. "Statistical Report on General Elections to the Lok Sabha – Volume 1." Government of India.

———. 1990a. "Statistical Report on General Election to the Legislative Assembly of Bihar." Government of India.

———. 1990b. "Statistical Report on General Election to the Legislative Assembly of Gujarat." Government of India.

———. 1990c. "Statistical Report on General Election to the Legislative Assembly of Madhya Pradesh." Government of India.

———. 1990d. "Statistical Report on General Election to the Legislative Assembly of Maharashtra." Government of India.

———. 1990e. "Statistical Report on General Election to the Legislative Assembly of Orissa/Odisha." Government of India.

———. 1991a. "Statistical Report on General Election to the Legislative Assembly of Tamil Nadu." Government of India.

———. 1991b. "Statistical Report on General Election to the Legislative Assembly of West Bengal." Government of India.

———. 1991c. "Statistical Report on General Elections to the Lok Sabha – Volume 1." Government of India.

———. 1993. "Statistical Report on General Election to the Legislative Assembly of the National Capital Territory of Delhi." Government of India.

———. 1994a. "Statistical Report on General Election to the Legislative Assembly of Andhra Pradesh." Government of India.

———. 1994b. "Statistical Report on General Election to the Legislative Assembly of Madhya Pradesh." Government of India.

———. 1994c. "Statistical Report on General Election to the Legislative Assembly of Sikkim." Government of India.

———. 1995a. "Statistical Report on General Election to the Legislative Assembly of Bihar." Government of India.

———. 1995b. "Statistical Report on General Election to the Legislative Assembly of Gujarat." Government of India.

———. 1995c. "Statistical Report on General Election to the Legislative Assembly of Maharashtra." Government of India.

———. 1995d. "Statistical Report on General Election to the Legislative Assembly of Orissa/Odisha." Government of India.

———. 1996a. "Statistical Report on General Election to the Legislative Assembly of Tamil Nadu." Government of India.

———. 1996b. "Statistical Report on General Election to the Legislative Assembly of West Bengal." Government of India.

———. 1996c. "Statistical Report on General Elections to the Lok Sabha – Volume 1." Government of India.

———. 1998a. "Statistical Report on General Election to the Legislative Assembly of Gujarat." Government of India.

———. 1998b. "Statistical Report on General Election to the Legislative Assembly of Madhya Pradesh." Government of India.

———. 1998c. "Statistical Report on General Election to the Legislative Assembly of the National Capital Territory of Delhi." Government of India.

————. 1999a. "Statistical Report on General Election to the Legislative Assembly of Andhra Pradesh." Government of India.

————. 1999b. "Statistical Report on General Election to the Legislative Assembly of Maharashtra." Government of India.

————. 1999c. "Statistical Report on General Election to the Legislative Assembly of Sikkim." Government of India.

————. 1999d. "Statistical Report on General Elections to the Lok Sabha – Volume 1." Government of India.

————. 2000a. "Statistical Report on General Election to the Legislative Assembly of Bihar." Government of India.

————. 2000b. "Statistical Report on General Election to the Legislative Assembly of Orissa/Odisha." Government of India.

————. 2001a. "Statistical Report on General Election to the Legislative Assembly of Chhattisgarh." Government of India.

————. 2001b. "Statistical Report on General Election to the Legislative Assembly of Tamil Nadu." Government of India.

————. 2001c. "Statistical Report on General Election to the Legislative Assembly of West Bengal." Government of India.

————. 2002. "Statistical Report on General Election to the Legislative Assembly of Gujarat." Government of India.

————. 2003a. "Statistical Report on General Election to the Legislative Assembly of Madhya Pradesh." Government of India.

————. 2003b. "Statistical Report on General Election to the Legislative Assembly of the National Capital Territory of Delhi." Government of India.

————. 2004a. "Statistical Report on General Election to the Legislative Assembly of Andhra Pradesh." Government of India.

————. 2004b. "Statistical Report on General Election to the Legislative Assembly of Chhattisgarh." Government of India.

————. 2004c. "Statistical Report on General Election to the Legislative Assembly of Maharashtra." Government of India.

————. 2004d. "Statistical Report on General Election to the Legislative Assembly of Orissa/Odisha." Government of India.

————. 2004e. "Statistical Report on General Election to the Legislative Assembly of Sikkim." Government of India.

————. 2004f. "Statistical Report on General Elections to the Lok Sabha – Volume 1." Government of India.

————. 2005. "Statistical Report on General Election to the Legislative Assembly of Bihar." Government of India.

———. 2006. "Statistical Report on General Election to the Legislative Assembly of Tamil Nadu." Government of India.

———. 2007. "Statistical Report on General Election to the Legislative Assembly of Gujarat." Government of India.

———. 2008a. "Statistical Report on General Election to the Legislative Assembly of Chhattisgarh." Government of India.

———. 2008b. "Statistical Report on General Election to the Legislative Assembly of Madhya Pradesh." Government of India.

———. 2008c. "Statistical Report on General Election to the Legislative Assembly of the National Capital Territory of Delhi." Government of India.

———. 2009a. "Statistical Report on General Election to the Legislative Assembly of Maharashtra." Government of India.

———. 2009b. "Statistical Report on General Election to the Legislative Assembly of Orissa/Odisha." Government of India.

———. 2009c. "Statistical Report on General Election to the Legislative Assembly of Sikkim." Government of India.

———. 2009d. "Statistical Report on General Elections to the Lok Sabha – Volume 1." Government of India.

———. 2010. "Statistical Report on General Election to the Legislative Assembly of Bihar." Government of India.

———. 2011a. "Statistical Report on General Election to the Legislative Assembly of Tamil Nadu." Government of India.

———. 2011b. "Statistical Report on General Election to the Legislative Assembly of West Bengal." Government of India.

———. 2012. "Statistical Report on General Election to the Legislative Assembly of Gujarat." Government of India.

———. 2013a. "Statistical Report on General Election to the Legislative Assembly of Chhattisgarh." Government of India.

———. 2013b. "Statistical Report on General Election to the Legislative Assembly of Madhya Pradesh." Government of India.

———. 2013c. "Statistical Report on General Election to the Legislative Assembly of the National Capital Territory of Delhi." Government of India.

———. 2014a. "Statistical Report on General Election to the Legislative Assembly of Andhra Pradesh." Government of India.

———. 2014b. "Statistical Report on General Election to the Legislative Assembly of Maharashtra." Government of India.

———. 2014c. "Statistical Report on General Election to the Legislative Assembly of Orissa/Odisha." Government of India.

———. 2014d. "Statistical Report on General Election to the Legislative Assembly of Sikkim." Government of India.

———. 2014e. "Statistical Report on General Elections to the Lok Sabha – Volume 1." Government of India.

———. 2015a. "Statistical Report on General Election to the Legislative Assembly of Bihar." Government of India.

———. 2015b. "Statistical Report on General Election to the Legislative Assembly of the National Capital Territory of Delhi." Government of India.

———. 2016a. "Statistical Report on General Election to the Legislative Assembly of Tamil Nadu." Government of India.

———. 2016b. "Statistical Report on General Election to the Legislative Assembly of West Bengal." Government of India.

———. 2017. "Statistical Report on General Election to the Legislative Assembly of Gujarat." Government of India.

———. 2018. "Statistical Report on General Election to the Legislative Assembly of Chhattisgarh." Government of India.

———. 2019a. "Statistical Report on General Election to the Legislative Assembly of Andhra Pradesh." Government of India.

———. 2019b. "Statistical Report on General Election to the Legislative Assembly of Madhya Pradesh." Government of India.

———. 2019c. "Statistical Report on General Election to the Legislative Assembly of Maharashtra." Government of India.

———. 2019d. "Statistical Report on General Election to the Legislative Assembly of Orissa/Odisha." Government of India.

———. 2019e. "Statistical Report on General Election to the Legislative Assembly of Sikkim." Government of India.

———. 2019f. "Statistical Report on General Elections to the Lok Sabha – Volume 1." Government of India.

———. 2020a. "Statistical Report on General Election to the Legislative Assembly of Bihar." Government of India.

———. 2020b. "Statistical Report on General Election to the Legislative Assembly of the National Capital Territory of Delhi." Government of India.

———. 2021a. "Statistical Report on General Election to the Legislative Assembly of Tamil Nadu." Government of India.

———. 2021b. "Statistical Report on General Election to the Legislative Assembly of West Bengal." Government of India.

Lokniti–CSDS. 1971. "National Post Poll Survey Findings 1971." Survey. National Election Studies. Lokniti-Centre for the Study of Developing Societies, New Delhi. https://www.lokniti.org/national-election-studies.

———. 1980. "CSDS-Pre-Poll Survey 1980—Findings." Survey. National Election Studies. Lokniti–Centre for the Study of Developing Societies, New Delhi. https://www.lokniti.org/national-election-studies.

———. 1995. "Bihar Pre-Poll Survey 1995." Survey. State Election Studies. Lokniti-Centre for the Study of Developing Societies, New Delhi. https://www.lokniti.org/state-election-studies.

———. 2001. "Tamil Nadu Postpoll Survey 2001—Survey Findings." Survey. State Election Studies. Lokniti–Centre for the Study of Developing Societies, New Delhi. https://www.lokniti.org/state-election-studies.

———. 2002. "Gujarat Postpoll 2002—Survey Findings." Survey. Lokniti–Centre for the Study of Developing Societies, New Delhi. https://www.lokniti.org/state-election-studies.

———. 2003. "Chattisgarh Postpoll 2003—Survey Findings." Survey. State Election Studies. Lokniti–Centre for the Study of Developing Societies, New Delhi. https://www.lokniti.org/state-election-studies.

———. 2004. "NES-Postpoll 2004—Findings (Weight by State Proportion and Actual Vote Share)." Survey. Lokniti–Centre for the Study of Developing Societies, New Delhi. https://www.lokniti.org/national-election-studies.

———. 2005. "Bihar Postpoll Survey 2005." Survey. Lokniti–Centre for the Study of Developing Societies, New Delhi. https://www.lokniti.org/state-election-studies.

———. 2006. "Tamil Nadu Prepoll Survey 2006—Survey Findings." Survey. State Election Studies. Lokniti–Centre for the Study of Developing Societies, New Delhi. https://www.lokniti.org/state-election-studies.

———. 2007. "Gujarat Prepoll Survey 2007—Survey Findings." Survey. State Election Studies. Lokniti-Centre for the Study of Developing Societies, New Delhi. https://www.lokniti.org/state-election-studies.

———. 2008. "Chattisgarh Postpoll 2008—Survey Findings." Survey. State Election Studies. Lokniti–Centre for the Study of Developing Societies, New Delhi. https://www.lokniti.org/state-election-studies.

———. 2009. "NES-Postpoll 2009—Findings (Weight by State Proportion and Actual Vote Share)." Survey. Lokniti–Centre for the Study of Developing Societies, New Delhi. https://www.lokniti.org/national-election-studies.

———. 2010. "Bihar Postpoll Survey 2010." Survey. State Election Studies. Lokniti–Centre for the Study of Developing Societies, New Delhi. https://www.lokniti.org/state-election-studies.

———. 2011a. "Tamil Nadu Postpoll Survey 2011—Survey Findings." Survey. State Election Studies. Lokniti–Centre for the Study of Developing Societies, New Delhi. https://www.lokniti.org/state-election-studies.

———. 2011b. "West Bengal Postpoll Survey 2011—Survey Findings." Survey. State Election Studies. Lokniti–Centre for the Study of Developing Societies, New Delhi. https://www.lokniti.org/state-election-studies.

———. 2012. "Gujarat Postpoll Survey 2012—Survey Findings." Survey. State Election Studies. Lokniti–Centre for the Study of Developing Societies, New Delhi. https://www.lokniti.org/state-election-studies.

———. 2013a. "Chattisgarh Prepoll 2013—Survey Findings." Survey. State Election Studies. Lokniti–Centre for the Study of Developing Societies, New Delhi. https://www.lokniti.org/state-election-studies.

———. 2013b. "Delhi Prepoll 2013—Survey Findings." Survey. State Election Studies. Lokniti–Centre for the Study of Developing Societies, New Delhi. https://www.lokniti.org/state-election-studies.

———. 2014. "NES Post Poll 2014—Findings (Weight by State Proportion and Actual Vote Share)." Survey. Lokniti–Centre for the Study of Developing Societies, New Delhi. https://www.lokniti.org/national-election-studies.

———. 2015a. "Bihar Postpoll Survey 2015." Survey. State Election Studies. Lokniti–Centre for the Study of Developing Societies, New Delhi. https://www.lokniti.org/state-election-studies.

———. 2015b. "Delhi Postpoll 2015—Survey Findings." Survey. State Election Studies. Lokniti–Centre for the Study of Developing Societies, New Delhi. https://www.lokniti.org/state-election-studies.

———. 2016a. "Tamil Nadu Prepoll Survey 2016—Survey Findings." Survey. State Election Studies. Lokniti–Centre for the Study of Developing Societies, New Delhi. https://www.lokniti.org/state-election-studies.

———. 2016b. "West Bengal Postpoll Survey 2016—Survey Findings." Survey. State Election Studies. Lokniti–Centre for the Study of Developing Societies, New Delhi. https://www.lokniti.org/state-election-studies.

———. 2018. "Telangana Prepoll 2018—Survey Findings." Survey. State Election Studies. Lokniti–Centre for the Study of Developing Societies, New Delhi. https://www.lokniti.org/state-election-studies.

———. 2019. "NES 2019 Prepoll—Survey Findings." Survey. Lokniti–Centre for the Study of Developing Societies, New Delhi. https://www.lokniti.org/national-election-studies.

———. 2020a. "Bihar Postpoll Survey 2020." Survey. State Election Studies. Lokniti–Centre for the Study of Developing Societies, New Delhi. https://www.lokniti.org/state-election-studies.

———. 2020b. "Delhi Election Eve Survey 2020—Findings." Survey. State Election Studies. Lokniti–Centre for the Study of Developing Societies, New Delhi. https://www.lokniti.org/state-election-studies.

———. 2021. "West Bengal Postpoll Survey 2021—Survey Findings." Survey. State Election Studies. Lokniti–Centre for the Study of Developing Societies, New Delhi. https://www.lokniti.org/state-election-studies.

———. 2024. "National Election Study: Social and Political Barometer Post Poll Study 2024—Survey Findings." Lokniti–Centre for the Study of Developing Societies, New Delhi.

———. N.d.a. "National Election Study Post Poll 1996—Findings (Weight by Actual Vote Share)." Lokniti–Centre for the Study of Developing Societies, New Delhi.

———. N.d.b. "NES Postpoll 2014." Survey. National Election Studies. Lokniti–Centre for the Study of Developing Societies, New Delhi. https://www.lokniti.org/national-election-studies.

Secondary Sources

Ahmed, Hilal. 2022. "The Problem—India 75 Years: A Symposium on the Idea of People." *Seminar*, no. 756 (August). https://www.india-seminar.com/2022/756/756-01%20The%20problem.htm (accessed January 18, 2025).

Akkerman, Agnes, Cas Mudde, and Andrej Zaslove. 2014. "How Populist Are the People? Measuring Populist Attitudes in Voters." *Comparative Political Studies* 47 (9): 1324–53.

Alam, Sanjeer. 2024. "Personal Financial Conditions Played Key Role in Voting Choice." *The Hindu*, June 6.

Alizada, Nafisa, Rowan Cole, Lisa Gastaldi, Sandra Grahn, Sebastian Hellmeier, Paulina Kolvani, Jean Lachapelle et al. 2021. "Democracy Report 2021: Autocratization Turns Viral." V-Dem Institute, University of Gothenburg.

AlRoy, Gil Carl. 1970. "Populism: Its Meaning and National Characteristics. Edited by Ghita Ionescu and Ernest Gellner. (New York: Macmillan. 1969.

Pp. 263.).” *American Political Science Review* 64 (3): 968–69. https://doi.
org/10.1017/S0003055400131880.

Ananth, V. Krishna. 2014. “Where Does the Aam Aadmi Party Stand?” *Economic
and Political Weekly* 49 (14): 14–15.

———. 2016. “Democratic Process Not Yet Lost in Tamil Nadu.” *Economic and
Political Weekly* 51 (22): 26–28.

Andrews, Matt, Lant Pritchett, and Michael Woolcock. 2017. *Building State
Capability: Evidence, Analysis, Action*. Oxford, UK: Oxford University
Press.

Ankit, Rakesh. 2018. “Caste Politics in Bihar: In Historical Continuum.” *History
and Sociology of South Asia* 12 (2): 115–36.

Arnimesh, Shankar, and Shikha Salaria. 2024. “Voter Disconnect, Motormouths,
Wrong Candidate Selection—What Review of BJP’s UP Results Found.” *The
Print*, July 10. https://theprint.in/politics/voter-disconnect-motormouths-
wrong-candidate-selection-what-review-of-bjps-up-results-found/2169063/
(accessed January 18, 2025).

Aslandis, Paris. 2017. “Populism and Social Movements.” In *The Oxford Handbook
of Populism*, edited by Cristobal Rovira Kaltwasser, Paul Taggart, Paulina
Ochoa Espejo, and Pierre Ostiguy, 305–25. Oxford: Oxford University
Press. https://doi.org/10.1093/oxfordhb/9780198803560.013.18.

Ayyangar, Srikrishna. 2007. “Cleaning the Augean Stables: Populism in Latin
America and India.” *SAIS Review of International Affairs* 27 (1): 93–101.
https://dx.doi.org/10.1353/sais.2007.0000.

———. 2024. “Populisms in India.” In *Three Faces of Populism in Asia*, edited by
Shiru Wang, 27–44. Hong Kong: Routledge.

Balagopal, K. 1999. “The Man and the Times.” *Economic and Political Weekly* 34
(26): 1654–58.

Barr, Robert R. 2017. *The Resurgence of Populism in Latin America*. Boulder: Lynne
Rienner Publishers.

Barrio, Astrid. 2020. “The Weakness of Populism in Spain.” *DEBATS—Annual
Review* 5: 197–209.

Bedi, Tarini. 2007. “The Dashing Ladies of the Shiv Sena.” *Economic and Political
Weekly* 42 (17): 1534–41.

Bertoa, Fernando Casal. 2023. “In Polarised Spain, Populists Win Even When
They Lose the Elections.” Who Governs Europe (blog). September 8.
https://whogoverns.eu/in-polarised-spain-populists-win-even-when-they-
lose-the-elections/ (accessed January 18, 2025).

Bhaduri, Amit and Arvind Kejriwal. 2005. "Reforming the Reformers." *Economic and Political Weekly* 40 (53): 5543–45.

Blair, Harry W. 1980. "Rising Kulaks and Backward Classes in Bihar: Social Change in the Late 1970s." *Economic and Political Weekly* 15 (2): 64–74.

Bora, Banasmita. 2004. "Pro-Incumbency Factor." *Economic and Political Weekly* 39 (51): 5536–44.

Bourke, Richard. 2016. "Introduction." In *Popular Sovereignty in Historical Perspective*, edited by Richard Bourke and Quentin Skinner, 1–14. Cambridge, UK: Cambridge University Press. https://www.cambridge.org/core/books/popular-sovereignty-in-historical-perspective/BD12523010A2069871EE40C25CD75170 (accessed January 19, 2025).

Brass, Paul R. 1992. *The Politics of India Since Independence*. New Delhi: Oxford University Press.

Brest, Paul, and Linda Hamilton Krieger. 2010. *Problem Solving, Decision Making, and Professional Judgment: A Guide for Lawyers and Policymakers*. New York: Oxford University Press.

Brubaker, Rogers. 2019. "Populism and Nationalism." *Nations and Nationalism* 26 (1): 1–23. https://doi.org/DOI: 10.1111/nana.12522.

Burakowski, Adam, and Krzysztof Iwanek. 2017. "India's Aam Aadmi (Common Man's) Party." *Asian Survey* 57 (3): 528–47.

Canovan, Margaret. 2005. *The People*. Cambridge, UK: Polity Press.

Castanho Silva, Bruno. 2018. "Populists Success: A Qualitative Comparative Analysis." In *The Ideational Approach to Populism: Theory, Method and Analysis*, edited by Kirk A. Hawkins, Ryan Carlin, Levente Littvay, and Cristobal Rovira Kaltwasser, 279–93. London: Routledge.

Chadda, Maya. 2013. "Integration through Internal Reorganization: Containing Ethnic Conflict in India." In *Handbook of Politics in Indian States: Regions, Parties, and Economic Reforms*, edited by Sudha Pai, 55–72. New Delhi: Oxford University Press.

Chakrabarty, Bidyut. 2016. "Defying the Pattern: The 2016 State Assembly Elections." *Economic and Political Weekly* 51 (43): 18–20.

Chakravarty, Sumit, Meher Engineer, Prashant Bhushan, Arvind Kejriwal, Amit Bhaduri, Sumit Sarkar, Manoranjan Mohanty, Ramaswamy R. Iyer, Madhu Bhaduri, and Achin Vanaik. 2007. "Shameful Events." *Economic and Political Weekly* 42 (45/46): 4.

Chandhoke, Neera. 2012. "Modi's Gujarat and Its Little Illusions." *Economic and Political Weekly* 47 (49): 10–11.

Chatterjee, Partha. 2012. "The Movement against Politics." *Cultural Critique* 81 (Spring): 117–22.

Chaudhari, Sritama. 2021. "From 'Amma Canteen' of Jayalalitha to 'Maa Kitchen' of Mamata Banerjee: A Saga of Food, Politics and Motherhood." Doing Sociology (blog). October 30. https://doingsociology.org/2021/10/30/from-amma-canteen-of-jayalalitha-to-maa-kitchen-of-mamata-banerjee-a-saga-of-food-politics-and-motherhood-sritama-chaudhuri/ (accessed January 19, 2025).

Chhotray, Vasudha, Anindita Adhikari, and Vidushi Bahuguna. 2020. "The Political Prioritization of Welfare in India: Comparing the Public Distribution System in Chhattisgarh and Jharkhand." *World Development* 128 (April): 104853. https://doi.org/10.1016/j.worlddev.2019.104853.

Cleen, Benjamin De. 2017. "Populism and Nationalism." In *The Oxford Handbook of Populism*, edited by Cristobal Rovira Kaltwasser, Paul Taggart, Paulina Ochoa Espejo, and Pierre Ostiguy, 342–62. Oxford: Oxford University Press. https://doi.org/10.1093/oxfordhb/9780198803560.013.18.

Collier, Ruth Berins, and David Collier. 2002. *Shaping the Political Arena: Critical Junctures, the Labor Movement, and Regime Dynamics in Latin America.* Notre Dame, IN: University of Notre Dame Press.

Dahrendorf, Ralf. 1990. "Europe's Vale of Tears." *Marxism Today*, May.

Deshpande, Prachi. 2007. *Creative Pasts: Historical Memory and Identity in Western India, 1700–1960.* New York: Columbia University Press.

Devasahayam, M. G. 2024. "For the First Time, India's Elections Are under International Scrutiny." *The Wire*, April 1. https://thewire.in/politics/for-the-first-time-indias-elections-are-under-international-scrutiny/?mid_related_new (accessed January 19, 2025).

Dhanagare, D. N. 1988. "Subaltern Consciousness and Populism: Two Approaches in the Study of Social Movements in India." *Social Scientist* 16 (11): 18–35.

Docx, Edward. 2021. "The Clown King: How Boris Johnson Made It by Playing the Fool." *The Guardian*, 18 March. https://www.theguardian.com/news/2021/mar/18/all-hail-the-clown-king-how-boris-johnson-made-it-by-playing-the-fool (accessed January 19, 2025).

Donthi, Praveen. 2014. "How KCR Became the Face of the Telangana Movement." *The Caravan*, 1 April. https://caravanmagazine.in/reportage/wedge (accessed January 19, 2025).

Dornbusch, Rudiger, and Sebastian Edwards. 1990. "The Macroeconomics of Populism in Latin America." *Journal of Development Economics* 32 (2): 247–77.

Dreze, Jean, and Reetika Khera. 2015. "Understanding Leakages in the Public Distribution System." *Economic and Political Weekly* 50 (7): 39–42.

Dusa, Adrian. 2019. *QCA with R. A Comprehensive Resource.* Cham, Switzerland: Springer International Publishing.

EPW Editorial Desk. 1989a. "How Tamil Nadu Was Won and Lost." *Economic and Political Weekly* 24 (4): 177.

———. 1989b. "Tamil Nadu Pointers." *Economic and Political Weekly* 24 (4): 167.

———. 2011a. "Fourteenth Assembly Election Results in Tamil Nadu." *Economic and Political Weekly* 46 (25): 138–42.

———. 2011b. "'National' State Elections." *Economic and Political Weekly* 46 (20): 7–8.

———. 2012. "From Lokpal to Lokniti: Can the New Political Party of Arvind Kejriwal and Company Mature into a Popular Political Force?" *Economic and Political Weekly* 47 (46): 8.

———. 2014. "2013 Legislative Assembly Elections, Delhi." *Economic and Political Weekly* 49 (6): 82–85.

Gandhi, Mohandas Karamchand. 1938. *Hind Swaraj or Indian Home Rule.* Ahmedabad: Navajivan Publishing House.

Geetha, V., and S. V. Rajadurai. 1991. "Dravidian Politics: End of an Era." *Economic and Political Weekly* 26 (26): 1591–92.

Gerring, John. 2011. "The Case Study: What It Is and What It Does." In *The Oxford Handbook of Comparative Politics*, edited by Carles Boix and Susan Stokes, 90–122. Oxford: Oxford University Press.

Goertz, Gary. 2006. *Social Science Concepts: A Users Guide.* Princeton, NJ: Princeton University Press.

Goertz, Gary, and James Mahoney. 2006. "Negative Case Selection: The Possibility Principle." In *Social Science Concepts: A User's Guide*, by Gary Goertz, 177–210. Princeton, NJ: Princeton University Press.

Gould, Harold A. 1980. "The Second Coming: The 1980's Elections in India's Hindi Belt." *Asian Survey* 20 (6): 595–616.

Gudavarthy, Ajay. 2023. *Politics, Ethics and Emotions in "New India."* New Delhi: Routledge.

Guha, Ayan. 2016. "West Bengal Elections: Unchanged amidst Change." *Economic and Political Weekly* 51 (41): 69–71.

Guha, Ramachandra. 2010. "Political Leadership." In *The Oxford Companion to Politics in India*, edited by Niraja Gopal Jayal and Pratap Bhanu Mehta, 288–98. New Delhi: Oxford University Press.

————. 2017. *India after Gandhi: The History of the World's Largest Democracy.* New Delhi: Pan Macmillan.

Gupta, Dipankar. 1980a. "The Appeal of Nativism: A Study of the Articulation and Perception of Shiv Sena's Ideology." *Sociological Bulletin* 29 (2): 107–41.

————. 1980b. "The Shiv Sena Movement: Its Organization and Operation: Part One." *Social Scientist* 8 (10): 22–37.

————. 1980c. "The Shiv Sena Movement: Its Organization and Operation: Part Two." *Social Scientist* 8 (11): 32–43.

Hansen, Thomas Blom. 2001. *Wages of Violence: Naming and Identity in Postcolonial Bombay.* Princeton, NJ: Princeton University Press.

Hauser, Walter. 1997. "General Elections 1996 in Bihar: Politics, Administrative Atrophy and Anarchy." *Economic and Political Weekly* 32 (41): 2599–607.

Hawkins, Kirk A. 2010. *Venezuela's Chavismo and Populism in Comparative Perspective.* New York: Cambridge University Press.

Hawkins, Kirk A., Ryan E. Carlin, Levente Littvay, and Cristobal Rovira Kaltwasser, eds. 2019. *The Ideational Approach to Populism: Concept, Theory and Analysis.* Routledge Studies in Extremism and Democracy. New York: Routledge.

Hawkins, Kirk A., Scott Riding, and Cas Mudde. 2012. "Measuring Populist Attitudes." The Committee on Concepts and Methods Working Paper Series 55. CIDE, Mexico City.

Hawkins, Kirk A., and Cristóbal Rovira Kaltwasser. 2017. "What the (Ideational) Study of Populism Can Teach Us, and What It Can't." *Swiss Political Science Review* 23 (4): 526–42.

Hawkins, Kirk A., Cristóbal Rovira Kaltwasser, and Ioannis Andreadis. 2020. "The Activation of Populist Attitudes." *Government and Opposition* 55 (2): 283–307. https://doi.org/10.1017/gov.2018.23.

Heuzé, Gérard. 2000. "Populism, Religion, and Nation in Contemporary India: The Evolution of the Shiv Sena in Maharashtra." *Comparative Studies of South Asia, Africa and the Middle East* 20 (1): 3–43.

Hlavac, Mark. 2022. "Stargazer: Well-Formatted Regression and Summary Statistics Tables." R Package. https://CRAN.R-project.org/package=stargazer.

Hoekstra, Kinch. 2016. "Athenian Democracy and Popular Tyranny." In *Popular Sovereignty in Historical Perspective*, edited by Richard Bourke and Quentin Skinner, 15–51. Cambridge: Cambridge University Press.

Howladar, Sumit. 2014. "Populist Politics and Electoral Democracy: A Study of Mamata Banerjee." *Journal of Political Studies* 9: 91–101.

———. 2016. "Trinamool, Politics and Poribarton: Comprehending the Ideological Connection." *Journal of Political Studies* 12 (March–October): 1–12.

Ionescu, Ghița, and Ernest Gellner. 1969. *Populism: Its Meaning and National Characteristics.* New York: Macmillan.

Irschick, Eugene F. 1986. *Tamil Revivalism in the 1930s.* Madras: Cre-A.

Isham, Jonathan, Thomas Kelly, and Sunder Ramaswamy. 2002. *Social Capital and Economic Development: Well-Being in Developing Countries.* Cheltenham, UK: Edward Elgar Publishing. https://doi.org/10.4337/9781781950388.

Jaffrelot, Christophe. 2008. "Gujarat: The Meaning of Modi's Victory." *Economic and Political Weekly* 43 (15): 12–17.

———. 2013. "Gujarat Elections: The Sub-Text of Modi's 'Hattrick'—High Tech Populism and the 'Neo-Middle Class.'" *Studies in Indian Politics* 1 (1): 79–95.

———. 2019. "Class and Caste in the 2019 Indian Election: Why Have So Many Poor Started Voting for Modi?" *Studies in Indian Politics* 7 (2): 149–60.

———. 2021. *Modi's India: Hindu Nationalism and The Rise of Ethnic Democracy.* New Delhi: Context.

———. 2024. *Gujarat under Modi: The Blueprint for Today's India.* New Delhi: Context.

Jaffrelot, Christophe, and Louise Tillin. 2017. "Populism in India." In *Oxford Handbook of Populism*, edited by Cristóbal Rovira Kaltwasser, Paul Taggart, Paulina Ochoa Espejo, and Pierre Ostiguy, 179–94. Oxford: Oxford University Press.

Jalal, Ayesha. 1995. *Democracy and Authoritarianism in South Asia: A Comparative and Historical Perspective.* Contemporary South Asia. Cambridge, UK: Cambridge University Press. https://doi.org/10.1017/CBO9780511559372.

Jayal, Niraja Gopal. 2016. "Contending Representative Claims in Indian Democracy." *India Review* 15 (2): 172–95.

———. 2019. *Re-Forming India: The Nation Today.* New Delhi: Penguin Random House.

Jenne, Erin K., Kirk A. Hawkins, and Bruno Castanho Silva. 2021. "Mapping Populism and Nationalism in Leader Rhetoric Across North America and Europe." *Studies in Comparative International Development* 56 (2): 170–96. https://doi.org/10.1007/s12116-021-09334-9.

Jeyaranjan, J., and M. Vijayabaskar. 2011. "Not by Patronage Alone: Understanding Tamil Nadu's Vote for Change." *Economic and Political Weekly* 46 (22): 13–15.

Jha, Dhirendra K. 2022. "Priest of Violence: Adityanath's Reign of Terror." *The Caravan*, January 1.

Jha, Himanshu. 2015. "Restive Voices for Change." *The New Indian Express*, February 11, Delhi edition.

Jose, Vinod K. 2011. "The Last Lear: Karunanidhi's Struggle to Cling to Power and Hold Together His Fractious Political Dynasty." *The Caravan*, April.

———. 2012. "The Emperor Uncrowned: The Rise of Narendra Modi." *The Caravan*, March 1.

Joshi, Dhananjai, and Praveen Rai. 2009. "Chhattisgarh 2008: Defeating Anti-Incumbency." *Economic and Political Weekly* 44 (6): 38–41.

Kadt, Emanuel de. 1970. "Populism: Its Meanings and National Characteristics." *International Affairs* 46 (1): 138–39. https://doi.org/10.2307/2614244.

Kaicker, Abhishek. 2020. *The King and the People: Sovereignty and Popular Politics in Mughal Delhi*. New York: Oxford University Press.

Kaltwasser, Cristóbal Rovira, Paul A. Taggart, Paulina Ochoa Espejo, and Pierre Ostiguy. 2017. *The Oxford Handbook of Populism*. Oxford: Oxford University Press.

Kannan, R. 2017. *MGR: A Life*. New Delhi: Penguin Random House India.

Kaviraj, Sudipta. 1986. "Indira Gandhi and Indian Politics." *Economic and Political Weekly* 21 (38/39): 1697–708.

———. 2018. *The Trajectories of the Indian State*. Ranikhet, India: Permanent Black.

Kedhar, Anusha. 2020. "Choreographing Tolerance: Narendra Modi, Hindu Nationalism, and International Yoga Day." *Race and Yoga* 5 (1): 42–58.

Kejriwal, Arvind. 2012. *Swaraj*. New Delhi: Harper Collins.

Kenny, Paul D. 2021. *Populism and Patronage: Why Populists Win Elections in India, Asia, and Beyond*. Populism and Patronage. Oxford: Oxford University Press. https://oxford.universitypressscholarship.com/view/10.1093/oso/9780198807872.001.0001/oso-9780198807872.

Kirk, Jason A. 2005. "Banking on India's States: The Politics of World Bank Reform Programs in Andhra Pradesh and Karnataka." *India Review* 4 (3–4): 287–325.

Kitschelt, Herbert, and Steven I. Wilkinson. 2007. "Citizen–Politician Linkages: An Introduction." In *Patrons, Clients and Policies: Patterns of Democratic Accountability and Political Competition*, edited by Herbert Kitschelt and Steven I. Wilkinson, 1–49. Cambridge: Cambridge University Press. https://doi.org/10.1017/CBO9780511585869.001.

Kohli, Atul. 1988. "The NTR Phenomenon in Andhra Pradesh: Political Change in a South Indian State." *Asian Survey* 28 (10): 991–1017. https://doi.org/10.2307/2644703.

———. 2006. "Politics of Economic Growth in India, 1980-2005: Part I: The 1980s." *Economic and Political Weekly* 41 (13): 1251–59.

Koole, Karin, and Barbara Vis. 2012. "Working Mothers and the State: Under Which Conditions Do Governments Spend Much on Maternal Employment Supporting Policies?" COMPASSS Working Papers 2012 (71). http://www.compasss.org/wpseries/KooleVis2012.pdf (accessed April 16, 2025).

Krishna, Vineeth. 2024. "This Month in Constitution-Making (January 1947): The Constituent Assembly Passes the Objectives Resolution." Constitution ofindia.Net (blog). January 1, 2024. https://www.constitutionofindia.net/blog/this-month-in-constitution-making-january-1947-the-constituent-assembly-passes-the-objectives-resolution/ (accessed April 16, 2025).

Kumar, Anup. 2011. *The Making of a Small State: Populist Social Mobilisation and the Hindi Press in the Uttarakhand Movement*. New Delhi: Orient Blackswan.

Kumar, Ashutosh. 2013. "Development Focus and Electoral Success at State Level: Nitish Kumar as Bihar's Leader." *South Asia Research* 33 (2): 101–21.

Kumar, Awanish. 2013. "Nitish Kumar's Honourable Exit: A Brief History of Caste Politics." *Economic and Political Weekly* 48 (28): 15–17.

Kumar, Sanjay. 2003. "Gujarat Assembly Elections 2002: Analysing the Verdict." *Economic and Political Weekly* 38 (4): 270–75.

Kumar, Sanjay, and Rakesh Ranjan. 2009. "Bihar: Development Matters." *Economic and Political Weekly* 44 (39): 141–44.

Laclau, Ernesto. 2005. "Populism: What's in a Name?" In *Populism and the Mirror of Democracy*, edited by Francisco Panizza, 48: 32–49. London: Verso.

Laclau, Ernesto, and Chantal Mouffe. 2014. *Hegemony and Socialist Strategy: Towards a Radical Democratic Politics*. Vol. 8. London: Verso Books.

Lakoff, George. 1987. *Metaphors We Live By: What Categories Reveal about the Mind*. Chicago: University of Chicago Press.

Lakshman, Abhinay. 2024. "Did a Constitutional Conscience Drive Much of the Dalit and OBC Vote?" *The Hindu*, June 28. https://www.thehindu.com/opinion/op-ed/did-a-constitutional-conscience-drive-much-of-the-dalit-and-obc-vote/article68341647.ece (accessed January 19, 2025).

Lama-Rewal, Stéphanie Tawa. 2019. "Political Representation in the Discourse and Practices of the 'Party of the Common Man' in India." *Politics and Governance* 7 (3): 179–88.

Lee, Daniel. 2016. "The Lex Regia: The Theory of Popular Sovereignty in the Roman Law Tradition." In *Popular Sovereignty in Early Modern Constitutional Thought*, 25–50. Oxford: Oxford University Press. https://doi.org/10.1093/acprof:oso/9780198745167.003.0002.

Levitsky, Steven, and Maxwell A. Cameron. 2003. "Democracy without Parties? Political Parties and Regime Change in Fujimori's Peru." *Latin American Politics and Society* 45 (3): 1–33. https://doi.org/10.1111/j.1548-2456.2003. tb00248.x.

Levitsky, Steven, and James Loxton. 2013. "Populism and Competitive Authoritarianism in the Andes." *Democratization* 20 (1): 107–36. https://doi. org/10.1080/13510347.2013.738864.

Levitsky, Steven, and A. Way Lucan. 2002. "Elections Without Democracy: The Rise of Competitive Authoritarianism." *Journal of Democracy* 13 (2): 51–65.

Levitsky, Steven, and Daniel Ziblatt. 2019. *How Democracies Die: What History Reveals about Our Future.* New York: Crown.

M. T. 2001. "Tamil Nadu: The Frequent Phoenix Factor." *Economic and Political Weekly* 36 (19): 1587–87.

Mackie, John L. 1965. "Causes and Conditions." *American Philosophical Quarterly* 2 (4): 245–64.

Mahoney, James. 2021. *The Logic of Social Science.* Princeton, NJ: Princeton University Press.

Mahoney, James, Erin Kimball, and Kendra L Koivu. 2009. "The Logic of Historical Explanation in the Social Sciences." *Comparative Political Studies* 42 (1): 114–46.

Malu, Bhasker, Santhosh Kareepadath Rajan, and Nikhita Jindal. 2023. "Regional Populism in India: A Case of Sikkim." In *Encyclopedia of New Populism and Responses in the 21st Century*, edited by Joseph Chacko Chennattuserry, Madhumati Deshpande, and Paul Hong, 1–6. Singapore: Springer Nature Singapore. https://doi.org/10.1007/978-981-16-9859-0_36-1.

Manor, James. 1980. "Pragmatic Progressives in Regional Politics: The Case of Devaraj Urs." *Economic and Political Weekly* 15 (5/7): 201–13.

———. 2004. "'Towel over Armpit': Small Time Political 'Fixers' in India's States." In *India and the Politics of Developing Countries: Essays in Honour of Myron Weiner*, edited by Ashutosh Varshney, 60–86. New Delhi: Sage.

———. 2010. "Beyond Clientelism: Digvijay Singh's Participatory Pro-Poor Strategy in Madhya Pradesh." In *Power and Influence in India: Bosses, Lords and Captains*, edited by Pamela Price and Arild Engelsen Ruud, 193–213. New Delhi: Routledge.

———. 2015. "An Odisha Landslide Buries Both National Parties: Assessing the State and Parliamentary Elections of 2014." *Contemporary South Asia* 23 (2): 198–210. https://doi.org/10.1080/09584935.2015.1019426.

Mantena, Karuna. 2016. "Popular Sovereignty and Anti Colonialism." In *Popular Sovereignty in Historical Perspective*, 297–319. Cambridge, UK: Cambridge University Press.

Marcos-Marne, Hugo, Homero Gil De Zuniga, and Porismita Borah. 2023. "What Do We Not (Know) about Demand-Side Populism? A Systematic Literature Review of Populist Attitudes." *European Political Science* 22 (3): 293–307.

Maringanti, Anant. 2010. "Telangana: Righting Historical Wrongs or Getting the Future Right?" *Economic and Political Weekly* 45 (4): 33–38.

Mashal, Mujib. 2023. "Why Is Narendra Modi So Popular? Tune In to Find Out." *The New York Times*, June 21.

Mehta, Pratap Bhanu. 2003. *The Burden of Democracy*. New Delhi: Penguin Books India Private Limited.

Melendez, Carlos, and Cristóbal Rovira Kaltwasser. 2019. "Political Identities: The Missing Link in the Study of Populism." *Party Politics* 25 (4): 520–33.

Mello, Patrick A. 2021. *Qualitative Comparative Analysis: An Introduction to Research Design and Its Applications*. Washington, DC: Georgetown University Press.

Mény, Yves, and Yves Surel, eds. 2001. *Democracies and the Populist Challenge*. London: Springer.

———. 2002. "The Constitutive Ambiguity of Populism." In *Democracies and the Populist Challenge*, edited by Yves Mény and Yves Surel, 1–22. New York: Palgrave.

Michelutti, Lucia. 2010. "Wrestling with (Body) Politics: Understanding 'Goonda' Political Styles in North India." In *Power and Influence in India: Bosses, Lords and Captains*, edited by Pamela Price and Arild Engelsen Ruud, 44–69. New Delhi: Routledge.

Misra, Surya Narayan. 2009. "Naveen Patnaik Authors a New Chapter for Orissa." *Economic and Political Weekly* 44 (39): 148–50.

Mitra, Ashok. 2012. "Lumpenland—The Cause of West Bengal's Gloom Lies in Its People's Naiveté." *The Telegraph Online*, April 5. https://www.telegraphindia.com/opinion/lumpenland-the-cause-of-west-bengal-s-gloom-lies-in-its-people-s-naivete/cid/425425 (accessed January 19, 2025).

Moffitt, Benjamin. 2016. *The Global Rise of Populism: Performance, Political Style, and Representation*. Stanford, CA: Stanford University Press.

Mohanty, Manoranjan. 2014. "Persisting Dominance: Crisis of Democracy in a Resource Rich Region." *Economic and Political Weekly* 49 (14): 39–47.

Mooij, Jos. 2007. "Hype, Skill and Class: The Politics of Reform in Andhra Pradesh, India." *Commonwealth and Comparative Politics* 45 (1): 34–56. https://doi.org/10.1080/14662040601135771.

Mottahedeh, Roy. 1985. *The Mantle and the Prophet: Religion and Politics in Iran.* New York: Simon and Schuster.

Mounk, Yascha. 2018a. *The People vs. Democracy.* Cambridge, MA: Harvard University Press.

———. 2018b. "The Undemocratic Dilemma." *Journal of Democracy* 29 (2): 98–112.

Mudde, Cas. 2004. "The Populist Zeitgeist." *Government and Opposition* 39 (4): 541–63.

———. 2007. "Introduction." In *Populist Radical Right Parties in Europe*, by Cas Mudde, 1–8. Cambridge, UK: Cambridge University Press. https://doi.org/10.1017/CBO9780511492037.001.

———. 2017. "Populism—An Ideational Approach." In *The Oxford Handbook of Populism*, edited by Cristobal Rovira Koltwasser, Paul Taggart, Paulina Ochoa Espejo, and Pierre Ostiguy, 34:27–47. Oxford: Oxford University Press. https://doi.org/10.1093/oxfordhb/9780198803560.013.1.

Mudde, Cas, and Cristobal Rovira Kaltwasser. 2017. *Populism: A Very Short Introduction.* New York: Oxford University Press.

Mudde, Cas, and Cristóbal Rovira Kaltwasser. 2013. "Exclusionary vs. Inclusionary Populism: Comparing Contemporary Europe and Latin America." *Government and Opposition* 48 (2): 147–74. https://doi.org/10.1017/gov.2012.11.

Muller, Jan-Werner. 2016. *What Is Populism?* London: Penguin.

Nag, Kingshuk. 2016. "Telangana Chief Minister Makes Cornwallis Turn in His Grave." *Economic and Political Weekly* 51 (44–45): 18–19.

Naidu, Chandrababu, and Sevanti Ninan. 2000. *Plain Speaking.* New Delhi: Viking.

Narayan, Deepa. 1999. "Bonds and Bridges: Social Capital and Poverty." Policy Research Working Paper 2167. Washington D.C.: The World Bank.

Nehru, Jawaharlal. 2004. *The Discovery of India.* New Delhi: Penguin Random House. https://penguin.co.in/book/the-discovery-of-india/.

———. 2022. "'The Light Has Gone Out of Our Lives': Nehru's Words on Gandhi's Assassination." *The Wire.* January 17. https://thewire.in/history/light-gone-lives-nehrus-words-gandhis-assassination (accessed January 19, 2025).

Nigam, Aditya. 2002. "In Search of a Bourgeoisie: Dalit Politics Enters a New Phase." *Economic and Political Weekly* 37 (13): 1190–93.

———. 2010. "Democracy and Capitalist Development: Reflections from the Indian Experience." *Transeuropéennes–International Journal of Critical Thought* (8 December).

———. 2011. "Democracy, Populism and the 'Middle Class': The Return of 'Anna Hazare.'" *Kafila*, August 5. http://kafila.online/2011/08/05/democracy -populism-and-the-'middle-class'-the-return-of-anna-hazare (accessed January 19, 2025).

———. 2013. "Winds of Change: Rise of the BJP and Challenge of an Alternative." *Economic and Political Weekly* 48 (52): 37–40.

Oana, Ioana-Elena, and Carsten Q Schneider. 2018. "Set Methods: An Add-on R Package for Advanced QCA." *The R Journal* 10 (1): 507–33.

Oana, Ioana-Elena, Carsten Q. Schneider, and Eva Thomann. 2021. *Qualitative Comparative Analysis Using R: A Beginner's Guide*. Cambridge, UK: Cambridge University Press.

Ostiguy, Pierre. 2017. "Populism: A Socio-Cultural Approach." In *The Oxford Handbook of Populism*, edited by C. Rovira Kaltwasser, P. Taggart, P. O. Espejo, and Pierre Ostiguy, 73–97. Oxford: Oxford University Press.

Ostiguy, Pierre, and Kenneth M. Roberts. 2016. "Putting Trump in Comparative Perspective: Populism and the Politicization of the Sociocultural Law." *Brown Journal of World Affairs* 23 (1): 25–50.

Palshikar, Suhas. 2004. "Shiv Sena: A Tiger with Many Faces?" *Economic and Political Weekly* 39 (14/15): 1497–507.

Pandey, Neelam. 2024. "'Sevaks Can't Be Arrogant' Remark Not for Modi, but RSS Cut up over Nadda Saying BJP Doesn't Need It." *The Print*, June 14. https://theprint.in/politics/sevaks-cant-be-arrogant-remark-not-for-modi -but-rss-cut-up-over-nadda-saying-bjp-doesnt-need-it/2131714/ (accessed January 19, 2025).

Pandian, M. S. S. 1989. "DMK's Miscalculations." *Economic and Political Weekly* 24 (48): 2628–29.

———. 2014. "The Rebirth of the Gandhi Cap: Anna Hazare, Arvind Kejriwal and the Aam Aadmi Party Have Given a New Lease of Life to the Very Humble Gandhi Cap." *Economic and Political Weekly* 49 (6): 96–96.

———. 2015. *The Image Trap: M.G. Ramachandran in Film and Politics*. New Delhi: SAGE Publishing India.

Pandian, M. S. S., and V. Geetha. 1989. "Jayalalitha: 'Sworn Heir.'" *Economic and Political Weekly* 24 (11): 551.

Pappas, Takis. 2016. "Modern Populism: Research Advances, Conceptual and Methodological Pitfalls, and the Minimal Definition." In *Oxford Research*

Encyclopedia, March 3. Oxford University Press. https://doi.org/10.1093/acrefore/9780190228637.013.17.

Parciack, Ronie, and Ilanit Loewy Shacham. 2018. "Divine Order, Social Disorder: Debating the Visual Representations of Lalu Prasad Yadav." In *India and Its Visual Cultures: Community, Class and Gender in a Symbolic Landscape*, edited by Uwe Skoda and Birgit Lettman, 278–302. India: Sage.

Patkar, Medha, Aruna Roy, P. M. Bhargava, E. A. S. Sarma, Sekhar Singh, Rajendra Singh, Arvind Kejriwal, and Sandeep Pandey. 2011. "Hyderabad Metro." *Economic and Political Weekly* 46 (16): 5–5.

Pinto, Ambrose. 1999. "Politics of Opportunism." *Economic and Political Weekly* 34 (36): 2544–47.

Pratim Basu, Sibaji. 2019. "Mamata Banerjee's Populist Politics." Mahanirban Calcutta Research Group. http://www.mcrg.ac.in/PP108.pdf (accessed January 19, 2025).

Przeworski, Adam. 1991. *Democracy and the Market: Political and Economic Reforms in Eastern Europe and Latin America*. Studies in Rationality and Social Change. Cambridge, UK: Cambridge University Press.

Puri, Raghav. 2012. "Reforming the Public Distribution System: Lessons from Chhattisgarh." *Economic and Political Weekly* 47 (5): 21–23.

Ragin, Charles C. 2008. *Redesigning Social Inquiry: Fuzzy Sets and Beyond*. University of Chicago Press.

———. 2014. *The Comparative Method: Moving Beyond Qualitative and Quantitative Strategies*. Oakland, CA: University of California Press.

Rai, Atul Krishna. 2015. "Bihar: Manjhi Refuses to Vacate CM House, Nitish Regime Fumes." *The Hindustan Times*, March 30, 2015. https://www.hindustantimes.com/india/bihar-manjhi-refuses-to-vacate-cm-house-nitish-regime-fumes/story-u42KkYGe9UE76C5twXnm9H.html (accessed April 16, 2025).

Ramanujan, A. K. 1989. "Is There an Indian Way of Thinking? An Informal Essay." *Contributions to Indian Sociology* 23 (1): 41–58. https://doi.org/10.1177/006996689023001004.

Rathore, Akash S. 2020. *Ambedkar's Preamble: A Secret History of the Constitution of India*. New Delhi: Penguin Random House.

Ray Chaudhury, Proma. 2022. "The Political Asceticism of Mamata Banerjee: Female Populist Leadership in Contemporary India." *Politics and Gender* 18 (4): 942–77. https://doi.org/10.1017/S1743923X21000209.

Reddy, G. Krishna. 2002. "New Populism and Liberalisation: Regime Shift under Chandrababu Naidu in AP." *Economic and Political Weekly* 37 (9): 871–83.

Roberts, Kenneth M. 1995. "Neoliberalism and the Transformation of Populism in Latin America: The Peruvian Case." *World Politics* 48 (1): 82–116.

———. 2017. "Populism and Political Parties." In *The Oxford Handbook of Populism*, edited by Cristobal Rovira Kaltwasser, Paul Taggart, Paulina Ochoa Espejo, and Pierre Ostiguy, 287–304. Oxford: Oxford University Press.

Rodgers, Jeffrey Pepper. 2018. "A Different Path to Journalism." The Maxwell Perspective, June 21.

Rodrigues, Valerian. 2014. "Political Power and Democratic Enablement: Devaraj Urs and Lower Caste Mobilisation in Karnataka." *Economic and Political Weekly* 49 (25): 62–70.

Rooduijn, Matthijs. 2014. "Vox Populismus: A Populist Radical Right Attitude among the Public?" *Nations and Nationalism* 20 (1): 80–92. https://doi.org/10.1111/nana.12054.

Rousseau, Jean Jacque. 1997. "Discourse on Political Economy" and "Of the Social Contract." In *Rousseau: The Social Contract and Other Later Political Writings*, edited by Victor Gourevitch, 1–38 and 39–155. Cambridge, UK: Cambridge University Press. https://doi.org/10.1017/9781316584606.

Rovira Kaltwasser, Cristóbal. 2021. "Bringing Political Psychology into the Study of Populism." *Philosophical Transactions of the Royal Society B* 376 (1822): 20200148.

Roy, Rajat. 2016. "Nothing Succeeds Like Success in West Bengal." *Economic and Political Weekly* 51 (22): 24–26.

———. 2019. "Populist Initiatives in a Competitive Democracy Chattisgarh: A Case Study." In Kolkotta: Mahanirban Calcutta Research Group. http://www.mcrg.ac.in/RLS_Populism/Populism_Abstract_Fullpaper/Rajat_Roy_Abstract.pdf (accessed January 19, 2025).

Rudolph, Lloyd I. 1961. "Urban Life and Populist Radicalism: Dravidian Politics in Madras." *The Journal of Asian Studies* 20 (3): 283–97. https://doi.org/10.2307/2050816.

Rudolph, Lloyd I., and Susanne Hoeber Rudolph. 1987. *In Pursuit of Lakshmi: The Political Economy of the Indian State*. Chicago: University of Chicago Press. https://press.uchicago.edu/ucp/books/book/chicago/I/bo5972167.html.

———. 2001. "Iconisation of Chandrababu: Sharing Sovereignty in India's Federal Market Economy." *Economic and Political Weekly* 36 (18): 1541–52.

Rueda, Daniel. 2021. "Is Populism a Political Strategy? A Critique of an Enduring Approach." *Political Studies* 69 (2): 167–84.

Rutten, Roel, and Claude Rubinson. 2022. "A Vocabulary of QCA." https://compasss.org.

Sadanandan, Anoop. 2012. "Bridling Central Tyranny in India: How Regional Parties Restrain the Federal Government." *Asian Survey* 52 (2): 247–69.

Samaddar, Ranabir. 2016. "West Bengal Elections: The Verdict of Politics." *Economic and Political Weekly* 51 (24): 23–25.

Sanders, Paul. 2020. "Populism Discourse and Trouble in Democracy: A Critical Approach." In *Leadership, Populism, and Resistance*, edited by Kristin M. S. Bezio and George R. Goethals, 8–28. Elgar Online. https://doi.org/10.4337/9781788979269.00008.

Sarangi, Asha. 2013. "States Reorganization Commission: A Critical Reading." In *Handbook of Politics in Indian States: Regions, Parties, and Economic Reforms*, edited by Sudha Pai, 40–54. New Delhi: Oxford University Press.

Sarkar, Swagato. 2011. "'Populism and the Anna Hazare Event." *Kafila.* September 1. https://kafila.online/2011/09/01/populism-and-the-anna-hazare-event-swagato-sarkar/ (accessed January 19, 2025).

Sartori, Giovanni. 1970. "Concept Misformation in Comparative Politics." *American Political Science Review* 64 (4): 1033–53.

———. 2005. *Parties and Party Systems: A Framework for Analysis.* Colchester, UK: ECPR Press.

Sathyamurthy, T. V. 1989. "Tamil Nadu Assembly Elections: Portents and Prospects." *Economic and Political Weekly* 24 (16): 883–92.

Schneider, Carsten Q., and Claudius Wagemann. 2012. *Set-Theoretic Methods for the Social Sciences: A Guide to Qualitative Comparative Analysis.* Cambridge: Cambridge University Press.

Schulz, Anne, Philipp Müller, Christian Schemer, Dominique Stefanie Wirz, Martin Wettstein, and Werner Wirth. 2018. "Measuring Populist Attitudes on Three Dimensions." *International Journal of Public Opinion Research* 30 (2): 316–26. https://doi.org/10.1093/ijpor/edw037.

Sen, Sarbani. 2007. *The Constitution of India: Popular Sovereignty and Democratic Transformations.* New Delhi: Oxford University Press.

Sharma, Alakh N. 1995. "Political Economy of Poverty in Bihar." *Economic and Political Weekly* 30 (41/42): 2587–602.

Shastri, Sandeep. 2024. "Modi Factor Seems to Have Stagnated over a Decade." *The Hindu*, June 6.

Shatrugna, M. 1985. "Repeat Performance." *Economic and Political Weekly* 20 (11): 442–42.

Silva, Bruno Castanho, Ioannis Andreadis, Eva Anduiza, Nebojša Blanuša, Yazmin Morlet Corti, Gisela Delfino, Guillem Rico et al. 2018. "Public Opinion Surveys: A New Measure." In *The Ideational Approach to Populism* edited by Kirk A. Hawkins, Ryan E. Carlin, Levente Littvay, and Cristóbal Rovira Kaltwasser, 150–78. London: Routledge.

Singh, Jagpal. 2015. "Karpoori Thakur: A Socialist Leader in the Hindi Belt." *Economic and Political Weekly* 50 (3): 54–60.

Singh, Prerna. 2016. *How Solidarity Works for Welfare: Subnationalism and Social Development in India*. Cambridge Studies in Comparative Politics. Cambridge, UK: Cambridge University Press. https://doi.org/10.1017/CBO 9781107707177.

Sinha, H. N. 1936. "Sovereignty in Ancient Indian Polity: A Study in the Evolution of Early Indian State." Doctor of Philosophy Theses, University of London. https://www.proquest.com/openview/a207b97b0ad3f07fe6d3153f b0f226b4/1?pq-origsite=gscholar&cbl=2026366&diss=y (accessed January 19, 2025).

Skocpol, Theda, and Margaret Somers. 1980. "The Uses of Comparative History in Macrosocial Inquiry." *Comparative Studies in Society and History* 22 (2): 174–97.

Srinivas, M. N., and M. N. Panini. 1984. "Politics and Society in Karnataka." *Economic and Political Weekly* 19 (2): 69–75.

Stavrakakis, Yanis. 2017. "Populism and Hegemony." In *The Oxford Handbook of Populism*, edited by Cristobal Rovira Kaltwasser, Paul A. Taggart, Paulina Ochoa Espejo, and Pierre Ostiguy, 535–53. Oxford: Oxford University Press.

Subbiah, Ar. 1991. "Reviving Shibboleths." *Economic and Political Weekly* 26 (34): 1938.

Subramanian, Narendra. 1999. *Ethnicity and Populist Mobilization, Political Parties, Citizens and Democracy in South India*. New Delhi: Oxford University Press.

———. 2007. "Populism in India." *The SAIS Review of International Affairs* 27 (1): 81–92.

Subramanya, Rupa. 2021. "Has India Become 'Lynchistan'?" ORF. July 1. https://www.orfonline.org/expert-speak/has-india-become-lynchistan/ (accessed January 19, 2025).

Suhrud, Tridip. 2008. "Modi and Gujarati 'Asmita.'" *Economic and Political Weekly* 43 (1): 11–13.

Syangbo, Genevive. 2010. "The Sikkim Democratic Front and the Politics of Popular Mobilisation in Sikkim (1993-2004)." Ph.D., University of North Bengal, Raja Rammohunpur, India.

Tiwari, Deeptiman. 2020. "Jagadanand Singh: Rajput Leader Who Has Lalu's Ear, Tejashwi's Back." *Indian Express*, 25 October. https://indianexpress.

com/elections/jagadanand-singh-bihar-elections-rjd-tejashwi-yadav
-profile-6881530/ (accessed January 19, 2025).

Tiwari, Ravish, and Rajkumar Jha. 2019. "Prime Minister Narendra Modi
Interview to Indian Express: 'Khan Market Gang Hasn't Created My
Image, 45 Years of Tapasya Has … You Cannot Dismantle It.'" *The Indian
Express*, May 13. https://indianexpress.com/elections/pm-narendra-modi-
interview-to-indian-express-live-lok-sabha-elections-2019-bjp-5723186/
(accessed January 19, 2025).

Torre, Carlos de la. 2017. "Populism in Latin America." In *The Oxford Handbook
of Populism*, edited by Cristóbal Rovira Kaltwasser, Paulina Ochoa Espejo,
Paul Taggart, and Pierre Ostiguy, 195–213. Oxford: Oxford University
Press. https://doi.org/10.1093/oxfordhb/9780198803560.013.8.

Tripathy, Jyotirmaya. 2017. "The Broom, the Muffler and the Wagon R: Aam
Aadmi Party and the Politics of de-Elitisation." *International Quarterly for
Asian Studies* 48 (1–2): 77–95.

Vaageeshan, H., and Ramya Chitrapu. 2021. "Springing a Surprise: Electoral
Politics in the State of Telangana." In *Electoral Dynamics in the States of India*,
edited by Sandeep Shastri, Ashutosh Kumar, and Yatindra Singh Sisodia,
322–34. New Delhi: Routledge India.

Vaasanthi. 2019. *The Lone Empress: A Portrait of Jayalalitha*. New Delhi:
Penguin.

Vajpeyi, Ananya. 2020. "Minorities and Populism in Modi's India: The Mirror
Effect." In *Minorities and Populism–Critical Perspectives from South Asia
and Europe*, edited by Kaul Volker and Ananya Vajpeyi, 17–28. Cham,
Switzerland: Springer. https://doi.org/10.1007/978-3-030-34098-8.

Varadarajan, Siddharth. 2014. "The Rise of Mango Man." *The World Today* 70 (2):
28–30.

Varshney, Ashutosh. 2013. *Battles Half Won: India's Improbable Democracy*. India:
Penguin Viking.

———. 2017. "India's Democracy at 70: Growth, Inequality, and Nationalism."
Journal of Democracy 28 (3): 41–51.

———. 2019a. "Modi Consolidates Power: Electoral Vibrancy, Mounting
Liberal Deficits." *Journal of Democracy* 30 (4): 63–77. https://doi.org/10.1353/
jod.2019.0069.

———. 2019b. "The Emergence of Right Wing Populism in India." In
Re-Forming India: The Nation Today, edited by Niraja Gopal Jayal, 327–45.
New Delhi: Penguin Random House.

———. 2021. "Populism and Nationalism: An Overview of Similarities and Differences." *Studies in Comparative International Development* 56 (2): 131–47. https://doi.org/10.1007/s12116-021-09332-x.

Varshney, Ashutosh, Srikrishna Ayyangar, and Siddharth Swaminathan. 2021. "Populism and Hindu Nationalism in India." *Studies in Comparative International Development* 56 (2): 197–222. https://doi.org/10.1007/s12116-021-09335-8.

Vis, Barbara. 2010. *Politics of Risk Taking: Welfare State Reform in Advanced Democracies*. Amsterdam: Amsterdam University Press.

Vittorini, Simona. 2022. "Modi a La Mode: Narendra Modi's Fashion and the Performance of Populist Leadership." *Journal of Commonwealth and Comparative Politics* 60 (3): 276–97.

Walker, Margaret Urban. 2015. "Making Reparations Possible: Theorizing Reparative Justice." In *Theorizing Transitional Justice*, edited by Claudio Corradeti, Nir Eisikovits, and Jack Volpe Rotondi, 211–22. London: Ashgate Press.

Weyland, Kurt. 1996. "Neopopulism and Neoliberalism in Latin America: Unexpected Affinities." *Studies in Comparative International Development* 31 (3): 3–31.

———. 2001. "Clarifying a Contested Concept: Populism in the Study of Latin American Politics." *Comparative Politics* 34 (1): 1–22.

———. 2002. *The Politics of Market Reform in Fragile Democracies: Argentina, Brazil, Peru and Venezuela*. Princeton, NJ: Princeton University Press.

———. 2017. "Populism: A Political Strategic Approach." In *The Oxford Handbook of Populism*, edited by Cristobal Rovira Kaltwasser, Paul Taggart, Paulina Ochoa Espejo, and Pierre Ostiguy, 48–73. Oxford: Oxford University Press. https://doi.org/10.1093/oxfordhb/9780198803560.013.2.

Winship, Christopher. 2006. "Policy Analysis as Puzzle Solving." In *The Oxford Handbook of Public Policy*, edited by Michael Moran, Martin Rein, and Goodin, 6:109–24. Oxford: Oxford University Press.

Witsoe, Jeffrey. 2011. "Corruption as Power: Caste and the Political Imagination of the Postcolonial State." *American Ethnologist* 38 (1): 73–85.

Wuytens, Chris, Bart Cambré, and Ans De Vos. 2020. "What Are the Necessary and Sufficient Conditions for Front-Line Employees' Need Fulfilment?" COMPASSS Working Papers 2020–94 (May). http://www.compasss.org/wpseries/WuytensCambreDeVos2020.pdf (accessed January 19, 2025).

Wyatt, A. K. J. 2002. "New Alignments in South Indian Politics: The 2001 Assembly Elections in Tamil Nadu." *Asian Survey* 42 (5): 733–53. https://doi.org/10.1525/as.2002.42.5.733.

Wyatt, Andrew. 2013. "Populism and Politics in Contemporary Tamil Nadu." *Contemporary South Asia* 21 (4): 365–81. https://doi.org/10.1080/09584935.2013.803036.

Zúquete, Jose Pedro. 2017. "Populism and Religion." In *The Oxford Handbook of Populism*, edited by Cristobal Rovira Kaltwasser, Paul Taggart, Paulina Ochoa Espejo, and Pierre Ostiguy, 445–66. Oxford: Oxford University Press.

Index